1850

The *Sun* Shines for All

The Sun
Shines for All

Journalism and Ideology in
the Life of Charles A. Dana

Janet E. Steele

Syracuse University Press

Library of Congress Cataloging-in-Publication Data

Steele, Janet E.
    The Sun shines for all: journalism and ideology in the life of
Charles A. Dana / Janet E. Steele.
        p.   cm.
    Includes bibliographical references and index.
    ISBN 0-8156-2579-0
    1. Dana, Charles A. (Charles Anderson), 1819–1897.
    2. Journalists — United States — 19th century — Biography.   3. Sun (New
York, N.Y. : 1833)   4. Press and politics — United States.
I. Title.
PN4874.D3S76   1993
070.4'1'092 — dc20
    [B]   92-33861

Manufactured in the United States of America

To my parents, Robert and Ellen Steele.

Janet E. Steele is an Assistant Professor, Department of Rhetoric and Communication Studies at the University of Virginia. She has published several articles on media history and criticism in journalism and communication journals and has written a number of entries for *The Biographical Dictionary of American Journalism*.

Contents

Illustrations

Table

Preface

When a dog bites a man, that is not news, but when
a man bites a dog, that is news.

New York Sun, 1882[1]

In January 1868, Charles Anderson Dana bought the *New York Sun*,
an undistinguished newspaper with a modest circulation and a
colorful past. Within a few years, he tripled the *Sun's* readership to
120,000 and transformed the morning daily into what Joseph Pulitzer called "the most piquant, entertaining, and without exception,
the best newspaper in the world."[2]

Dana helped to shape the metropolitan press for nearly fifty years.
As the managing editor of Horace Greeley's *New York Tribune* between 1849 and 1862, he assisted in making that paper the most influential daily in America and the voice of the nascent Republican
party. When Dana died in 1897, after thirty years as editor of the
New York Sun, his contemporaries described him as "the last of the
old-time great editors" and the *Sun* as "the acme of dignified, pol-
ished journalism."[3] Dana knew nearly everyone of significance in
American public life, and he was on friendly terms with an astonishing array of nineteenth-century intellectuals and politicians, including George Ripley, Horace Greeley, Abraham Lincoln, Ulysses S.
Grant, Karl Marx, Walt Whitman, Elizabeth Cady Stanton, and William Dean Howells.

Charles Dana was a man of striking contradictions. He was one
of the greatest innovators in nineteenth-century American journal-

ism; his *New York Sun* was famous for its style, its literary character, and its fresh definition of "the news." Yet Dana stubbornly refused to install modern typesetting machines in the *Sun's* shop, and he claimed to see no value in either illustrations or advertisements. As editor of the *Sun*, Dana could be idealistic. His paper championed the rights of the working class, he attacked frauds and humbugs, and he hated shams. Yet he could also be an unprincipled opportunist and a hypocrite, driven by self-interest and by lust for power and influence. And while those who worked for Dana nearly always described him as warm, generous, and good-natured, he was also spiteful, petty, and enormously vain.

Despite his remarkable achievements, Charles Dana has been ignored by historians.[4] It is a sign of this neglect that while nearly all historians and journalists recognize the famous man-bites-dog definition of "news," virtually no one remembers that it first appeared in the pages of the *New York Sun*.[5]

There are several explanations for this scholarly neglect of Dana and the *Sun*. First, there are no surviving records from the *Sun:* the business files of the paper are long gone, and the circulation data are sketchy at best. Moreover, neither Dana nor his descendants saved the editor's private correspondence. (As Dana explained in 1895: "It has not been my practice to preserve letters after the subjects on which they were written have been disposed of."[6]) To date, the most comprehensive study of the *New York Sun* is Candace Stone's 1938 *Dana and the Sun*. Stone used the *Sun's* files at the "new" Sun building on the northeast corner of Broadway and Chambers streets at a time when the paper was still a healthy business. Today the *Sun's* morgue, disorderly and uncataloged, is crumbling to dust in the Forty-third Street annex of the New York Public Library. Though Dana's *Sun* is readily available on microfilm, there is no index to ease the task of the historian who attempts to reel through thirty years' worth of daily papers.[7]

The second reason for the neglect of Dana and the *Sun* stems from what has become the hegemonic explanation of the history of American journalism. According to this familiar story of the rise of the modern newspaper, a process of natural selection was at work in the way that newspapers "progressed" or "evolved" from partisan political papers to "objective" commercial dailies.[8] Until recent years, historians have thus tended to focus on newspapers such as Joseph

Pulitzer's *New York World*, or Adolph Ochs's *New York Times* —
seemingly modern nineteenth-century newspapers that appear to be
harbingers of the mass-produced, commercial media of today. The
fallacy in this "Whig" view of journalism history is that it traces a
single path of development and ignores or distorts the significance
of papers that followed other routes.[9] The neglect of Charles Dana's
New York Sun is a particularly vivid example of this intellectual myo-
pia. Despite the *Sun's* large circulation and widely recognized literary merit, it has received almost no scholarly notice in the last fifty
years, losing out to studies of newspapers that seemed to usher in the
journalism of our own time.

    If Charles Dana's newspaper has suffered at the hands of histo-
rians, then the editor's fate has been even worse. Though Dana's earlier life is usually considered noteworthy because of his years at the
utopian socialist community Brook Farm, most scholars have followed
the lead of progressive historian Vernon Louis Parrington, who called
Dana a "disillusioned intellectual" and described his success at the
Sun as "a cynical commentary on the changing spirit of America
from the days of Brook Farm to the days of Mark Hanna."[10] In more
recent years, labor and social historians have continued to overlook
the *Sun* — though it was widely read by New York City's working
classes — because they have uncritically accepted Parrington's conclusion that "[with] the great success of the *Sun* [Dana] became the
apologist and defender of capitalism."[11]

    I initially chose to study Dana because of what appeared to be
the contradiction between the editor's early interest in radical reform
and his later reputation as a conservative and malicious cynic. It was
through what began as an intellectual biography of Dana that I came
to realize that the facts of the editor's life simply did not support the
conventional view of his post–Civil War disillusion and cynicism. It
also became clear that historians had overlooked Charles Dana and
the *New York Sun* because neither one fit the prevailing theoretical
framework of the political culture of the Gilded Age.

    Charles A. Dana's voice was a discordant one. He was usually
out of step with his contemporaries, and he was a thorn in the side
of politicians and public figures. Yet despite this contrariness, from
the time that Charles Dana purchased the *New York Sun* he went
about building a newspaper that would ultimately reach the largest

and most diverse audience in the United States. Dana's relationship with that audience is the key to understanding both the man and his newspaper. The *Sun's* motto, It Shines for All, captured Dana's broadly democratic vision. This book explores the relationship between Dana and his readers by first tracing the development of Dana's "producer" ideology, then analyzing the way in which his values were reflected in the *New York Sun*.

A good place to begin the task of reconstructing the *Sun's* relationship with its readers is the paper's coverage of the January 13, 1874, Tompkins Square "riot." In this bloody incident, two-thirds of New York City's police force attacked seven thousand unemployed workers in a public park. Both the riot and the resulting newspaper coverage exposed the social fissures of a deeply divided city. Of all the leading newspapers in New York City, only one came out squarely on the side of the unemployed laborers. It would have surprised Dana's latter-day progressive critics to learn that this paper was the *New York Sun*.

Janet E. Steele

Charlottesville, Virginia
October, 1991

Acknowledgments

I have relied on many teachers, friends, and colleagues in writing this book. My greatest thanks go to John Higham, who initially led me to Charles Dana and then gave unstinting support to this project. Not only was he generous with his time and insights into American history and culture, but he also forced me to examine critically the truisms of journalism history. In retrospect, I see that John Higham knew the potential importance of this study well before I did; I hope that the work comes close to what he imagined. Ronald G. Walters also read the manuscript closely in its early stages, and I benefited enormously from his thoughtful suggestions and his insistence that I enter the computer age.

A fellowship from the Gannett Center for Media Studies at Columbia University in New York City (now the Freedom Forum Media Studies Center) gave me a wonderful year in which to revise the manuscript and to explore media studies with some of the best scholars in the field. Director Everette E. Dennis provided me with advice and encouragement in my efforts to merge media studies with cultural history. Mrs. Marion Wilson gave me invaluable support at a critical moment, along with a gift that enabled me to spend a summer of research in New York City. For other financial assistance, I am grateful to the University of Virginia Research Grants Committee and the Media Studies Project of the Woodrow Wilson Center, Washington, D.C.

Daniel Schiller, Sally Griffith, and Douglas Gomery each read and commented on earlier drafts of this manuscript and helped me to sharpen its focus. I am grateful also to the participants in the Commercial Culture Seminar at the New York Institute for the Humanities for comments on an earlier version of chapter 7.

William Lee Miller and Bernard and Regina Carlson have given me both encouragement and intellectual sustenance at the University of Virginia; James D. Goodyear, Michael Lapp, and Elizabeth Bowen always provided friendship and support when I needed it. I would also like to thank James Baughman for sharing with me his commitment to excellence in the field of journalism history.

Robert Cross carefully read the whole of the manuscript and offered valuable suggestions for improving the text. Martin Schram also read and marked up the entire manuscript, and I am grateful for both his insights into Charles Dana and his frequent reminders that newspaper editors are motivated by more than ideology. Steven Finkel's exceptionally close reading helped me to polish the manuscript at its final stage and to clarify my arguments at several key points.

I am indebted to Duncan Longcope, Charles Dana's great-grandson, who enthusiastically gave of his time, his knowledge of the Dana family, and the use of previously unpublished photographs. Mr. Longcope's hospitality at Cornhill Farm in Lee, Massachusetts, was unquestionably the highlight of my work on this book.

I am particularly indebted to Gerald Macdonald, who knows more about Charles A. Dana than any geographer should have to. Not only did he generously take time out from his own work to comment on successive drafts of this manuscript, but he also forced me to wrestle with the theoretical issues underlying Dana's intellectual development. For his unwavering faith in this project, I owe him more than I can possibly say.

And, finally, I am grateful to the New-York Historical Society, the New York Public Library, and the Library of Congress for permission to use the illustrations in this book and to Bix for taking the photographs.

The *Sun* Shines for All

1

Zenith

The *New York Sun* and the
Ideology of Producerism

𝕴t was bitterly cold in New York City on January 13, 1874. An icy
wind penetrated the threadbare coats of the unemployed workers who massed in Tompkins Square Park that morning, while leaden
skies darkly threatened afternoon snow.[1] The depression of 1873 had
thrown thousands of northeastern laborers out of jobs, and in New
York City desperate and hungry workers had gathered in the Lower
East Side park to press for public employment.

The rally on January 13 was organized by the Committee of
Safety, an amorphous group that included socialists, trade unionists,
and antimonopolist reformers. The organizers had run into problems
from the start, as rivals competed for leadership and city authorities
threw obstacles in the way of a proposed march from Tompkins Square
to City Hall. On the evening of January 12, the Police Board had can-
celed the committee's permit to meet in the park. Word of the last-
minute change failed to spread, however, and on the morning of the
thirteenth the unemployed crowded into Tompkins Square. Meanwhile, the Mulberry Street Police Board Office had mustered its men
and stationed two-thirds of the city's entire police force between Tompkins Square and City Hall.

The fighting began when the police tried to disperse the crowd,
and it ended with what trade unionist Samuel Gompers called "an
orgy of brutality," as the police attacked the workers with drawn sticks.[2]
By late afternoon the "rioters" had been subdued and Tompkins Square

was quiet, covered with four inches of fresh snow. Forty-six protesters were in jail.

News of the attack spread quickly, as street corner newsies hawked special editions of the city's newspapers. That night, safe from the below-freezing temperatures in the warmth of their homes, middle-class New Yorkers read with horror of the events in Tompkins Square Park. The *New York World* dismissed the protesters as "sham work-ingmen" and "dangerous fools." The *New York Tribune* described them as "insane and enthusiastic foreigners," and called their demand for jobs and food "criminal and foolish talk."[3] It was hard for the respect-able classes to forget the role that workers and immigrants had played in the bloody days of the 1863 draft riots.[4] More recently, the Paris Commune of 1871 had raised fears of revolutionary convulsions and violence.[5] Having little daily contact with the workers, most of New York City's upper classes probably agreed with their papers' conclu-sions that the "rioters," driven by "idleness, ignorance, and vice," had been pacified only by the "logic . . . of force."[6] In the words of a *New York World* editorialist, "The right of the people peaceably to assemble and petition for a redress of the constitution does not mean the right of a rabble of blackguards, mostly foreigners, to brandish red rags in public squares and breathe out threatenings [*sic*] against decent people."[7]

Yet one major New York City newspaper did not join the near-universal condemnation of the protestors: Charles A. Dana's *New York Sun* was both sympathetic to the unemployed workers and highly critical of the actions of the police.[8] Its four pages contained vivid accounts of the violence and of the confusion and panic of the mostly peaceable demonstrators as they ran for cover from the horses of the 1st Mounted Squad: "Men tumbled over each other . . . into the gut-ters or clambered up high stoops to get out of the way of the chargers. The horsemen beat the air with their batons and many persons were laid low. There seemed to be a determination on the part of the mounted police to ride over somebody, and they showed no mercy."[9]

In the days following the rally in Tompkins Square, *Sun* edito-rials blamed city authorities for their "want of judgment." The paper pointed out that most New York City laborers were "industrious" and "orderly," and it argued that "at a time when such suffering prevails . . . it is natural that the unemployed should have a curiosity to hear what men who profess devotion to their interests have to say." In fact, the *Sun* suggested that the police were ultimately responsible for the melee:

> In the crowd which assembled on Tuesday, it is not probable that there were one hundred men who would have favored any act of violence. But the police, without any notice, and in what cannot be described as other than a brutal manner, charged upon the mass of unemployed mechanics and laboring men who had peaceably assembled to learn if any measures were to be taken for their relief and clubbed them unmercifully. . . . This is not a proper way to treat American Citizens.[10]

In sharp contrast to the editorial comments of New York City's other newspapers, the *Sun* not only blamed the city for its unwillingness to create public employment for the relief of the jobless, but it also accused public officials of callousness. The *Sun* concluded that "the city authorities do not seem to have manifested any real sympathy for the distress which exists among the workingmen, or to have even thought about taking any effectual measures to mitigate the hardship of their condition."[11]

For the next few days, letters to the *Sun's* editor, reflecting the "widespread circulation of [the *Sun*] among the working classes," congratulated the paper for its courageous stand and roundly condemned the Police Board. As the writer of a typical letter commented, "Your sensible and true remarks in today's *Sun* concerning the troubles in Tompkins Square of Tuesday last are just what the honest workingmen expected from you."[12]

The significance of the *Sun's* lone defense of the Tompkins Square protesters cannot be overemphasized. In broad terms, what was being contested in Tompkins Square on January 13, 1874, was the future of the city of New York and the right of workers to participate in defining that future. After all, as historian Thomas Bender has pointedly remarked, "the police prevented workers from holding a public meeting in the largest public space on the Lower East Side."[13]

The Tompkins Square melee occurred at the beginning of the decade of the *Sun's* greatest popularity; just a few days earlier, the paper had announced that its daily circulation had reached 120,000

— or 50,000 more than that of its nearest competitor, James Gordon Bennett's *New York Herald*.[14] The rhetoric with which Charles Dana's *New York Sun* defended the unemployed protesters who rallied in Tompkins Square drew upon two themes familiar to the paper's predominantly Democratic, working-class readers. The first was the language of "equal rights," a radical egalitarian tradition that had reached its pinnacle in the politics of the "Locofoco" (or Equal Rights) party of the 1830s.[15] The *Sun* invoked this tradition when it emphasized that the city's most "wretched" inhabitants had the same right as its wealthiest citizens to assemble and publicly express their grievances: "With trembling lips the poor, emaciated beings . . . asked why they should not be permitted to assemble in public and discuss 'Capital and Labor,' and why they should not be allowed to march through the streets and show the public who and what they are and bring to the very faces of the people the fact that they are able and willing to work, and that they must have employment or starve."[16]

The second theme that Dana's paper developed in its defense of the Tompkins Square protesters was the dignity of labor and the centrality of the human need to engage in productive work. As a *Sun* editorial argued, "It is a sad thing that thousands of honest, industrious men, able and willing to work, should be in this city without means to provide for their starving families."[17] By repeatedly stating that the protesters were "unemployed mechanics and laboring men" who merely wanted jobs and relief from hardship, Charles Dana's *New York Sun* drew upon a set of ideas that had deep roots in antebellum America.

Of all the contradictions of Charles A. Dana, the most intriguing is the division between Dana the Utopian Socialist and Dana the editor of the Gilded Age. The key to understanding Dana as an intellectual lies in the ideas that he developed at Brook Farm, that evolved into the Free Soil crusade of the 1850s, and that permeated the pages of the *New York Sun* in the 1870s and early 1880s. Dana's paper offered its readers an interpretation of urban life grounded in what I call an ideology of "producerism." Producerism divided society into two moral categories: producers and nonproducers. Producers were those who created all wealth yet owned nothing but their labor; nonproducers were those who extracted the income of the "industrious classes" in the form of rent, interest, and the profits gained from buying labor at one price and selling it at another.[18]

In the United States, producerism was rooted in the ideology of artisan republicanism that dated back to the Revolutionary War era.[19] The term *producer* did not refer only to the working class, but rather to an unstable alliance of classes that identified the interests of the craftworker and laborer with those of the shopkeeper and clerk.[20] In this worldview, "honest" mechanics and "honorable" employers were joined in their opposition to the corrupting and monopolistic influences of capitalists, bankers, and large merchants and manufacturers. The vision they shared was a republic of autonomous producers united in a cooperative commonwealth. They favored a society made up of individuals who could set the price of their own labor, free from the fetters of competitive capitalist production.

As managing editor of Horace Greeley's *New York Tribune*, Dana was well known to the circle of bourgeois reformers who made up the intellectual wing of the New York workingmen's movement. In fact, Charles Dana had risen to prominence as the author of a remarkable series of letters from Europe in which he defended the rights of the Parisian craftworkers who took to the streets in the revolution of 1848. The *Sun*'s coverage of the 1874 Tompkins Square riot suggests that twenty-five years later Dana continued to champion the urban working class and its demand to put the question of the right to work on the political agenda.[21]

Charles Dana's *New York Sun* invoked both the antebellum "producerism" of Brook Farm and the Free Soil ideology of Horace Greeley's *New York Tribune* to explain metropolitan life in the Gilded Age.[22] Charles Dana saw the *Sun*'s largely Democratic, working-class readers as producers, whose identity was bound up with the labor they performed. Dana defined the interests of his readers in the rhetoric of antebellum workingmen's associations, emphasizing cooperation, mutual aid, and self-help.[23] His producer orientation was reflected in the *Sun*'s political outlook: its championing of labor unions, producers' cooperatives, and Tammany Hall.[24] Dana's vision was democratic, rooted in the traditions of urban artisans and mechanics and nurtured by both the perfectionism of Brook Farm and the antislavery crusade of the 1850s. At its best it celebrated toleration, diversity, and a broad commitment to social justice. The success of Dana's *Sun* suggests that the liberal reform movements of the 1840s produced an urban legacy extending well into the 1870s and 1880s.

The *Sun's* popularity can also give new insight into the political rhetoric of the postwar Democratic party, as it struggled to define itself in terms of something other than racism.[25] Though Dana usually claimed that the *Sun* was politically independent, it was widely recognized that he supported the interests of the Democratic party.[26] If Democratic officials sometimes despaired of the *Sun's* idiosyncrasies at midcentury, the success of the paper suggests that the ideology of the Free Soil wing of the antebellum party persisted well into the postwar years. The intellectual thread that runs from Brook Farm to *Tribune* Republicanism to the ideology of the postbellum Democratic party suggests a basic continuity in nineteenth-century American political culture.[27] Charles Dana's political views were forged in the context of antebellum workingmen's culture. The large circulation of the *New York Sun* in the 1870s is testimony to the persistence of that ideology in the Gilded Age. This book will trace the development of such ideas, thereby providing insight into a worldview that has been forgotten today.

When Charles Dana died in 1897, he was one of the wealthiest and most powerful newspaper editors in the United States. Yet the man who would end his career as the editor of the *New York Sun* began his life in poverty. Charles Dana's struggle to overcome his humble origins would not only help to shape his ideology of producerism; it would also lead to his almost visceral sympathy with the working people of New York City.

2

"Heaven on Earth"

Brook Farm and the Harmony of
Interest Between Labor and Capital

Though Charles Anderson Dana attended Harvard College, he was not a Harvard graduate.[1] Poverty and humble origins held him back, truncating his studies and forcing him to leave the college after completing only one full year. Harvard made Dana feel like an outsider. This experience had a profound effect on the development of his political ideology, leading him to attack wealth and privilege and to identify with the interests of the "producing classes." Though Charles Dana eventually found friends and compatible associates at Brook Farm, he continued to view himself as "the house servant of humanity" and to criticize the acquisitive society that had shut him out.[2] At Brook Farm, Dana became a self-styled radical, a Fourierist with a mission of nothing less than the creation of "heaven on earth."[3]

Charles Dana was born on August 8, 1819, in Hinsdale, New Hampshire. He was the eldest of the four children of Anderson and Ann Dennison Dana.[4] Anderson Dana was a small-time merchant, a man who failed at nearly every business to which he put his hand. He was distantly related to the wealthy and prominent descendants of colonial settler Richard Dana, and his children grew up keenly aware of their family's diminished social status.

Anderson Dana was largely to blame for the unsettled home life of his wife and children. Plagued by financial troubles, he moved frequently from job to job, and one business after another ended in failure. Life was difficult for the Dana children, and their hardscrabble existence held little promise of a better future.

In 1828 catastrophe struck in the form of an epidemic that swept through western New York and claimed Ann Dennison Dana as one of its victims. Unwilling to accept the responsibility of raising a family, Anderson Dana scattered his children among relatives, sending nine-year-old Charles to live with an uncle, David Dennison. More than fifty years later, Charles Dana still recalled these events as "the saddest and most shocking" of his life.[5] Not only had he lost his mother; he had also been abandoned by his father. Biographer James Harrison Wilson minced no words in his assessment of Anderson Dana as a self-centered ne'er-do-well: "[Charles's] father, who appears to have always been something of a dreamer and never a successful or forehanded man . . . married again and [raised] . . . a new family. . . . He had done nothing for his first set of children . . . nor was he ever afterwards able to give them any help whatever. Charles, like the rest, was therefore forced to depend absolutely upon himself and such assistance as he could secure from his friends."[6]

These traumatic events not only affected Dana's childhood but also left their mark on his adult personality. As an adult, Dana was ambitious, driven by hunger for recognition and financial independence. Despite his outward geniality, Dana was touchy and quick to take offense. Critics accused him of too much concern about the opinions of others. It seems likely that the events of his boyhood made Dana particularly sensitive to questions of loyalty and obligation. Dana placed a high premium on friendship and was coldly unforgiving whenever his trust was betrayed.

Despite the tragic disruptions of his boyhood, Dana showed considerable promise at school. According to Wilson, his biographer, Dana did the work of boys who were six to eight years his senior. When Charles Dana's guardians moved him to Buffalo, New York, in 1831, they assumed that the boy's education was complete. It was expected that he would live in the home of his uncle William Dana and clerk in the family dry goods store, Staats and Dana.

Buffalo opened new worlds to the twelve-year-old boy. Despite its sizable population of twenty-five thousand, Buffalo was still a frontier town. Located at the western outlet of the newly completed Erie Canal, it was perched between the wilderness and the great commer-

cial pipeline heading east. As the nephew of a prosperous business-
man, Dana came into contact with a number of Buffalo's leading
citizens. He was ambitious and managed to win the friendship of older
men, among them Dr. Austin Flint, a Harvard graduate and medical
doctor. Flint was the first of several influential men to whom Dana
turned for encouragement and patronage.

To nearly all who knew him in Buffalo, Charles Dana showed
exceptional promise. He spent most of his evenings studying languages, literature, and history. One of his uncle's clerks later remembered him as "a quiet, studious boy who loved nature and books, and
although a good salesman, rather prone to spend too much time in
the adjoining book-store looking over volumes he could not buy."[7] His
literary diet was varied; he enjoyed both the English classics and the
works of Tom Paine. Dana was particularly adept at languages. In
addition to learning Greek and Latin, he also mastered the local Sen-
eca dialect.

The panic of 1837, which undermined the dry goods firm of Staats
and Dana, paradoxically presented Charles A. Dana with a great opportunity. Along with thousands of poor young men from declining
agricultural communities, Dana escaped economic hardship in advanced education. The rocky soil and depressed economy of the old
Northeast pushed a generation of indigent young men to the colleges
of New England.[8] Some hoped to find work in the cities. Most expected to become teachers or, in the wave of religious conversions
following the Second Great Awakening, to enter the ministry.

Characteristically, Dana chose not to attend one of the inexpensive provincial colleges. Instead he set his sights on Harvard, which
was at that time the stronghold of the Boston elite.[9] Charles Dana's
matriculation at Harvard in 1839 was an astonishing achievement,
given his economic and social background. While it is likely that Dr.
Flint had helped Dana apply to his own alma mater, that assistance
alone was no guarantee of success. When Dana set off for Harvard
College at the age of twenty, he took with him $200 in savings but
no aid from his family.[10]

Dana completed only one full year of study at Harvard. He
entered the college as a freshman in September 1839 and at the end
of the term ranked seventh in a class of seventy-four. Though he began the fall terms of 1840 and 1841, he was forced to take a leave of

absence each year to earn money by "keeping school." He probably had charge of a rural, one-room school in which discipline was more important than learning—a depressingly familiar scenario for poor young scholars. During the first half of the nineteenth century, at least one-third of all New England college students left their studies to earn a living, their lack of financial resources adding a vagabond-like quality to student life.[11] To make ends meet, Dana taught school in Scituate, New York; boarded with an uncle in Guildhall, Vermont; and frequently stayed with friends in Lancaster, New Hampshire— all while formally affiliated with Harvard College.[12]

In May of 1840, Dana received a letter from C. C. Fenton, a professor of Greek who later became Harvard's president, advising him "by all means" to return to college, and even suggesting that a loan might be available to help with the expenses.[13] It was an impressive offer; loan funds, like all other forms of scholarship aid, were dwindling.[14] Harvard had undergone a dramatic shift toward exclusivity during the 1830s.[15] While the college estimated in 1835 that a year of study would cost $185, real expenses amounted to about $300, far more than any but the wealthy could afford. At the same time, Harvard reduced the length of its winter vacations, thus preventing the needy from earning money by keeping school. Tougher admission requirements also tended to keep out those who had not had extensive private preparation. Given these obstacles, it is impressive that Dana survived at Harvard for as long as he did.

Dana was an outsider at Harvard. The demands of keeping school and the extensive reading necessary to catch up with his better-prepared classmates took their toll. In 1841 his eyesight deteriorated from the strain of studying by gaslight, and he had to ask others to read to him. He later remembered having had little spare time to engage in the pleasures of the more privileged. Transcendentalist minister Theodore Parker had students like Dana in mind when in 1846 he wrote: "The poor man's son . . . struggling for a superior education, obtains his culture at a monstrous cost; with the sacrifice of pleasure, comfort, the joys of youth, often of eyesight and health. . . . The rich man's son needs not that terrible trial. . . . All the outward means of education, refining, elevating a child, are to be had for money, and money alone."[16]

Dana's struggle to obtain a Harvard education revealed determination and strength of character. Harvard educated the elite who would people New York's literary establishment in the Gilded Age. Dana's financial troubles meant that he was not part of their circle at Harvard, nor would he be thirty years later as editor of the *New York Sun*. Dana, in fact, would use the *Sun* as a platform for attacking the kind of privilege that money and power conferred.

Dana received a remarkable education in Cambridge, Massachusetts, perhaps because of the obstacles that the college threw in his path. He enrolled at Harvard one year after Ralph Waldo Emerson had delivered his controversial Divinity School address there, a manifesto that was still reverberating throughout the academic community. Dana's background of economic hardship made him receptive to these appeals for religious and social reform. When he described the Transcendentalist ministers Emerson and George Ripley to friends in Buffalo, he suggested that Cambridge was giving him an education having little to do with what Emerson had denounced as the "corpse cold Unitarianism of Harvard College and Brattle Street."[17] Dana, in a word, was radicalized.

Not all of the ministers who revolted against Unitarianism were motivated solely by religious zeal. Some, like George Ripley, were drawn to Transcendentalism by an interest in social reform.[18] The young Charles Dana was particularly impressed with Ripley's radical social views, as he explained in a letter to Dr. Austin Flint: "Apropos of Mr. Ripley, he leaves his church [Purchase Street Church, Boston] on the 1st of January as I am informed. He is to be one of a society who design to establish themselves at Concord, or somewhere in the vicinity, and introduce, among themselves at least, a new order of things. Their object is social reformation. . . . With these men are my sympathies."[19]

George Ripley was one of a second generation of Unitarian rebels against Calvinism; by the time he dedicated his first church in 1826, the feud was more than twenty years old.[20] Though the Unitarians had departed from Calvinist orthodoxy over the doctrine of the Trinity, the real conflict had been the nature of human beings and their contribution to their own salvation. Unitarians believed that human reason was a gift from God and that man had an infinite capacity for good. Even more controversial was their rejection of the idea that some sinners were predestined to damnation. Ironically, by the 1830s, when Ripley, Emerson, Theodore Parker, and Orestes Brownson organized the Transcendentalist Club, Unitarianism had calcified into the church of the Boston establishment.[21] Transcendentalists rejected what they felt was unnecessary formalism in the Unitarian faith. They believed that God touched men and women through human intuition, rather than by centuries-old revelation in sacred books.

Not surprisingly, the Transcendentalists found it hard to agree on a host of philosophical matters, including the problem of social responsibility and reform. For Emerson, the solitary self was all-important; others, including George Ripley, believed that the misery of the Boston slums demanded greater attention to social justice. The pull of the secular world was eventually more than Ripley could withstand, and in May 1840 he abandoned the ministry. He hoped to organize a community that would practice radical economics based on Christian principles. As he wrote to Emerson, this community would "insure a more natural union between intellectual and manual labor . . . combine the thinker and the worker [and] guarantee the highest mental freedom by providing all with labor adapted to their tastes and talents, and securing to them the fruits of their industry."[22] This idea would take shape as Brook Farm.

Ripley bought Brook Farm at West Roxbury, Massachusetts, in the winter of 1840 and moved his family and fifteen others into the farmhouse the following April. Shortly thereafter he invited Dana to join them, and the young Harvard student moved to Brook Farm in September. As a Brook Farmer, he would be a member of Boston's most self-conscious community of radicals and intellectuals — a participant in what many believed was the most daring social experiment of the day.

By all accounts, Brook Farm's setting was idyllic. Located in the rolling Massachusetts countryside, the farm was tucked between a pine forest and a brook. Residents could see the Charles River from a sprawling two-story farmhouse known as the Hive. Two terraced embankments between the Hive and the brook were planted with shrubs, flowers, and mulberry and spruce trees. Sophia Ripley, George Ripley's wife, described the farm as rich with "birds, trees, sloping green hills, and lazy fields as far as the eye can reach."[23]

Shortly after his arrival at Brook Farm, Dana wrote to his sixteen-year-old sister, Maria, that he had joined the community "for the purpose of living purely and justly and of acting from higher principles than the world recognizes."[24] Charles Dana had seen his only sister one year earlier for the first time in more than eight years. His affection for his sister was obvious, particularly in his concern for her education. He told a friend how happy he had been to see her and added that "to her young mind I may be of some assistance."[25] To Maria he described his farming and teaching duties, and commented on the "excellent society" and "warm sympathy" of his friends. Before long he had persuaded her to join the community, thus re-creating—at least in part—the family his father had shattered nine years earlier.

Dana's initial financial investment in Brook Farm poses a mystery. When he joined the community in September 1841, he purchased three of the twenty-four shares of stock at $500 each and was elected trustee and director of finance.[26] How did twenty-one-year-old Dana, a student with no evident assets, not only manage to find $1,500 to invest in the joint-stock company but also happen to be appointed director of community finances? Unfortunately, there is no clear answer. Perhaps Dana impressed a patron with his talent and ambition, as it is unlikely that he was able to borrow the money commercially.[27] If so, it was only one of the many instances in which he managed to win financial backing at the most unlikely of times. Maybe Dana's six years of business experience made him stand out as a man of great practical abilities, particularly in a group of social reformers drawn from the ranks of the Unitarian ministry.

Although George Ripley may have been the undisputed spiritual leader of Brook Farm, he was dependent on the energy and skills of Charles Dana for help in everyday matters.[28] According to Ripley's biographer, Dana was second in command and controlled the daily operations of the enterprise.

In addition to his role as Ripley's lieutenant, Dana also taught Greek and German at the Brook Farm School. Journalist and transcendentalist philosopher Margaret Fuller described the school as a place where children would learn "to distinguish between truth sublime and the dead dogma of the past."[29] To the less poetically inclined, it was a preparatory academy with a progressive curriculum emphasizing modern languages and literature. Still, it was a far cry from the school Dana had "kept" in Scituate, New York. A newspaper advertisement announced: "Pupils of different ages and of both sexes are received; a constant maternal care [is] exercised over the youngest; and the more advanced [are] subject to the friendly counsel and assistance of the teachers, without the restraints of arbitrary discipline."[30] It has been suggested that of all the teachers at the Brook Farm School, only Dana used any disciplinary restraints whatsoever; one pupil later recalled that an unlearned lesson invited greater shame in Mr. Dana's class than in any other.[31] The Brook Farm School was an unqualified success. By the end of 1842, thirty boys and girls had been enrolled, among them George William Curtis, who later became editor of *Harper's Weekly*.

Dana's nickname at Brook Farm was "the Professor." Quiet and perhaps a bit aloof, he had a "natural dignity [that] kept him from many of the extravagances into which some of the others fell."[32] Dana was not a frivolous young man. Yet despite his steady decorum, he was jovial and affectionate, with a "vigorous stride [and] hearty laugh."[33] Dana's sense of humor is evident in this story of his chance meeting with an itinerant preacher who offered to "save" the sinners of Brook Farm.

> The visitor announced that his mission was to save souls by delivering a warning to sinners in immediate danger of eternal punishment, a task which required that all Brook Farmers be assembled for castigation. Dana, without looking up from his work cheerfully replied: "You can, but they have a way of not listening sometimes. I'll tell you what, if you are able and willing to preach a sound, old-fashioned, blue blazes and brimstone sermon, you will get an audience. I would like to hear a real scorcher once more."[34]

One frequent visitor to Brook Farm was *New York Tribune* editor Horace Greeley. Though Greeley did not join the community, he took an active interest in its development. Almost certainly Dana first met Greeley at Brook Farm, thus beginning a volatile relationship that lasted until Greeley's death in 1872.

Only eight years older than Dana, Greeley had also been something of a prodigy, establishing the *New York Tribune* in 1841 at the age of twenty-nine. Horace Greeley became increasingly involved in the affairs of Brook Farm during the winter of 1842, as Ripley and others grew more interested in Fourierism, a system of social reform that had originated in France with Charles Fourier. Charles Dana would become one of Fourierism's most enthusiastic devotees.

In August 1842, Horace Greeley wrote to Dana suggesting that the Brook Farm experiment proved that Christian philanthropy was not enough to transform society, because idlers could always live off the work and earnings of others. Greeley argued that, lacking the "science" of Fourierism, Brook Farm was suited only to those of angelic temperament, and "the entrance of one serpent would be as fatal as in Eden of old." In the editor's view, Fourierism would counteract the poison of selfishness: "I think Fourier's system avoids this danger, by having a rampart of exact Justice behind that of Philanthropy. With this no one will be tempted to say — why shall I labor, when another in wanton idleness consumes the product? Why shall I assume unpleasant functions when others avoid them and in secret laugh at my easy good nature?"[35]

Dana shared Greeley's enthusiasm for economic and social reform and, as one Brook Farmer remembered, took to Fourierism with "ardor and systematic energy."[36] During the 1840s Dana became a leading publicist for "Association," as the Fourierist cause was generally called in the United States. Albert Brisbane had transplanted Fourierism to America, and Horace Greeley popularized it in the *New York Tribune*. Fourierism was a curious combination of economic theory and fanciful futurology that supposedly described "scientifically" the workings of society. It started with the premise of human perfectibility and, working through a complex system of numerology and "passional attractions," concluded with the coming of a millennial kingdom of material well-being. Though much of Fourierism sounds absurd today, it nonetheless had the very serious aims of reconciling the individual with the community, creating harmony between labor and capital, and bringing about a more humane society through economic reorganization.[37]

In the United States, Fourierism drew upon deeply rooted values of democracy, Christianity, and self-help, and it appealed to reformers of widely different persuasions.[38] To Horace Greeley, for example, Fourierism was nothing more than a system of producer-owned and -operated cooperatives. He argued in favor of Fourierism on the basis of the system's practicality. Others, such as radical Democratic editor Parke Godwin, were attracted by Fourierism's libertarian elements of equal rights and minimal coercion. Some, like George Ripley, found in Fourierism an ethical system similar to what would later be known as the Social Gospel. That three such different men — a Whig, a radical Democrat, and a Unitarian minister — could all be committed Fourierists suggests the wonderfully amorphous character of Fourierism in America.

For all its emphasis on harmony, the introduction of Fourierism into the Brook Farm community deepened an already existing rift. From the beginning, Brook Farm had attracted two types of reformers: those like Emerson who were primarily concerned with the regeneration of individuals, and those like Ripley and Dana who were more interested in reforming society. For this reason, some historians have claimed that Fourierism was the hidden snake in the idyll of Brook Farm.[39] Actually, the "conversion" of Brook Farm to Fourierism was smooth, and those who disliked the new emphasis on social reform simply drifted away.[40] Ripley favored the introduction of Fourierism because he believed the community would benefit from a more coherent social philosophy, as well as from being part of a larger movement.

In June 1845, the Brook Farmers began to publish the *Harbinger*, a weekly newspaper intended to advance the cause of Association. Dana quickly became one of its leading contributors, along with George Ripley, Albert Brisbane, and former Unitarian minister John Dwight. Working without pay, they wrote more than three-fourths of the articles. Though the circulation of the *Harbinger* at no point exceeded two thousand, the weekly's influence was greater than this number would suggest. Dozens of editors lifted material from its pages, and many copies circulated from hand to hand.[41]

Though Charles Dana contributed articles to the *Harbinger* on a variety of topics, most of his writing focused on the social problems brought about by the rapid acceleration of factory production. He acknowledged that the mechanization of industry had increased national wealth and lowered prices through new economies of scale, but his articles reminded readers of what he called "the other side of the picture"— the "increasing poverty of the producing classes."[42]

The rhetoric of the *Harbinger* can be understood only by looking at the context of industrializing America in the 1830s and 1840s. As factory production accelerated in the decades preceding the Civil

War, the demand for consumer goods in greater quantities, at lower prices, replaced traditional patterns of production, broke down the apprenticeship system, and widened the gap between master artisans and workers. As lower wages, sweated labor, piecework, and high-volume production came to characterize industries like shoemaking, tailoring, masonry, and furniture making, all of the trades were affected by the expanding American market. Journeymen who started work in hopes of achieving master status found that they were fast becoming a class of permanent wage earners. As historian Sean Wilentz has shown in the case of New York City, between 1825 and 1850 metropolitan industrialization challenged assumptions about the "cardinal ideas of the artisan republic," or independence, virtue, equality, cooperation, and a share in the work process.[43]

Charles Dana's writing for the *Harbinger* addressed this breakdown of traditional patterns of production. According to Dana, even the model cotton mills of Lowell, Massachusetts robbed workers of their traditional rights: "The existing system of labor and the relations between the workmen and their employers are full of the foulest wrongs. . . . That gloomy era approaches — in our manufacturing towns we see more than mere premonitions of its coming,— when the pale sky of New England shall look down on men, women, and children ground to the very dust by feudal monopoly."[44]

Charles Dana claimed that individualism was the poisonous fruit produced by the acquisitiveness and selfish competition of modern industrial society. Dana had personally experienced the ill-effects of the burgeoning market economy — first in his father's repeated business failures and later in the collapse of the dry goods firm of Staats and Dana. As he observed, "Intimate acquaintance of many years with commercial life . . . [has] constrained [me] to believe that in commerce, absolute and complete honesty . . . is impossible. . . . The Savior was right to throw the merchants out of the temple."[45]

Dana's description of commerce suggests a striking component of the rhetoric of American Fourierism: its connection with the deeply rooted sensibility of New England Congregationalism. Most of the Brook Farmers, including Dana, had been brought up in Congregational orthodoxy, and the community drew its leaders from the ranks of the ministry. Brook Farm had a strong spiritual orientation; its members easily equated the Fourierist utopia with the coming of the

Christian millennium. As Dana wrote in 1844, "In Association, then
. . . the promise of Christianity is to be fulfilled — fulfilled by making the incarnation of the great law of love an actual and universal
fact."[46] The imagery that Dana used in his *Harbinger* articles held
special significance for those readers weaned on Congregationalism, as did the apocalyptic language he used to describe industrial
conditions.

Dana and other American Fourierists often used the angry
rhetoric of the radical workingmen's associations but did not share
their aims or tactics. Instead of encouraging strikes and industrial
conflict, Fourierists proposed to eliminate unproductive labor and
waste. Fourierism called for harmony. According to Dana, the misery
of the producing classes would not be alleviated by stopgap measures
such as wage-and-hour legislation, but rather by "a peaceful and complete reform which shall bring labor and capital into unity."[47] In a
cooperative economy, labor and capital would both benefit from the
increase in productivity that would occur after wasteful competition
was eliminated. In Dana's words, material well-being could be
achieved without sacrifice: "In offering abundance to all, [Associa-
tion] invades the established rights of none. . . . It is pacific and not
destructive."[48]

Fourierism found few adherents among workers in the 1840s;
it was for the most part a movement made up of New England's intellectuals and reformers. Private correspondence among Brook
Farmers and other Associationists suggests one explanation. Like later
generations of progressive reformers and Social Gospelers, Dana and
his friends were all too eager to explain to the workers what their
real interests were. In an 1844 letter to Parke Godwin, Dana described
reforms that would be carefully directed by Fourierist intellectuals,
and he expressed patronizing skepticism of labor's ability to act in
its own best interest:

> The workingmen's movement . . . grows promising for us. I think
> we can hardly fail to have it in our hands. . . . We are in fact
> the only men who can really point out their course for them and
> they can hardly help looking to us for their advisors. . . . We
> preach the guarantees to them without touching much upon the
> means by which they can be attained. That will come in its own

time. Let the people be awakened to a knowledge of their real rights and a demand for them and the work will be very near its accomplishment.[49]

Impassioned? Yes. But radical, no. Though Dana clearly felt a great sympathy for the misery of the "producing classes," the reforms he advocated were modest ones, not incompatible with the existing capitalist structure of the 1840s.

Associationists not only agitated tirelessly for reform in the relations between labor and capital; they also challenged the most sacred of nineteenth-century institutions, the family. At Brook Farm, men and women shared the domestic chores; Charles Dana supervised the community kitchen in addition to his duties at the Brook Farm School. Like other American Fourierists, Dana was careful to distance himself — at least in public — from Fourier's more advanced theories of "passional attractions" in sexual relations. The Brook Farmers were extremely cautious in the appearance they presented to their West Roxbury neighbors, wanting to avoid the charge that they were practicing "free love."[50] Despite their care, hostile newspaper attacks frequently forced them to publish statements like the following, written by Charles Dana: "We wish to have most distinctly understood that we do not adopt either the theories or the statements of Fourier as to the relations of the sexes, nor are we in any way responsible for them. And indeed we might reply at once to all the charges of our opponents, by saying that we simply advance *industrial association.*"[51]

This denial, although useful, was not quite accurate. Some Brook Farmers promoted changes in marital relations by espousing the standard Fourierist view that the "isolated family" was wasteful and a burden to women. In an 1844 lecture, Dana asserted that the family was anything but civilization's greatest triumph. He ventured the unorthodox opinion that nine-tenths of the homes in Christendom were characterized by boredom, unhappiness, and selfishness; and he concluded that the traditional family restricted the individual, binding all in an "endless round of petty cares, and narrow and monotonous duties."[52] In an ideally cooperative society, every branch of industry, art, and science would be open to women. He concluded with the radical statement that only a complete reformation of society would raise the status of women and "render [them] in all respects

. . . independent being[s] and not mere appendage[s] to man."[53]

There is no evidence that Charles Dana followed this advice within his own marriage, which began in New York City on March 6, 1846, when he exchanged vows with Eunice MacDaniel, another Brook Farmer. The MacDaniel family—Eunice, her mother, and her sister Fanny—had moved from Baltimore to join Brook Farm in 1844. Osborne MacDaniel, Eunice MacDaniel Dana's brother, was also an indefatigable Fourierist who later married Maria Dana, Charles Dana's sister.

Dana's marriage to Eunice MacDaniel apparently came as an "unpleasant" surprise to the others at Brook Farm, although the reason for their displeasure is unclear.[54] George Ripley wrote that "the whole matter calls forth some amazement" and called it "an injudicious step on the part of Charles."[55] The Brook Farmers may have believed that Dana was still in love with another woman—Mary Lovering, who, while never having lived at Brook Farm, seems nonetheless to have been closely associated with the community.[56] Dana's own surviving letters do little to clear up the mystery; even the explanation he gave to one of his closest friends left questions unanswered.

> You will be surprised at this and indeed when you left it was entirely unexpected to me. The marriage itself took place in New York before I came home but for obvious reasons connected with E's private movements which then seemed to require her to stay for some time in New York it was entirely private. . . . We desired to make it known when E. came home which was to have been in the summer but as this present crisis in Brook Farm affairs brought her home it is made public of course. These explanations are for *yourself* and not the world in general.[57]

Why such a sudden marriage? Was Eunice MacDaniel Dana pregnant and did she go to New York to have an abortion? The truth may never be known. The Danas' first child, a girl, was born on March 4, 1847, almost exactly a year after the wedding. The parents had difficulty in naming the baby, and six months after the child's birth, the two had still not made a decision. In a jocular note to his friend Hannah Ripley, Dana wrote: "By the way send us a name for the youngster."[58] The Danas ultimately named their daughter Zoe.

In the months before the Danas were married, the Brook Farmers, with justifiable pride in their experiment, had high hopes for the future. Work was progressing well on the "phalanstery," the new building that would signal the community's final transition into a Fourierist "Phalanx." On March 6 (the day of the Danas' wedding) a fire broke out at Brook Farm, and the nearly completed, uninsured building burned to the ground. There was no realistic hope of reconstruction. When the newlyweds returned to the farm almost immediately after their wedding, they found the building in ruins and the inhabitants despondent.[59]

Three groups emerged from the crisis: those who wished, however unrealistically, to rebuild Brook Farm to what it had been before the fire; those who wanted to salvage the farm operations regardless of what happened to Fourierism; and those who believed that the Fourierist movement should be saved at all costs. Dana belonged to the third group, arguing for drastic retrenchment and an end to all extraneous expenses save the *Harbinger* and the Brook Farm School. Many of the Brook Farmers began to lose interest and drifted away. Dana, realizing that the farm would not be rebuilt, accepted a full-time job at Horace Greeley's *New York Tribune*, and moved with his wife to New York City.

Although the Brook Farm experiment had literally gone up in smoke, Fourierism survived, and Dana continued to agitate on its behalf. The *Harbinger* limped along at a financial loss throughout the remainder of 1846. Each of the editors volunteered his time, and Dana pledged to raise $150 for the publication of the fourth volume.[60] Correspondence between the former Brook Farmers continued, and despite the movement's dire financial straits, Dana seemed convinced that the future of Association was still bright.[61]

Almost everyone who has written about Charles Dana has concluded that the breakup of Brook Farm signaled an end to his youthful idealism, thrusting him into the commercialism of New York City, where he developed a cynical and conservative edge. It is true that Charles Dana began to devote more of his energies to the *Tribune*, particularly after February 1847, when Greeley appointed him city editor. While Dana continued to contribute to the *Harbinger*, his articles reflected an increasing interest in political matters. Eventually, his contributions dwindled to a regular column on foreign affairs.

Yet far from signaling an end to his commitment to Association, Dana continued to draw upon Fourierist principles to explain everything from the "barbarous war" in Mexico to the European revolutions of 1848. Dana interpreted the ferment in Europe as a fevered crisis that would bring about a purged and purified new society. In words reminiscent of Brook Farm millennialism, he asked, "What is this power which thus tears away the old fastness and lays new foundations for all human things? It is the power of human destiny. It is that living force which will hereafter cover the now convulsed earth with glory and joy inexpressible."[62]

Nowhere was Dana's idealism more evident than in his joy at the "February Days" of revolution in France. Dana saw the abdication of Louis-Philippe and the proclamation of the Second Republic as a "providential" sign of the progress of history. Congratulating the French for shaking off the "oppressions of arbitrary, irresponsible power," he warned that the experience of the United States had proved that republican institutions alone would not guarantee either the well-being of the people or true social reorganization. Dana praised the French for their experiments in the organization of labor, and he expressed hope that the nations of the world would see in France a model with the face of the future.[63]

With revolution erupting across Europe and radical social experiments taking place in Paris, Charles Dana was more eager than ever to visit the Old World. In the spring of 1848, he made arrangements with the publishers of five newspapers to send him to Europe as a foreign correspondent. A letter from Horace Greeley to *Tribune* publisher Thomas McElrath suggests, however, that not everyone viewed Dana's new assignment with equal enthusiasm. Evidently one of the *Tribune*'s stockholders had pointed out that a salary increase might induce Dana to stay in New York, where his services were considered necessary. Greeley explained to McElrath that such an increase "at an irregular time and on a seeming compulsion" would not only set a bad example but was also unwarranted. He added, "[Dana] may be worth something now, but I don't feel sure of it; and I think, looking at the whole case, his salary is too liberal. . . ." Greeley argued that Dana's trip to Paris was unnecessary because the *Tribune* already had a capable correspondent stationed there.

It may suit Dana well to spend the next winter in Paris, but I don't intend to have him go there if he crosses the ocean. . . . If Dana goes at all, I mean to have him go to Liverpool as Telegraph Agent for the A.P., paying him beside to write us letters and make up foreign news for each steamer. If he does that well, we can afford to pay him well for it, and I shall feel that he is nearly as useful to us as he would be here. Otherwise we shall differ about his compensation in Europe.[64]

Dana ignored Greeley's wishes—a harbinger of the later conflicts that would emerge between the two men. Leaving his wife and fifteen-month-old daughter in New York, Dana set sail for Paris via Southampton on June 10, 1848.[65]

Dana arrived in Europe on June 23, in the midst of the violent "June Days," which began when Parisian workers took to the streets in response to the dissolution of the National Workshops. American reaction to the worker insurrection was universal condemnation; even an article in the Fourierist *Harbinger* distinguished between the Paris uprising, which it called "a vulgar appeal to the lowest prejudices" and the social class cooperation advanced by Fourier.[66] Greeley likewise distanced the *Tribune* from the opinions of its new European correspondent. A note accompanying Dana's first dispatch explained:

However many may condemn [Dana's] undisguised sympathy with the laborers who were driven by their own miseries and the arts of intriguers into so dreadful a rebellion, his lucid analysis of the origin and nature of the conflict must commend itself to the thoughtful appreciation of all. Hitherto the published accounts have united in depicting the insurgents as miscreants and unprovoked assassins. All who reflect must realize that this is not the whole truth—that such a carnage could not have been utterly causeless.[67]

In contrast to Greeley's careful statement, Dana's first letter from Paris, dated June 29, 1848, was warmly on the side of the workingmen. "In a word, they [the workers] revolt against the employers and the institutions by which one makes others the tools of his own profit."[68] Though he condemned acts of violence, Dana told his readers that the true causes of the insurrection were starvation, lack of jobs, and the faint-heartedness of the Republican government. He wrote that Americans should hardly rejoice at the victory of the bourgeoisie, and he defended the vitality of the workers' ideals. In Dana's words, "Socialism is thus not conquered nor obscured in France by this desperate attempt . . . but strengthened."[69]

Dana was in France not only to interpret the struggles of workers in the Second Republic; he was also there as an informal agent of the American Union of Associationists.[70] His letters to the *Harbinger* included sketches of leading French Fourierists, a description of the Phalanstery at Condé, and details of the organization and constitution of a Carpenters' Association. After a visit to the offices of the French Fourierist newspaper, Dana described the journal's independence and "eloquent humanity" and explained its Fourierist division of labor. Clearly believing that he was helping to set an agenda for American Associationists, Dana asked in one letter, "Cannot some hints be gathered for operations in America?"[71]

Although Dana functioned as a transatlantic agent of American Fourierism, the events of 1848 brought subtle challenges to his perception of the world. The violence of the June Days caused him to question the possibility of harmonious relations between labor and capital. The bloody events seem to have forced Dana to the realization that some of Fourier's notions were too fanciful to be taken seriously by the working men and women behind the barricades.[72]

Dana's observation of developments in the National Assembly and on the streets of Paris also led him to distinguish between various manifestations of "socialism," and to explain these differences to his American audience. Dana was torn, able on the one hand to see the irrelevance of the Fourierist ideal of class cooperation, yet unwilling on the other to accept an ideology based on violent class conflict. In letter after letter, he provided lucid analyses of the distinctions between the followers of Fourier, Proudhon, and the "communists," noting with approval that the Fourierists were set apart by their "pacific tendencies" and their "constant defense" of the right to private property. Dana also condeded, however grudgingly, that Proudhon's "extremist" doctrines reflected the force of popular misery and despair among the producing classes.[73] These distinctions marked a sophisticated departure from Dana's earlier observations on the progress of the "spirit of the age," in which all progressive reform moved toward the same glorious end.

The events of 1848 contributed to the unraveling of Dana's view of the historical process. Abandoning the Fourierist rhetoric of harmony, Dana increasingly described events in terms of class struggle. In August 1848, he wrote from Paris: "The duration and painfulness of this struggle must depend on the party that by position, instinct, and interest, resists the movement. The innovation proceeds from the people; the resisting party is the Bourgeoisie; in '89 the innovation proceeded from the Bourgeoisie, and the resisting party was the Aristocracy."[74]

By arguing that class struggle rather than cooperation propelled historical change, Dana showed his awareness of the Marxist ideas that were beginning to circulate throughout Europe in 1848. In fact, Dana may have derived this language directly from Karl Marx. The two met in Cologne in October 1848, while Dana was en route to Berlin.[75] Marx had published the *Communist Manifesto* a few months earlier, first in English, then translated into French. Dana was evidently impressed with the relatively unknown social theorist. Three years later, as managing editor of the *New York Tribune*, he would ask Marx to write for the newspaper.

Despite Dana's flirtation with Marxist notions of the role of class struggle in bringing about social change, the disappointments of 1848 led him and other American intellectuals to retreat from radicalism. When he returned to New York in March 1849, he had both a new commitment to gradual reform and a renewed appreciation of the republican institutions that flourished on American soil. As historian John Higham has suggested, a pall descended on social reformers in the 1850s: "the very idea of revolution lost much of its lustre." To the majority of Americans who had understood revolution as meaning the triumph of republicanism over aristocracy, the threat of socialism evident in the violent class struggles of 1848 brought about a shift in attitude.[76] The role of Charles A. Dana in changing the opinions of American radicals has never been fully recognized. Those who looked to the *New York Tribune* for sympathetic coverage of the European revolutions read the words of Charles Dana, and with him experienced the disappointment of watching revolutionary hopes dashed in the wake of military despotism. The evidence that class relations throughout Europe were marked by bitter struggle brought an end to many of their radical enthusiasms.

Dana's final letter from Paris demonstrated that despite his ardent sympathies with the aspirations of the working class, he would remain safely entrenched within the mainstream of American reform, a believer "in the nobility of work and labor within the relatively safe confines of a romanticized artisan tradition."[77] Abandoning revolutionary rhetoric, Dana began instead to emphasize that producers' cooperatives alone could gradually bring about social change.

> The practical movement of Labor Reform is wider and profounder than is generally imagined. The principle of cooperation is surely, as I believe supplanting that of competition. Here in Paris there are now in operation some fifty associations of workmen, and they are springing up in other places also. . . . In five years the greater part of the labor done in Paris will be so done that the workman will be his own master, and receive the full fruit of his toil. This will settle the question for the whole of Europe.[78]

Charles Dana returned from Europe with a new appreciation of the exceptionalism and social fluidity of the American experience. Unwilling to concede that the revolutions had been complete failures, Dana expressed guarded optimism that despite their lack of positive results, they had "open[ed] wide the way of progress."[79] Hoping that the relations between capital and labor might someday be reformed, he emphasized that republican institutions had been established in several European capitals and that this small beginning might yet lead to great reforms. Concluding that "universal suffrage is the utmost limit of political Democracy," he went home with a new appreciation of American republicanism.[80]

With his wanderlust satisfied, Dana began the new decade by returning to a job at the *New York Tribune*, the newspaper that many considered to be at the apex of urban journalism. Not one to ruminate on the past, Dana faced the future with confidence and enthusiasm. Writing to his old friend Hannah Ripley, Dana reflected that while "there was something providential about our Brook Farm, with all that was glorious and all that was absurd in it," he was happy with his life: "My best ambition has open to it the widest sphere of action and influence, a sphere congenial to my taste, and daily giving new development to my faculties."[81]

Within a few months of his return to New York City, Dana's faculties as well as his ambitions would be tested by what he soon came to regard as a dangerous new threat to the independence and dignity of the producing classes: the attempt by the Southern "Slave Power" to undermine the free-labor traditions of the North.

3

Apprenticeship

The *New York Tribune* and
the Tradition of Free Labor

For a young writer in the 1850s, there was no better place to work
than the *New York Tribune*. With a voice that never wearied in
its calls for reform, the *Tribune* was the most influential newspaper
in America. As nineteenth-century historian James Parton observed,
"The republicanism of the Continent [came] to a focus at the corner
of Nassau and Spruce Streets."[1] *Tribune* editor Horace Greeley — vain,
self-important, and unabashedly partisan — exhorted readers daily with
his own version of the Whig gospel. With a love of humanity that
led him to endorse every nineteenth-century fad from Fourierism to
vegetarianism, Greeley reached a national audience. If anything, the
New York Tribune was more influential outside the metropolis than
within. By the mid-1850s the weekly edition of the *Tribune* had an
estimated circulation of fifty thousand readers, most of them living
far beyond the rivers that bounded Manhattan.[2]

Horace Greeley was erratic, hard to work with, and almost impossible to please, yet he managed to bring together journalists of
stunning ability. *Nation* editor E. L. Godkin did not exaggerate when
he remarked that an appointment to the staff of the *Tribune* gave
a journalist a lifelong "patent of literary nobility."[3] The *Tribune*
housed an assembly of some of America's most luminous intellectuals:
literary editor George Ripley (Dana's mentor at Brook Farm), travel
writer Bayard Taylor (poet and translator of Goethe), essayist George
William Curtis, and Transcendentalist Margaret Fuller — in addition

29

to correspondents Albert Brisbane, Henry C. Carey, and Karl Marx. When Dana returned to New York in February 1849, he had every reason to be confident about the future. He was coming home to what he assumed would be a long career at the *Tribune*, and he could take pride in the reception of his analyses of the revolutions of 1848. Even the frequently peevish Greeley acknowledged the brilliance of Dana's writing when he created a new position for the thirty-year-old correspondent: managing editor, second only to Greeley himself. In 1849 Dana faced the future with self-assurance, knowing he had the talent and skill necessary for great success. Thirteen years later, Greeley would shatter Dana's plans by unceremoniously firing him. In doing so, Greeley would break up what for Dana had been an almost familial community of friends and colleagues, many of whom had been together since the days of Brook Farm. Dana, once ejected from their group, would never again join such a circle. He would prefer being an outsider to running the risk of another betrayal.

Like Greeley, Dana was ambitious, stubborn, vain, and an opportunist. Though Dana understood from the start that he could advance his career by an association with the *Tribune*, the benefits of the arrangement were far from one-sided. Horace Greeley, aware of his own limitations as a manager, recognized the need for a lieutenant able to direct the daily operations of the paper. In Dana he believed he had found his man. Greeley was initially responsible for Dana's meteoric rise in New York journalism, and he had high expectations for his protégé. Not only did Dana share Greeley's lofty ideals; he also had practical skills that promised to make him a valuable asset to the *Tribune* organization. Dana had proven to be an accomplished writer and a good manager; in short, he was an ideal candidate to run the paper during Greeley's frequent absences from New York.

Horace Greeley had entered the world of journalism as a printer, a start far more typical of the eighteenth century than of the nineteenth. Like Dana, Greeley had been born in rural New Hampshire and was separated from his family when his father suffered financial ruin.[4] He became an apprentice to a Vermont newspaper printer in 1826. When that venture collapsed, he made his way to New York City. After several lean years as a journeyman printer, he convinced friends to help him start a low-priced literary magazine called the *New-Yorker*. Unlike Dana, Greeley was entirely self-educated.

The panic of 1837, which ruined the dry goods firm of Staats and Dana, also crippled Greeley's *New-Yorker*. The magazine lasted long enough, however, to attract the attention of Thurlow Weed, editor of the *Albany Evening Journal*. Weed, the powerful boss of the New York state Whigs, in 1838 was looking for a politically compatible editor to run a Whig newspaper. Greeley was perfect for the job. The union of Weed and Greeley led to several short-lived weeklies that promoted Whig candidates. By 1841, Greeley had persuaded his influential friend to help him launch a project of which he had long dreamed — a Whig daily in New York City, to be sold for only a penny a copy. His hopes were realized on April 10, 1841, when the first issue of the *New-York Daily Tribune* was published.[5]

Though known for his idealism, Greeley had enough shrewd Yankee practicality to offer Thomas McElrath a partnership in the *Tribune* and to make him the paper's publisher. McElrath was an accomplished lawyer with newspaper experience. A year earlier, musing on the failure of the *New-Yorker*, Greeley had ruefully admitted to former colleague Henry J. Raymond that in future ventures he would find a reliable business associate who would stick "close to the office" and keep "all the books entirely himself." He added that anyone seeking to establish a newspaper should assume a crusading stance that would secure the support of its readers: "I believe I have erred in making my paper too Catholic. . . . Remember this, and if you ever become an editor, attach yourself to some distinct interest, not noisily, but in such a manner as to secure its support."[6] Greeley would follow his own advice in editing the *Tribune*.

On New Year's Day, 1849, Greeley reorganized his partnership with McElrath into the Tribune Association, a joint-stock company based loosely on the cooperative principles of Fourierism. The trustees divided the stock into one hundred equal shares and sold them under a complex set of provisions designed to enable company employees to become owners of the enterprise.[7] One of the first of the new proprietors was Thomas Rooker, the foreman of the compositors.[8]

By the 1850s the *Tribune* could be described as a Whig newspaper with a progressive outlook. In style, organization, and politics, it was an ideal place for young and reform-minded journalists to work. The *Tribune*'s primary crusade was the Free Soil movement, to which Charles Dana was drawn immediately upon his return from Europe.[9]

Throughout the 1850s, the *New York Tribune* directed its energies against what Ohio Congressman Salmon P. Chase had named the "Slave Power," a group of slaveholders allegedly seeking to establish political supremacy by unconstitutional means. The *Tribune* was the nation's leading proponent of free-labor ideology, which had implications reaching far beyond the single issue of opposition to slavery.[10] According to the *Tribune*, the extension of slavery into the territories would subvert the tradition of free labor that had made the nation strong.[11] Free labor was a powerful symbol that crystallized many Northern fears and hostilities. It connected ideas as potent as the dignity of labor and the Protestant work ethic. Its broad definition of "labor" was similar to that of the Brook Farmers, in that it left out only those nonproducers who lived off the earnings of others. The ultimate goal of the Free Soil movement was economic independence, not class consciousness. At its heart was the small producer, hardworking and suspicious of those who had acquired great wealth.

The economic genius behind the *Tribune's* ideology of free labor was Henry C. Carey, whom Karl Marx once called "the only North American economist of any note."[12] Some of Carey's views echoed those of the Fourierists, particularly his notion of the harmony of interest between labor and capital. Carey argued, for example, that economic growth would equally benefit all classes. Today's labor was tomorrow's capital; capital was "the accumulated labor of past times."[13] Carey believed that a tariff would protect the American worker from the threat of cheap foreign labor, an idea that the founders of the Republican party were to embrace. He envisioned a decentralized society of small towns and family farms similar to that which already existed in the North.

There was irony in the *Tribune's* promotion of Carey's vision of the small, local economy. The *Tribune* was a leading newspaper in the nation's largest metropolitan area. It stood for a strong, centralized government capable of Westward expansion and internal improvements. "Natural gravitation" would, as Dana put it, eventually center the entire Western Hemisphere on the United States. The transcontinental railroad and industrial expansion — aided by a high protective tariff — would bring about this "manifest destiny."[14]

What accounted for Dana's ready acceptance of the *Tribune's* political agenda? The connection between the utopian socialism of the 1840s and the antislavery impulse of Northern radicals of the 1850s is an interesting one.[15] There was an important parallel between what Dana saw as the force of reaction taking hold in Europe and his belief that the Slave Power was threatening the essence of American civilization. Dana had been drawn to Fourierism not only by his emotional affinity for the producing classes but also by his distrust of concentrated power, the vaguely defined "competitive capitalism" that had driven men like his father into bankruptcy and misery. To Dana, the Slave Power was the political expression of a similarly overwhelming economic power.

Yet there was a difference. As a Fourierist, Dana had called for the creation of a new society based on cooperation. In fighting the Slave Power, Dana *defended* a tradition, the free-labor tradition of the North. American democracy, with its supposed absence of classes, fluid social structure, and economic mobility for all, had recently won Dana's respect. In 1850 he believed that the Slave Power was conspiring to undermine the foundation of American society.

While it is Horace Greeley's name that is generally associated with the *New York Tribune* of the 1850s, Charles Dana contributed far more to the newspaper than nearly anyone but *Tribune* writers have recognized. Greeley was frequently absent from New York City, leaving Dana in charge of the paper. The role of being second in command was familiar to the managing editor, who until 1846 had been George Ripley's lieutenant at Brook Farm. Horace Greeley was recognized as the *New York Tribune*'s leading intellectual light, but it was Dana who ran the paper—at least, as *Tribune* writers saw it. As Mayo Hazeltine, who later followed Dana to the *Sun*, concluded: "It is no secret to those familiar with the inner history of that journal that the extraordinary circulation and influence attained by it during the decade preceding the Civil War was largely, if not mainly, due to the development of Mr. Dana's aptitude for his vocation."[16] Beman Brockway, who joined the *Tribune* in 1853, pointed out that few of the paper's readers appreciated how frequently Greeley was absent from New York City, and how much of the paper was the work of Charles A. Dana.[17]

Dana immediately took a commanding role at the *Tribune*. In his first few years as managing editor, he instituted a rotating system of night editors, reorganized the proofreading department, and cut down the number of police reports to "cases of importance." Dana negotiated with Nathaniel Hawthorne, Charles Dickens, and the Brontë sisters for the rights to original works. At Greeley's request, he also assumed the editor's responsibility for firing *Tribune* writers. In 1851, he urged the proprietors to enlarge the paper to the size of the London *Times*, to charge for advertisements by the word rather than by the line, and to purchase new presses that would print both sides of a page at once.[18]

Dana pioneered in journalism's move to delineate between news and advertisements. Because the *Tribune* sold for only two cents a copy, it earned most of its revenue from advertisements rather than from subscriptions. Like the other cheap dailies, it was notorious for mingling advertisements with news and editorial material. In 1852, Dana introduced the first guidelines at the *Tribune* for the separation of paid "puffs and announcements."

> No puffs or announcements of any private establishment or business shall be admitted into the editorial columns of the Tribune except with the word "Advertisement" over the same; from this rule are excepted statements which are news and regular criticisms or editorial comments, which in no case are to be paid for. Speeches and reports which the editor shall judge to be of sufficient *public interest* may be published for pay without the word advertisement[19] (italics in original).

Greeley was so pleased with the work of his deputy that in 1853 he suggested to the trustees that ten dollars a week be taken from his salary and added to Dana's. They unanimously agreed.

The proprietors of the paper had good reason to support Dana. The *Tribune* was making money; every six months the trustees declared dividends of $100 to $225 per share. As Dana proudly noted to Washington correspondent James S. Pike, "[The *Tribune*] is not bad property. Besides, it is growing prodigiously." He concluded casually that even in the unlikely event of Greeley's death, the paper would "go ahead conquering. . . . Nothing is needed but energetic direction and the judicious expenditure of money to put the thing through forever."[20]

Dana's private feelings toward Greeley were complex. Dana was often vexed by the man who had given him a start in big-city journalism. Confident of his own ability to manage the paper, Dana sometimes chafed under Greeley's yoke. He relished the editor-in-chief's frequent absences from New York. In April 1851, he wrote to Pike of Greeley's plans to spend the summer in Europe, adding, "I hope you'll send me up a rocket occasionally during the summer to flash up in our sky and save the country, not to speak of saving me from making a stupid paper. You see it must be *better* than when the old man is home, or they'll say Dana's a failure! Which God forbid!"[21]

One of Dana's more remarkable accomplishments as managing editor of the *New York Tribune* was his acquisition of Karl Marx as a regular correspondent.[22] In 1851, the *Tribune* needed a European correspondent and military analyst. Karl Marx needed money. Exiled in Britain, Marx wrote to Dana inquiring about the possibility of becoming a correspondent for the *Tribune*.[23] Dana responded by suggesting that the political economist write a series of articles about the German revolution of 1848–49. Marx, who had meanwhile become busy with other work, asked Friedrich Engels to write the series. The resulting letters were written in German, translated into English by Dana, and published over Marx's signature. (Evidently Dana never knew who the true author was.) When that series was completed, Marx and Engels continued to send articles to Dana, averaging two each week for the next ten years.[24] Dana paid tribute to the abilities of his correspondent in 1853, prefacing one article with this comment: "Mr. Marx has very decided opinions of his own, with some of which we are far from agreeing; but those who do not read his letters neglect one of the most instructive sources of information on the great questions of current European politics."[25]

The *Tribune* frequently edited Marx's correspondence, either making insertions or printing his work as unsigned editorial leaders. It was rumored in New York that Gen. Winfield Scott was the secret author of Engels's controversial analysis of the Mexican War.[26] Sometimes Marx seems to have enjoyed his anonymity; in 1853 he wrote to Engels, "The *Tribune* is making a great splash with your articles, poor Dana, no doubt, being regarded as their author. . . . For 8 weeks past, Marx-Engels have virtually constituted the editorial staff of the *Tribune*."[27]

Dana was happy at the *New York Tribune*. Along with George Ripley, George William Curtis, Parke Godwin, and Bayard Taylor, he was part of a self-conscious coterie of journalists, poets, and other writers who viewed themselves as a literary intelligentsia. Meeting informally at the Century Club and at the offices of *Putnam's Monthly* and the *New York Tribune*, this circle of writers and critics shared literary news as well as friendly rivalries.[28] For example, in one of his many letters to *Tribune* writer Bayard Taylor, Dana passed along gossip about mutual friends and *Putnam's Monthly*:

> [Richard Henry] Stoddard has a place in the Customs worth $975 a year, which helps out mightily I reckon. He has just published . . . an awfully long poem . . . wherein he confesses in detail all the sins and foibles of his youth, childhood, infancy, not to mention those committed earlier. I told him it was very poor, he thinks it very good. Ripley agrees with me, and so I suspect will the public if it reads. The length however makes it safe. . . . Curtis is sick, brain bothered with over work, so that for two months he has written nothing, and *Putnam's* suffers greatly in consequence. He is much the best writer in that magazine.[29]

As managing editor of the *Tribune*, it was Dana's job to keep up with the paper's more far-flung correspondents. Surviving letters from Dana to Washington correspondent James S. Pike and travel writer Bayard Taylor provide an uncharacteristically rich record of both his work and his domestic life during the 1850s. In the letters, Dana cultivated a tone of jovial manliness, showing both affection for his wife and four children and a persistent concern about money.

The Dana family lived on New York City's Clinton Place (now East Eighth Street, near University Place), in a neighborhood of Greek Revival houses and tree-lined streets. Imposing Colonnade Row, home to the Astors, was a short block away. In the 1850s, the neighborhood at the intersection of Clinton and Astor Places was beginning to change, as old residences gave way to new institutions of commerce and popular entertainment. Charles Dana's home was little more than a mile up Broadway from the *Tribune* office.[30]

Despite the slightly faded elegance of their surroundings, money was often tight for the Danas. During several lean years the family took in boarders. On one occasion Dana borrowed $1,500, a considerable sum for the day, from James Pike. With characteristic humor, Dana wrote, "What sweet and delightful emotions you benevolent old fellows must feel, when you come, with capital in your pouches to relieve the distresses of meritorious and promising young men like myself. Now for the 1st time I appreciate the compensation nature has in reserve for aged persons [to whom] the joys of love and the excitements of active life no longer appeal."[31] When the principal of the loan came due, Dana was unable to pay it and ruefully admitted, "The fact is the bills for last six months' household expenses pile up awfully for a young father of a family."[32]

Despite financial worries, Dana was a cheerful, hearty man, who delighted in his wife and children.[33] Marriage agreed with Dana. His letters were lusty, full of references to the "felicity" of love. He advised Pike, a bachelor, to "take the advice of friendly experience and get married this fall. No use waiting and wasting the vigor of youth."[34] Or, "You know old King David, when he got a little past your age, got a fresh and juicy young girl to warm him up, and I advise you to employ the same method."[35] Dana was quick to admit the perils of an unhappy marriage, however, particularly one as notoriously difficult as Greeley's. "Greeley's wife is going to Europe to spend the winter. She don't like Chappaqua—the children just don't thrive there. Poor old G—isn't he bedeviled!"[36]

In the summers, Eunice MacDaniel Dana and the children escaped the city's stifling heat by vacationing in Westport, Connecticut, "a nice refined place on the very edge of the salt water." Though he missed them, Dana reported: "Health is in all their cheeks and the consumption of butcher's meat is tremendous. The wife too, revives and blooms in that genial and wholesome air." Upon his wife's return he noted casually: "Wife is well, sends her special regards—mighty glad the boarders are gone, she says. The children are in the country . . . E and I sit alone at the table. Quite like a new married couple."[37]

Perhaps most of all, Dana loved his children.

I have been busy going to Westport to see my children—driving them about in old Bradley's one-horse wagon, rowing and sailing with them on the bay and sound, gathering shells on the shore with them, lounging on the grass, gazing in to the sky with the whole tribe about me!

There's no delight like that in a pack of young children. . . . Love is selfish, friendship is exacting, but this other affection gives all and asks nothing. The man who hasn't half a dozen young children about him must have a very mean conception of life.[38]

Dana had evidently reconsidered his Fourierist view that the "petty cares and monotonous duties" of domestic chores and rearing children were a burden to women and that the isolated family inevitably led to boredom and unhappiness.

Of the rest of Charles Dana's family—his father, his sister Maria, and her husband, Fourierist Osborne MacDaniel—almost nothing more is known.[39] Dana did oblige his brother-in-law with a letter of introduction to pro-tariff economist and speculator Henry C. Carey in 1857; evidently Osborne MacDaniel had a financial interest in "the new automatic oven lately introduced at Brooklyn," and he had hopes of establishing it in Philadelphia. Though household appliances were out of Dana's area of expertise, he "cheerfully complied with Mr. MacDaniel's request for an introduction" and relayed his impression "after a careful examination, that the matter is in every way worthy of attention."[40]

In addition to his duties at the *Tribune*, Dana began two major literary projects during the 1850s. He put together the *Household Book of Poetry* in 1857 and followed it one year later with the first volume of what would become the sixteen-volume *American Cyclopaedia*. The *Cyclopaedia* was "a popular dictionary of general knowledge," which Dana edited with George Ripley. The two had long shared the idea of publishing a reference work, and the contributors they gathered made up an impressive array of nineteenth-century intellectuals.[41] One of the writers was Karl Marx, who, with Friedrich Engels, contributed at least eighty-one articles on history and the military.[42]

The series was a great success. Ripley's biographer, Charles Crowe, states that by 1880 the *Cyclopaedia* had sold nearly 1.5 million copies, bringing Dana and Ripley more than $180,000 and assuring them of an annual income of several thousand dollars.[43] Though the panic of 1857 cut into the proceeds from the two works and the income did not in fact materialize until after the war, the intangible rewards of editing the series were immediate. In working on the *Cyclopaedia*, Dana communicated with some of the country's most prestigious men and cemented his reputation as a man of letters.[44]

In the view of *New York Tribune* managing editor Charles A. Dana, a newspaper should be lively. It should expose conspiracies and keep its readers entertained and informed. The columns of James S. Pike, the *Tribune*'s Washington correspondent, certainly met these criteria. Though Pike had such strong antislavery views that he eventually advocated disunion, in 1850 his exposés of the political arm of the Slave Power earned high praise from Dana: "They were great and good, and stirred up the animals, which you as well as I recognize as one of the great ends of life."[45] In 1852 Dana teased Pike, "What a desert void of news you keep at Washington! For goodness sake kick up a row of some sort. Fight a duel, defraud the treasury . . . get Black Dan [Webster] drunk, or commit some other excess that will make a stir."[46]

Unlike the cautious Horace Greeley, Dana liked to "stir up the animals." In the mid-1850s, Dana and Greeley came to have sharp differences, fueled by what Greeley viewed as Dana's impetuous actions during the senior editor's absences from New York. Significantly, the tensions between Dana and Greeley did not stem from fundamental political disagreement, rather from differences in style and temperament. In addition, Greeley's insatiable lust for political office contributed to the mounting tension between the two men. Understanding the source of this friction requires a brief look at the formation of the Republican party, particularly in its relation to the *New York Tribune*.[47]

The Kansas-Nebraska Act of 1854 struck at the heart of the Free Soil program. It repealed the provision of the 1820 Missouri Compromise that had restricted slavery north of 36°30'. Greeley believed that the legislation, introduced by Illinois Senator Stephen A. Douglas, was a gigantic swindle perpetrated by the Slave Power. According to historian Jeter Allen Isely, Greeley "jettisoned other reforms in which he was interested, marched with screaming headlines against the apologists for human bondage, and helped inaugurate the Republican party."[48] Greeley urged mass protest meetings in February and March, and he hoped to organize an antislavery, anti-rum movement that might ultimately sweep him into the governor's office.[49]

Greeley's antislavery agitation raised a host of problems for the *Tribune.* The editor's "partnership" with Thurlow Weed had been based on maintaining the New York state Whig organization, not on opposing the extension of slavery. Though Weed and U.S. Senator William Seward eventually convinced Greeley that the state's best interest lay in returning Seward to the Senate, the decision did not rest easily with the editor. Greeley saw himself as representing a national constituency and believed he was being held back by provincial Albany Whigs. Meanwhile, the rival *New York Times,* founded by Henry J. Raymond in 1851, threatened to usurp Greeley's place within the Whig machine.

The man who received the Whig gubernatorial nomination that Greeley coveted in 1854 was Myron Clark, who was also the candidate of the Know-Nothing nativist American party. Even more galling to Greeley, the nominee for lieutenant governor was *Times* founder and editor Henry J. Raymond. Clark's election revealed the chaotic state of New York politics, as the nativists emerged big winners from the breakdown of the old party system. With his political ambitions thwarted by the Whigs, Greeley would become an ardent supporter of the nascent Republican party, a move that would have profound implications for the *New York Tribune.*

The *Tribune* began to lose money as a result of its opposition to the Kansas-Nebraska Act. Advertisers left the paper for the more conservative *New York Times.* With production costs exceeding subscription and advertising revenue, the stockholders pressured Greeley to raise the price to three cents per copy. At the proprietors' meeting in June 1854, Greeley gave notice that he was planning salary reductions. The stockholders voted to send Dana to Henry J. Raymond of the *Times* and James Gordon Bennett of the *Herald* with a proposal for a simultaneous price increase to three cents.[50] The *Times* proprietors, as well as those of the *Herald,* favored the increase. According to Dana, it was Raymond who scuttled the plan.[51]

Though the *Tribune* stockholders voted on August 24 to reduce the size of the paper by taking two ems from each column, it continued to lose money. Dana explained to Pike, "The enormous consumption of paper for the weekly has cost some $15,000 more than the entire receipts."[52]

Dana and Pike were more politically radical than Greeley, who, as if suddenly aware of the consequences of his inflammatory rhetoric, feared further alienating the South. These differences became an issue between the two men in 1855, when Greeley went to Washington to promote Nathaniel Banks as a candidate for Speaker of the U.S. House of Representatives. Greeley believed that only a conservative approach would bring Democrats and nativist Know-Nothings into the Republican fold. Nathaniel Banks seemed a perfect candidate: he was an antislavery Know-Nothing and a former Democrat.[53] Greeley hoped that electing Banks would build up Republican strength in the House and thereby pressure President Franklin Pierce into protecting free-state settlers in the Kansas and Nebraska territories. During the struggle to elect a Speaker, which took nine weeks and 132 ballots, Dana had charge of the newspaper.

Greeley was not happy with Dana's management of the *Tribune* during his absence from New York City in the winter of 1855–56. He urged Dana "not to allow anything to get in which seems impelled by hatred of the South."[54] Greeley was provoked to exasperation by Dana's apparent lack of judgment in attacking congressmen with whom he was on friendly terms. On February 3 he pleaded, "Please don't attack any other member of Congress. . . . Pray allow me to judge with regard to what is passing under my own eyes and not under yours."[55] He accused Dana of costing Banks an easy election and threatened: "I write once more to entreat that I may be allowed to conduct the *Tribune* with reference to the mile that stretches either way from Pennsylvania Avenue. It is but a small space, and you have all the world besides. . . . If you are not willing to leave me entire control with reference to this city, both men and measures, I ask you to call the proprietors together and have me discharged."[56]

Were Greeley's complaints justified? Dana indeed took liberties with Greeley's orders, once printing details of a sensational divorce case rather than two congressional speeches that Greeley considered vital.[57] Greeley believed that Dana had usurped his authority during the winter of 1855–56 and that Dana's editorials had contributed to Southerners' growing hatred of the *Tribune*. According to Greeley, Dana was overconfident and sometimes careless. He warned Indiana Republican Schuyler Colfax, "I wish you would keep Dana advised in my absence. . . . He is shrewd, but green in politics, and don't keep his eye close enough to the field. . . . There will be occurrences that need to be seized on the instant, and Dana may be at Appleton's [bookstore] or the Opera when he should be studying dispatches."[58]

One of Dana's colleagues later found evidence of the managing editor's "sly humor" at Greeley's expense in the series of letters between Washington and New York. As he pointed out, "There is no reason to believe that Dana was doing all these things which irritated Greeley so intensely without full knowledge of what they portended."[59] Thus in the winter of 1855–56, Dana refused to defer to Greeley whenever he questioned the judgment of the senior editor. One thing was becoming clear: Charles A. Dana did not make a good subordinate.

While Dana was sniping at Greeley, the *Tribune*'s partisanship was growing. Charles Dana, so meticulous about separating news from advertisements, was more than willing to use the *Tribune* to raise funds for politics and armaments. The paper's vehement opposition to popular sovereignty and its reports of violence in "bleeding Kansas" have since suggested to one historian that "[Greeley's] staff had no concern for accuracy with regard to the Kansas of 1856."[60] Beyond provocative editorials, the *Tribune* also provided material assistance to the free-state settlers. In June the trustees voted unanimously to subscribe $1,000 each to "the general movement for Free Kansas" and the Republican National Committee.[61] Dana explained to Pike, "Money is now being raised for arms to Kansas. Boston has furnished $5,500 for Sharp's rifles, and Colt's revolvers, and $2,500 is wanted here. I suppose I may put you down for $50 at least. The guns have gone forward, and one of these days we shall certainly have a good fight there."[62]

The 1860 Republican presidential nominating convention found Greeley and Dana united in their opposition to William Seward. Dana believed that Seward was too radical to win the general election in November; as early as September 1859, he had written to Pike, "There can be no question that if we are to be beaten, Seward is the best man to run."[63] Greeley feared that Seward's nomination would block the drive to make Republicanism a national movement. This fear, coupled with a personal grudge against the New York senator, led Greeley to support Edward Bates, a conservative old-line Whig from Missouri.

Dana was not present in Chicago at the 1860 Republican convention, where the battle between Seward and Bates led to the surprise swing to compromise candidate Abraham Lincoln. He quickly became a Lincoln supporter, however, lecturing to local "Wide-Awake Clubs" in favor of the Republican candidate. He observed to Henry C. Carey, "It is certain to my judgment that if S. had been nominated, we should have been beaten to nothing."[64]

The *Tribune* printed a number of special election supplements during the campaign, a lavish expenditure that led some of the trustees to call a special meeting to complain of the cost.[65] In an unusual joint show of force, Dana and Greeley argued that publishing up-to-the-minute reports was the most important duty of the *Tribune*. Dana contended that if the paper were to retain its status as one of the nation's leading journals, "we must print all the news whether it requires a supplement once a month, or once, twice, or thrice a week." Greeley told the trustees that perhaps the *Tribune* "did not print supplements enough." The meeting ended with the trustees voting to adopt Dana's resolution that supplements should be published whenever the editors deemed necessary.

Shortly after Lincoln's election, the *Tribune*'s trustees anticipated that many of New York"s Southern sympathizers would blame Greeley's paper for Lincoln's victory—and what was fast becoming the threat of war. On December 27, one week after South Carolina seceded from the Union, the trustees appointed a committee to strengthen the door of the Tribune press room "in such a manner . . . that [it] would withstand sudden mob violence."[66]

Until the secession of South Carolina, Dana and Greeley had disagreed less over political issues than over matters of temperament and style. As Dana would later point out, for years he had swallowed his own ambition out of deference to Greeley, once turning down an attractive offer of "very liberal terms" from a group intending to establish a newspaper outside of the city, because, as he put it, "I don't think I could leave New York. The *Tribune* has made me, and to it I belong."[67] The secession crisis made it impossible for the two men to reconcile their views. After years of urging the containment of slavery, Greeley lost his nerve; he believed that compromise was still possible even as the South was threatening to secede. As Dana saw no room for compromise, a collision was inevitable.

When Greeley left New York on his annual winter lecture tour in January 1861, he still thought there were a large number of nonslaveholding Republican sympathizers in the South. He furthermore accepted the legality of peaceable secession, provided that it was duly voted upon in a constitutional convention. Dana, however, like most Republicans, believed that secession was unconstitutional and would lead to war. While Greeley was out of town, Dana raised the banner: "No Compromise! No concessions to traitors! The Constitution as it is!"[68]

Significantly, when Greeley returned from his winter lecture tour he neither removed Dana's controversial banner from the *Tribune's* masthead nor reversed the paper's belligerent policy toward the South. In fact, historian Jeter Allen Isely has concluded that by the end of February, Dana's "optimistic strategic outlook" had convinced Greeley that the national government must display a show of force.[69]

On April 12, 1861, when the Palmetto Guard of South Carolina opened fire on Fort Sumter, Greeley deferred to what he believed was his managing editor's superior understanding of military affairs.[70] It was at Dana's urging that on June 26, 1861, the *Tribune* proclaimed:

THE NATION'S WAR-CRY
Forward to Richmond! Forward to Richmond!
The Rebel Congress must not be allowed to meet
there on the 20th of July!
BY THAT DATE THE
PLACE MUST BE HELD BY THE NATIONAL ARMY![71]

The *Tribune* was blamed when the untrained Union troops were soundly defeated at the disastrous battle of Bull Run, and *Tribune* staffers believed that Horace Greeley held Dana responsible.[72] Even the usually confident managing editor admitted that he'd been overwhelmed with "work and trouble," and that "Bull Run has knocked the Republican party pretty badly."[73]

Following this episode, Dana's relationship with Greeley deteriorated rapidly, despite his later claim that their relations remained as "cordial as ever" during the winter of 1861–62. In February, Greeley lost his temper at Dana's "infernal carelessness" in letting an "absurd paragraph" about Lincoln's inaccessibility slip into the paper.[74] Then, on March 27, 1862, Greeley exploded. According to Dana's version of the events, Greeley gave the stockholders notice that one or the other of them must leave the paper.[75] Dana resigned. He later wrote to Pike that he was as "astounded" as if he had been told that he was "to be shot for treason."[76]

Despite the protest of Dana's friend George Ripley, the stockholders voted on March 28 to accept the resignation.[77] Dana later wrote that he had run into Greeley at the *Tribune* office on the night of his resignation. The editor took "special pains" to speak with him "in a manner even more confidential [than usual]" on everything other than what had just happened.[78] The next morning Greeley called a meeting of the trustees and, with characteristic evasiveness, denied that he had set afoot the movement to oust Dana. Indeed, Greeley claimed the whole thing was a "damned lie," and sent Dana word that he wished him to remain in the office as an editorial writer. When Dana asked one of the trustees what to make of these new developments, he was told that Greeley's offer to keep him on at the *Tribune* had been made in good faith. The trustee added that there was "no doubt," however, that Greeley "is much better pleased that you did not [accept]."[79]

Dana was shocked and angry at what he referred to as his "expulsion" from the *Tribune*. In the words of newly appointed managing editor Sydney Gay, "[Dana] avoids us all, is very dark, wounded, and is very bitter in his complaints."[80] Dana believed he had been betrayed by his friends and that the real cause was Greeley's vanity. He explained to Pike, "Mr. Greeley was weary of seeing letters sent to me by leading men, Senators, Congressmen, Cabinet ministers, etc. . . . He was weary also of seeing other papers speak of me as an essential part of the *Tribune*."[81] Dana repeated this version of the events to Carey, adding bitterly that no complaint had ever been made of his conduct that was not "frivolous."

My own impression is that Mr. Greeley was really the prompter of the secret intrigue to turn his confidential partner and nearest friend out of a business which he had spent the fifteen best years of his life in building up. . . . His reason I cannot fathom. I had rendered him great services and had never stood in his way. Political advancement for myself I had always refused, so as not to interfere with his ambition. . . . I dare say too he was weary of having it supposed that anybody but himself could be necessary to the *Tribune.*[82]

Although Dana was probably correct in claiming that his growing reputation posed a threat to Greeley's vanity, there was a disturbing lack of self-knowledge in this analysis. Dana had been ignoring Greeley's orders since 1848, when he had sailed for Paris despite his editor's opposition. He had been deliberately insubordinate as Greeley's managing editor. He had printed articles that Greeley opposed. He had promoted policies in the *Tribune* that Greeley had believed would lead to war. What Dana interpreted as betrayal, the stockholders viewed as a sound business decision. Regardless of their personal feelings for Dana, the paper could have only one editor. In the words of Sydney Gay, Dana left the stockholders with little choice but to let him go. "The action here was unanimous, excepting Mr. Ripley. . . . The rest of us are sincerely sorry for Mr. Dana, but while we regret the necessity, saw that it was imperative inasmuch as Dana is Dana, and Greeley, Greeley. Even if it were possible to change the former's will, it was clearly impossible to bestow upon him the gift of *judgement.*"[83]

As wounded as Dana felt, he must have found a certain satisfaction in selling his ten shares of *Tribune* stock, which according to Gay, "flooded the market" and threatened to have repercussions throughout the newspaper industry.[84] Once buyers were found, Robert Bonner of the *New York Ledger* wrote to Greeley, "I am glad that Mr. Dana's stock has been taken [so promptly]. . . . I was not exactly *anxious* about the sale . . . still I think it would have had a bad effect if it had been raised about that Dana could not sell his stock, after leaving the paper."[85] Bonner had his own interest in the sale. He had lent money to two or three other stockholders with *Tribune* certificates as collateral.

Dana learned two galling lessons from his experiences at the *New York Tribune.* In his eyes, his "expulsion" was above all a betrayal by friends, a violation of trust that reaffirmed his view of himself as an outsider. As he explained in a frosty letter to Bayard Taylor (who had declined to vote against accepting his resignation), "I have my own opinion of the conduct of some persons in the concern whom I loved as friends for years and whom for years I zealously served."[86] Moreover, Dana's resignation marked the end of his apprenticeship in the newspaper business and forced him to recognize that in the future he would have to be his own boss. He wrote, "I . . . shall [never] go back to the *Tribune* in any manner. I have sold all my interest . . . and shall be slow to connect myself again with any establishment where there are twenty masters."[87]

When Dana found another newspaper job, it would indeed be as his own "master"; in 1865 he would be named editor in chief of the *Chicago Republican*. But in 1862, the country was at war, and Dana would spend the next three years doing an entirely different kind of reporting. In an interlude from journalism, Dana would serve as the assistant secretary of war, acting as the eyes and ears of the president of the United States.

4

Interlude

The Civil War

Dana . . . always looked upon his services near [Grant, Sherman, and MacPherson] with unalloyed satisfaction, and never failed to congratulate himself upon the good-fortune that had brought him into such close and cordial relations with them. He was far from being an emotional man, but he made no effort to conceal the feelings of affection and respect with which he looked upon these splendid soldiers.[1]

— James Harrison Wilson,
Life of Charles A. Dana

The Civil War came at a fortunate time for Charles A. Dana. Out of a job and uncertain about the future, Dana was forty-three years old in 1862. No longer young, he had reached the age at which most men are well settled into careers. Suddenly unemployed, and with a wife and four children to support, he needed to make fast decisions about the future. The Civil War was an interlude in Dana's newspaper career, one that allowed him to postpone making such decisions. At the same time, the war gave him the chance to come into his own as a major player on the national stage: as a mediator between Ulysses S. Grant and Abraham Lincoln.

Since Lincoln's inauguration in 1861, Dana had worked at establishing close ties with key members of the president's cabinet. Perhaps he suspected that a break with Greeley was inevitable and was hedging his bets in the event that he might soon be looking for another job. Among his correspondents were radical Republican Salmon P. Chase, now secretary of the treasury; Secretary of State William Seward; and War Democrat Edwin Stanton, who in January 1862 had replaced Simon Cameron as secretary of war.[2] Any one of these men was in a position to offer lucrative wartime jobs.

After his resignation from the *New York Tribune*, Dana gave only desultory consideration to finding another job in journalism. According to biographer James Harrison Wilson, Secretary of War Stanton asked Dana to enter the service of the War Department "at once" upon the announcement of his resignation, and Dana accepted. He agreed despite "intimations" from the secretary of state that a diplomatic position would be forthcoming and a firm offer from Treasury Secretary Chase.[3] Evidently, Dana's strategy of keeping his options open had paid off.

In the spring of 1862, the war was not going well for the Union. With decisive victory still elusive in the year since the rout at Bull Run, it had become clear that the rebellion would not be put down by one swift battle. In Washington, Lincoln's congressional rivals hammered the administration with charges of incompetence and corruption. It was these accusations of venality that led Secretary of War Edwin Stanton to appoint Charles A. Dana to a special commission "to examine and report upon all unsettled claims against the War Department at Cairo, Illinois."[4]

Cairo was the supply depot for the Union Army quartermaster; munitions and supplies intended to outfit troops stationed in Missouri, Kentucky, and elsewhere along the Mississippi were dispersed from the river town. Dana was sent to Cairo to find out whether army contractors were cheating the U.S. government. The investigators reported that they found little evidence of corruption. By the time Dana returned to New York City one and one-half months later, he had taken advantage of the opportunity to meet every important army commander stationed along the banks of the Mississippi. Of these men, the most intriguing was the recent hero of Fort Donelson and Shiloh, Maj. Gen. Ulysses S. Grant.

Dana met Grant on July 4, 1862, during a celebration in Memphis. At first impression, he found the general "pleasant . . . a man of simple manners, straightforward, cordial, and unpretending."[5] Dana realized, however, that despite his recent victories, Grant was still "under a cloud."[6] Though a West Point graduate of the class of 1843, Grant had done little to distinguish himself. After credible service in the Mexican War, a peacetime stint on the Pacific coast had ended in disaster for him. Boredom, loneliness, and heavy drinking had led Grant to resign his commission in 1854, possibly to avoid a court-martial. Even after his desperately needed victory at Shiloh — notable for recording more casualties in two days than the battles of all previous American wars combined — Grant was cursed with powerful enemies and had few influential friends. Worse, he seemed unable to dispel his reputation as a hard-drinking mediocrity.

Dana saw a very different kind of person in Ulysses S. Grant. The very qualities on which Dana remarked to Stanton — simplicity, directness, and lack of pretense — stood in marked contrast to the way one might describe the mercurial, vain, and occasionally treacherous Horace Greeley. Whereas Greeley was visionary, Grant was a man of action. Greeley was an idealistic crusader; Grant, nothing if not pragmatic. In short, Dana was weary of men who were brilliant but unreliable. Greeley's fiery oratory had inflamed the crisis of the 1850s into a war for which he was not prepared. In 1862 Grant was known for his brevity and for a stolid willingness to live with the consequences of other men's words.

In September 1862, Dana's eagerness and ambition almost proved to be his undoing when he received word that Stanton was going to offer him the post of assistant secretary of war. With remarkable lack of discretion, Dana told a friend of the appointment before it was formally made. When the story appeared in the New York City newspapers the following morning, Stanton was forced to withdraw the offer.[7]

Relations between the two men remained cordial, however. Still postponing major career decisions, Dana sought to make some quick money in commerce. When Dana informed Stanton of his intention to trade in cotton between Union and Rebel lines, the secretary agreed to write letters of introduction to Union generals along the Mississippi.

Once again Dana had thrust himself into controversy. There were fortunes to be made in selling much-needed Confederate cotton to

Northern manufacturers, and Dana joined Roscoe Conkling in one such venture. Meanwhile, General Grant, struggling with the Mississippi campaign, lashed out at merchants so intent on getting to the cash crop that they refused to keep to the rear of the army. In December Grant ordered that all speculators be thrown out of the Department of the Mississippi. Among these speculators was Charles A. Dana.

Grant's biographer, William S. McFeely, has called Dana "a convert to rectitude" for his actions shortly after Grant issued his order. Dana wired Stanton of "the mania of sudden fortunes made in cotton" and recommended that all commercial intercourse with the Rebels be prohibited. He explained, "My pecuniary interest is in the continuance of the present state of things, for while it lasts there are occasional opportunities of profit to be made by a daring operator; but I should be false to my duty did I, on that account, fail to implore you to put an end to an evil so enormous, so insidious, and so full of peril to the country."[8]

Dana's disingenuous cable was effective as tangible proof of his value to the War Department. Shortly thereafter, Secretary Stanton gave Dana another job, this time appointing him special commissioner to investigate the pay service in the Western Armies.

Dana's new title was misleading. Stanton was in fact sending him to Vicksburg, secretly charged with the task of spying on General Grant and reporting on his conduct to Abraham Lincoln. The president and his secretary of war were still not entirely convinced of the general's steadiness.

Before Dana left for the western front, he wrote to James S. Pike that while he had "not made much money" by his travels of the preceding year, he was still better off financially than if he had stayed at the *Tribune*. Of that paper and its editor, Dana added with obvious satisfaction:

> The paper has lost greatly in character and prestige during the last few months by Horace's demagoguery first in favor of mediation and then in favor of abandoning the war and making peace. . . . At Washington especially and among the members of Congress his consideration has sunk very low, while at home the proprietors of the paper have come very near making a serious row

with him. They have obliged him to change his course and have come to the conclusion that he is a mighty unsafe man, liable at any moment to dash off into some foolish and fatal eccentricity.[9]

Dana was delighted with his new duties as special commissioner for the War Department. Energetic, athletic, and a fine horseman, he yearned to be in the thick of the war. While his poor eyesight had ruled out the possibility of active military duty, his new job put him at the heart of the war effort.

Dana joined General Grant in Mississippi in April 1863. According to topographical engineer (and future Dana biographer) Brig. Gen. James Harrison Wilson, "there was never the least misunderstanding" about Dana's supposedly secret mission. Grant's staff members were unusually close. Wilson recalled that he and John Rawlins, Grant's chief of staff, agreed "it would be better for all concerned" should Dana "be taken into complete confidence . . . without any reservation whatsoever." The general, probably making a virtue of necessity, received Stanton's special emissary "cordially."[10] Grant's aides' instincts in giving Dana free access to the general were good. Almost immediately, according to Grant"s biographer, William S. McFeely, "the spy became one of Grant's strongest advocates."[11]

What turned Dana, ostensibly the agent of the secretary of war, into an unbridled champion of Ulysses S. Grant? As was typically the case with Dana, the motive was opportunism mixed with genuine admiration. Dana was obviously impressed with the general's quiet confidence. Beyond that, he was energized by the excitement of war, the company of other men, and the break with domesticity. It is impossible to read either Dana's cables to Stanton or his personal correspondence without becoming convinced of Dana's sincerity.

Yet politics were never far from Dana's mind. The erstwhile newspaperman had learned an important lesson from Horace Greeley, who had profited well from his ties with the Whig "firm" of New York State politicians William Seward and Thurlow Weed. In 1863, Dana used the strategy that Greeley had elevated to an art: he cultivated Grant in hopes of furthering his own career.

The collaboration between the loquacious journalist and the taciturn general was an odd one, but it worked. Though Dana supported Ulysses S. Grant throughout the war, he was most critical to the general's success during the costly and drawn-out siege at Vicksburg.

Grant's campaign to take Vicksburg was vital to the war effort. By controlling the tiny river town, the Confederates controlled the Mississippi. One unexpected obstacle Grant faced was the rivalry of Gen. John McClernand, an Illinois War Democrat and friend of the president who had raised his own army of volunteers to take the heavily fortified town. Dana quickly sized up the situation, and on April 25, he informed Stanton of the corruption and "apparent confusion" among the staff at McClernand's headquarters. On May 23, he added that, in his own opinion, "McClernand has not the qualities necessary for a good commander, even of a regiment."[12]

According to James Harrison Wilson, Dana's support of Grant was effective; he "exercised a controlling influence in preparing the mind of the Secretary of War" for the removal of McClernand.[13] In response to Dana's cable, Stanton told his assistant to inform Grant that he had "full and absolute authority to enforce his own commands, and to remove any person who, by ignorance, inaction, or any cause, interferes with or delays his operations."[14] Grant's receipt of the dispatch "sealed the friendship of Dana and Grant."[15] When Grant relieved General McClernand of his command of the Thirteenth Army Corps in June, Dana's cable to Stanton defended the action.[16] The spy was no longer a bit player; he was now a powerful force mediating between Grant and the secretary of war.

In addition to reporting on the generals, Dana wrote candidly of other controversies, among them Grant's use of black troops. Most Americans—including many abolitionists—doubted that black men would make good soldiers, but Dana thought otherwise. On June 22, after a battle at Milliken's Bend in which more than half the casualties were black, he pointed out to Stanton that the bravery of the black soldiers had "revolutionized" the army. He concluded that even "prominent officers, who used in private to sneer at the idea, are now heartily in favor of it."[17]

The siege of Vicksburg ended with a Union victory on July 4, 1863. Shortly thereafter, U.S. troops captured Port Hudson, and the Confederacy was cut in two. At some time during the last few days of the siege, Edwin Stanton named Charles A. Dana assistant secretary of war. Later that summer Dana wrote to James S. Pike of what he called Grant's "very great chances" of becoming president. He reasoned: "The elements of popularity in his case are much like those of old Zack [Taylor] 16 years ago, and Grant is more of a man than that ancient hero."[18]

Dana loved being in the field. After the fall of Vicksburg he went home to New York City and, with typical exuberance, wrote to James S. Pike (then American minister to Holland), "Campaigning I found very agreeable and very wholesome, and came back from my 3 months experience in tents and on horseback in much better health than I went."[19]

Dana mentioned that New York City's draft riots of the summer had added nothing to the value of his Clinton Place home, which he was still trying to sell. The rioters had attacked the *New York Tribune* building, and Dana wrote generously that Horace Greeley had "behaved with great coolness and courage." Of a chance meeting with Greeley on lower Broadway, he wrote, "Horace I never want to see. I have met him once since our explosion, and then he looked to the other edge of the sidewalk. His idea of settling our difficulties . . . I will never forgive him for."[20]

Dana also sent to Pike photographs of his daughters, noting affectionately that "none of them is very like the original." Referring to Pike's newly luxurious life in Europe, he concluded, "Boast as you will of [your] yachting . . . there can't be any more fun in it than I find in a 15 ft sailboat full of children."[21]

When Dana returned to Washington to take up his duties as assistant secretary of war, there was considerable curiosity about Grant, with much of the interest centering on his drinking habits. Though Dana often damned other officers as "drunk and disorderly," he made no such criticisms of Grant. As he wrote to Illinois Senator Elihu Washburne, "My impressions concerning Grant do not differ from yours. I tell everybody that he is the most modest, the most disinterested, and the most honest man I have ever known. I have met hundreds of prominent and influential men to whom I have said that and other things in the same direction. To the question they all ask, 'Doesn't he drink?' I have been able from my own knowledge, to give a decided negative."[22]

This was a lie. Dana had first-hand knowledge of the general's drunkenness at Vicksburg.[23] The episode had occurred on the Yazoo River, on the steamer *Diligent*, when Grant and his staff were on an inspection tour to Satartia, Mississippi. Dana was on board the boat, as was *Chicago Times* reporter Sylvanus Cadwallader. According to Cadwallader's version of the story, when two officers refused to put the drunken general to bed, he did the job himself. Dana's own *Recollections of the Civil War* euphemistically states that "Grant was ill and went to bed soon after he started."[24]

Later that night, naval officers on a U.S. gunboat warned the *Diligent* that it was unsafe to proceed. The general had to be notified, as the naval officers wanted him to decide whether to turn back. According to Dana, however, Grant was "too sick" and said, "I will leave it with you." Dana ordered the boat turned back to Haynes's Bluff.

At breakfast the next morning, Grant, "fresh as a rose," said, "Well, Mr. Dana, I suppose we are at Satartia now." Dana had to tell him no, that they were actually twenty-five miles to the southwest, at Haynes's Bluff. Grant continued drinking the next day and almost injured himself during a reckless ride on a horse named Kangaroo. James Harrison Wilson, who was also present, makes cryptic reference to the incident in his biography of Dana, concluding, "Without repeating details, the subject may be dismissed with the statement that it completed Dana's knowledge of Grant's character and habits from actual observation in a way which no man could gainsay."[25] Wilson was more direct in his pocket diary, noting on June 7, 1863, "Genl. G. intoxicated."[26]

When the episode was over, Cadwallader decided not to file the story, probably because — like Dana — he enjoyed being on intimate terms with the general and his staff. Dana, perhaps wisely, chose to regard the general's occasional drunkenness as having little bearing on his worth as either a soldier or a leader of men. To Secretary of War Stanton he dismissed reports of Grant's alcoholism by writing, "Whenever he commits the folly of tasting liquor, Rawlins can be counted on to stop him."[27] Dana had shown Grant and his men that he, too, could be relied upon.

After spending one month in Washington, D.C., Dana was ordered by Stanton to Chattanooga to investigate Gen. William S. Rosecrans's command of the Army of the Tennessee in September 1863. Finding evidence of disorder and negligence, Dana indicated to the secretary that he agreed with those observers who doubted General

Rosecrans's abilities. He urged that George H. Thomas, the hero of Chickamauga, replace Rosecrans as commander of the Army of the Cumberland, and that the Western armies be consolidated and placed under a single command. On September 27, he suggested, "If it be decided to change the chief commander also I would take the liberty of suggesting . . . some Western General of high rank and prestige . . . Grant for instance."[28]

Perhaps as a result of Dana's urging, Ulysses S. Grant arrived at Chattanooga on October 21, 1863, newly appointed commander of the Military Division of the Mississippi. With relish the assistant secretary of war notified Stanton: "The change in command is received with satisfaction by all intelligent officers so far as I can ascertain. . . . The change at headquarters here is already strikingly perceptible — order prevails instead of universal chaos."[29]

One month later, Grant's troops won at Missionary Ridge, thereby securing Chattanooga and delivering the mountains of eastern Tennessee into Union hands. Shortly thereafter, Ulysses S. Grant was promoted to lieutenant general, the first U.S. officer since George Washington to hold that honor.

After Grant's victories in Tennessee, Dana made a brief trip to New York City, where he managed to rent his Clinton Place home before returning to Washington, D.C. He wrote to Pike: "The family are all in Westport. The house in Clinton Place has been leased to a Scotch pork packer. There is some doubt as to whether he will be agreeable to the aristocratic society of the neighborhood, but as the rent is safe, I will let the aristocracy take care of themselves."[30]

Dana spent the next five months in Washington, untangling the red tape of army supply contracts. On May 6, 1864, shortly after the battle of the Wilderness, the president of the United States personally asked the assistant secretary of war to join Grant in Culpeper, Virginia. Feeling out of touch with the general, who was less than seventy miles away, Lincoln wanted details of what would become the final campaign against Gen. Robert E. Lee's Army of Northern Virginia.

This new liaison with the president of the United States was of no small consequence to the ambitious Charles A. Dana. For years afterwards, he liked to tell the story of Lincoln's particular concern for the safety of his assistant secretary of war. Dana recalled how, just as he was to board the Maryland Avenue train from Washington to Alexandria, Virginia, he received word by special messenger that the president wished to see him at the War Department. According to Dana, the president said he had second thoughts about sending Dana to the Wilderness.

> "You can't tell," continued the President, "just where Lee is or what he is doing, and Jeb Stuart is rampaging around pretty lively in between the Rappahannock and the Rapidan. It's a considerable risk, and I don't like to expose you to it."
>
> "Mr. President," I said, "I have a cavalry guard ready and a good horse myself. If we are attacked, we probably will be strong enough to fight. If we are not strong enough to fight, and it comes to the worst, we are equipped to run. It's getting late, and I want to get down to the Rappahannock by daylight. I think I'll start."
>
> "Well, now, Dana," said the President, with a little twinkle in his eyes, "if you feel that way, I rather wish you would. Good night, and God bless you."[31]

This story — perhaps embellished — seems to show the friendly, personal nature of Dana's relationship with the president. He would often repeat it.

For the next year, Dana moved back and forth between Washington, D.C., and Grant's headquarters, as the weakening Confederate forces held on. Finally, on April 3, 1865, Stanton informed Dana that Richmond had surrendered. He ordered Dana to join Grant at City Point, Virginia, from where he could report on the evacuation of the Confederate capital. Even the usually unperturbable assistant secretary of war was shocked by the devastation of the city and the misery of its starving inhabitants. After Lee's surrender, Dana alluded to the painful process of bringing the former Confederates back into the Union, reporting that "among the men there is no sentiment but submission to the power of the nation, and a returning hope that their individual property may escape confiscation."[32] Two days later, as Grant prepared for his triumphal return to the nation's capital, Dana sent the secretary of war one final cable. Clearly appreciating his new source of power, he informed Stanton, "General Grant is going to Washington today, and unless I receive contrary orders I propose to go with him."[33]

Dana's wartime experiences had little impact on his intellectual development. In ideological terms, he ended the war much as he began it — in the radical wing of the Republican party. The war did not change Dana's ideas; it changed his life. No longer dependent on powerful men, he had become an important actor in his own right. The Civil War was an interlude that marked the end of Dana's apprenticeship on a personal level. Within the next few years, he would step into master status as a journalist.

5

Experience

The *Chicago Republican* and Radical Republicanism

"Don't pay any attention to the nonsensical claims of
that Windy City."
— Charles A. Dana[1]

The four years between Lincoln's assassination and Grant's inauguration in 1869 were pivotal ones for Charles A. Dana. Characterized by a rapid succession of high expectations and deep disappointments, these years marked the beginning of his career as an independent newspaper editor. For most of his life, Dana had depended upon the patronage of powerful men: George Ripley, Horace Greeley, Edwin M. Stanton, and Ulysses S. Grant. Though he had frequently chafed under their restraint, he had counted on them to advance his career. At the end of the Civil War, he was ready to forge ahead on his own.

While keeping a weather eye on the political horizon, Dana devoted the spring of 1865 to looking for a peacetime job. Despite occasional references to establishing himself in business, it is clear that Dana never seriously considered any occupation other than journalism.[2] On May 10, 1865, he confided to Pike: "I have various offers of a more or less attractive character. Among the best are 2 or 3 relating to newspapers in the West, and I rather think that in one or the other of those ways I shall get out of public employment and return to the dignity of a private citizen within the present month."[3] The best offer that Dana had came from a committee of Republican businessmen in Chicago. These financiers hoped to establish a newspaper that would rival the powerful *Chicago Tribune*, and they offered to make Dana its editor. Impatient to play an independent role, he accepted. In doing so, he took on an almost impossible task.

The *Chicago Tribune*, founded in 1847, was the foremost Republican paper in the Midwest. It had gone through some troubled times during the Civil War years, however, as its stockholders were sharply divided over the policies of the Lincoln administration. These problems had peaked in 1864 when *Tribune* editor Joseph Medill opposed Lincoln in the Illinois State Republican nominating convention. Medill resigned — temporarily, as it turned out — in 1865. According to the *Tribune's* historian, the paper was so "independent" in the immediate postwar period that "it almost fell into opposition to the Republican party which Medill had helped to found."[4]

The Chicago businessmen who approached Dana in the spring of 1865, unhappy with the *Tribune's* political idiosyncrasies, had bought the *Chicago Post*. They reorganized it as the *Chicago Republican*. There was an element of intrigue in the establishment of the *Republican*, though Dana certainly exaggerated its unsavory aspects in a letter to his distant cousin Richard Henry Dana, author of *Two Years Before the Mast*.

> I am, by and by, going to Chicago to take a hand again in public affairs as a newspaper writer. I return to that profession with hesitation and some reluctance. Much hard work makes me shrink from the necessity of drudgery and though, in the abstract, the business of a journalist is good and noble, there is a good deal that is revolting in its circumstances and details. But on the whole, there is nothing to which I can turn my hand that seems so useful or so satisfactory.[5]

Dana was less fastidious in other letters. For example, he advised his friend Charles Nordhoff to join him in the new venture in Chicago. To Nordhoff, who was torn between offers from Dana, the *New York Evening Post*, and a newspaper in Wilmington, Delaware, Dana prophesied, "Wilmington is a one horse place, and never can be anything else. You will always be overshadowed there by the newspapers of Philadelphia and Baltimore both. Chicago is a big town, bound to be bigger, and you can have in it, along with me, just as big a place as you want."[6]

Dana was right. The young city of Chicago had experienced a boom in the 1850s and 1860s, generated by immigrant labor and an explosion of railroad building. Its population soared from twenty-eight thousand in 1850 to more than two hundred thousand in 1865. Chicago's profusion of railroad terminals had made the city the chief supplier of the Union Army during the Civil War. Its postwar future looked bright, as eastern capitalists invested in stockyards, warehouses, and grain elevators. Despite its luxuries, getting there was not always easy, as Dana's biographer Wilson noted unflappably in his diary. "Train on which I was travelling precipitated down rr embankment, nearly 20 feet, when within 50 miles from Chicago. I escaped uninjured. Found Mr. Dana and family at home."[7]

When Dana signed a five-year contract with the owners of the *Chicago Republican* in June 1865, the terms sounded ideal. He would be editor in chief, with complete responsibility for the paper, its personnel, and its advertisements.[8] The first issue of the *Chicago Republican* appeared on May 30, 1865. While it listed Charles A. Dana as editor, it apologized that he would not take charge until the end of July, when he had completed his duties in Washington, D.C. Dana assumed editorial control on July 23, 1865.[9]

Before Dana took over, the *Republican* had the dubious distinction of being the largest "blanket sheet" newspaper in the United States. A single sheet was folded into four pages, with ten columns to a page. The first page carried wire stories, general news, and several columns of advertisements. Three editions were available by subscription: daily, triweekly, and weekly.

One of Dana's first acts upon taking charge of the paper was to eliminate the page 1 advertisements. He also gave notice that no payment would be accepted for placing anything in the editorial columns.[10] With rhetoric calculated to please his Republican stockholders, Dana declared in a signed editorial that the paper would be devoted to the Republic, the Union, and the flag, as well as to industrial and commercial interests. He promised to give President Andrew Johnson "cordial but independent and discriminating support" and to furnish readers with "the earliest, the most accurate, the most complete, and the most authentic news of the day."[11] By emphasizing efficiency, industrial development, and devotion to the Union, Dana made it clear that his paper would be as Republican in outlook as it was in name.

Dana ran a tight and well-edited journal. During his ten-month tenure at the *Republican,* he experimented constantly, adding human interest stories, women's features, and a daily weather report. On November 1, 1865, he completely altered the paper's format, expanding it from four to eight pages and reducing the number of columns on each page from ten to six. The new version was better organized and much easier to read. City notices and news from Washington, D.C., appeared on page 1, editorials on page 4. Page 3 was devoted to market and financial reports. The first half of the paper consisted entirely of news, and advertisements were banished to the last four pages. An editorial boasted of the *Republican*'s use of the latest technology, including new Hoe presses and a supposedly unprecedented number of telegraphic reports. Dana announced that "the most lavish expenditure will constantly be called into play to insure for the *Republican* an honorable place among the most enterprising and best informed newspapers of the world."[12]

Under Dana's leadership, the *Chicago Republican* became increasingly critical of the conservative Unionists led by Andrew Johnson and adopted "the most advanced sentiments of the most advanced wing of the [Republican] party."[13] It took a hard line on the readmission to the Union of the former Confederate states, insisting they repudiate their right of secession and ratify the Thirteenth Amendment abolishing slavery. The *Republican* demanded swift justice for the leaders of the Rebellion: "There is but one right way to dispose of these unequalled criminals. . . . Why should Jefferson Davis or any of his peers be pardoned when an assassin, a burglar, or a horsethief is subjected to the regular operation of the law?"[14]

Dana's radical views were most obvious in the *Chicago Republican*'s treatment of the inflammatory issue of suffrage for blacks. Most Northerners were unwilling to consider enfranchising Southern blacks, let alone those African-Americans within their own state borders. It took considerable moral courage to support Negro suffrage. When the state of Wisconsin voted down universal suffrage in November 1865, the *Republican* called it "disagreeable . . . evidence of the pertinacity

with which barbarous prejudices may govern an enlightened community."[15] Again in February 1866, the paper proclaimed, "We fail entirely to perceive either the rightfulness or the policy of legislation
which withholds from the black man, on account of his color alone,
what is conferred upon the white without question or condition."[16]

The *Chicago Republican* was pro-business, and pro-development.
On city issues, it called for a free library, public health measures to
stem a potential cholera epidemic, and equal pay for women's work.
A typical editorial argued the merits of railroad development, suggesting that private individuals should step aside in the interest of
the public good — as defined by the needs of railroad corporations.
"The city has a deep interest in every railroad making this point its
centre of business, and . . . the general interests of the city should
not be injured from mere motives of hostility to corporations. . . .
Should a railroad be excluded because lotholders along a certain street
object? Should the city stand still until John Smith can sell his lots
at a profit?"[17] The classified advertisements likewise reflected the boom-
ing economy and the needs of the paper's business readers; help-wanted
notices announced the need for agents, investors, and professional services. Only a handful of classifieds advertised for domestics or laborers.

Dana experimented with a number of techniques at the *Republican* that he would later use at the *New York Sun*. Although the two
papers served very different readers, they shared a similar style. Short,
pithy paragraphs, a deft editorial touch, and breezy humor domi-
nated the *Republican*. In August 1865, Dana published an editorial
on James Gordon Bennett's *New York Herald* that almost reads as a
blueprint for the kind of journalism he would later perfect as editor
of the *New York Sun*. To explain the *Herald's* extensive circulation
and influence, Dana pointed to that paper's humor and skeptical tone.
"In its treatment of every topic a joke is always in order, in fact you
never know when it is not joking, though you may be sure it never
jests without a purpose."[18]

What Dana described as Bennett's "joking" voice and ambiguous
meaning was characteristic of a style of urban journalism that was
uniquely suited to the needs of large, diverse audiences at midcentury. In the 1860s, New York and Chicago were made up of neighborhoods sharply divided by barriers of race, class, and ethnicity. Like
the dime museums and vaudeville theaters that originated in the years

after the Civil War, newspapers sought to widen their markets by bridging the social chasms that separated city dwellers. As historian William Taylor has explained, these institutions provided a new "commercial culture of pastiche" that allowed for interclass mingling, even though it was vicarious rather than face to face. Taylor has suggested that newspapers achieved this end by using formats that subjected them "to multiple interpretations by different groups within the city's population."[19] Humor was one means of offering something for every social class and taste. Dana's use of humor opened the columns of his paper to multiple interpretations. If, in Dana's words, readers "never know when [a newspaper] is not joking," they are less likely to take offense at any particular item. Dana's apparent willingness to be misinterpreted was thus a highly successful marketing technique. In the 1870s, it would also become his journalistic trademark.

Charles Dana's *Chicago Republican* gave readers a feisty alternative to the staid *Tribune*. The *Republican* was fun to read. For example, Dana loved to needle Joseph Medill, the erstwhile editor of the *Chicago Tribune*. Though Medill had resigned as editor in 1865, he continued to hold a financial interest in the paper. This situation delighted Dana, who frequently printed editorial leaders asking who, in fact, was the editor of the *Chicago Tribune*. A column entitled "The Medillian Vagaries" mocked, "It is none of our business who is or who is not the editor of the *Chicago Tribune*. . . . But as [it] is constantly advertising the editor-in-chief . . . it is no breach of good manners for the other papers . . . to form and express opinions on the matter."[20]

If these jabs failed to provoke Medill, Dana hit home with his parody of Medill's enthusiastic proposals for orthographic reform, a new system of spelling based on phonetics. The *Republican* began referring to Medill's system as "fonetix" or "foneticks," and suggested that the *Tribune*'s proprietors ought to consider using Medill's "fonetix" in the paper. "We have no doubt that it will be so published, because the giant mind that has stamped that paper so often with the indelible marks of its genius, cannot fail in the end to make it the pioneer paper in the spread of the reformation in spelling."[21]

Medill went for the bait. Wounded, he sent a private letter to Dana, addressed to "Editor Republican," chiding the *Republican* for failing to take orthographic reform seriously. Unable to resist the final word, Dana published his own answer: "'Editor Republican' is a clumsy and inelegant formula, which might answer for an ordinary ill-educated mortal, but is not credible in a great orthographist. You might as well address the distinguished chief magistrate of this State 'Governor Illinois,' or the editor and chief proprietor of the leading newspaper of this city as 'Joe Medill Tribune.'"[22]

In November 1865, Dana sent James S. Pike a bundle of newspapers from Chicago, proudly pointing out the changes he had made in the *Republican*'s format. He wrote of the "absorbing work" connected with establishing the paper, and described the difficult task of moving his family to Chicago and getting them settled. Enthusiastic about the city, he called it a "great seaport." He added, "The *Republican* is doing surprisingly well. We pay our expenses, and they are heavy, and we gain daily in circulation and prestige. . . . If the financial crash holds off a year or two, it will find us entirely out of the woods."[23]

Despite these promising developments, Dana left the *Chicago Republican* after only ten months for reasons that are not entirely clear. The official word later published by the *New York Sun* was that Dana had been "so embarrassed by the restraints and changing views of the publishers that he gave up his editorial charge and returned to New York."[24] Frederick Hudson, in his 1873 study, *Journalism in the United States*, attributed the collapse of the newspaper to bad financial management and imperious stockholders who hamstrung Dana. Hudson concluded, "On making an investigation as to the causes that led to this apparent failure, it was ascertained that the *Republican* had more than one head, and no paper can succeed brilliantly with more than one."[25] Dana's biographer James Harrison Wilson claimed that the editor had left the *Chicago Republican* because the paper lacked capital. To support this claim, Wilson cited a letter that Dana had written less than a month before his resignation. "I have been . . . much disturbed by difficulties in the *Republican*. These difficulties are serious, and how they will end I don't know. I shall get out of the concern if I can, unless it is put on a different basis, and means are raised by the capitalists who have invested in it to carry it through in a satisfactory manner."[26]

Yet there was more to the incident than the paper's uncertain financial footing. Dana's contemporaries believed that the editor was forced out because of a disagreement with the paper's stockholders over President Andrew Johnson. It was a conflict that developed out of Dana's unseemly pursuit of a political appointment, and it came at a time when Dana's paper was increasingly critical of the president.

In December 1865, *Chicago Republican* editor Dana wrote to *New York Times* editor Henry J. Raymond asking for advice. He raised a subject that he claimed he had "not before thought of"—offering himself as a candidate for the collector of the Port of New York. Coyly stating that he would never have conceived of this idea on his own, he described how it had been urged on him by certain members of the New York delegation in the U.S. House of Representatives. After mentioning his unique qualifications for the position, Dana offered an immodestly concealed quid pro quo in exchange for Raymond's recommendation: "I shall take it as a great kindness if you will give me your views freely and fully. Of course it is hardly necessary to say that if I were in the office, I should expect, whenever the occasion might offer, to render you every [possible] service of a friendly nature."[27]

The collectorship was what one historian has called "the most important patronage plum among all Federal offices."[28] During the 1860s, the collector appointed and controlled a staff of more than one thousand employees—nearly all of whom were, in the words of one Treasury official, "in the habitual receipt of emoluments from importers or their agents."[29] The opportunities for both political power and private gain were staggering.

With encouragement from a number of New York Republicans, particularly Roscoe Conkling, Dana formally requested the post from President Andrew Johnson on January 20, 1866. His letter left no doubt as to his desire for the office.

> Some of my friends in the New York delegation in Congress want me to be Collector of New York. I shall be glad to have that office, and accordingly address myself to you. I have been a resident of New York City for nearly twenty years, til a few months hence, when I came here on leaving the War Department. I know New-York, its merchants, and its politicians, but by reason of my connection with the War Department, I have been absent, so as

to be free from all identification with the political factions and personal controversies by which the Union party there had been much divided. I believe that there is no person of any prominence in the party whose appointment would give greater general satisfaction than mine.[30]

Dana seemed to anticipate disappointment. On January 27, he wrote nervously to New York attorney William Bartlett, "I have sent the paper to the lady's lodgings [a bizarre reference to Johnson]. She has taken some sort of miff against me, as also against many of her other friends. If I were to present the matter to her, I fear she should be more likely to refuse than otherwise. . . . Mr. Conkling was beating the bush."[31]

Johnson turned down Dana's application. Even more galling to the editor, the White House released Dana's letter of application to the press, making his desire to leave Chicago public knowledge. Unfriendly newspapers charged that in spite of Dana's reputation as a Radical Republican, he was "bowing before the chief enemy of radicalism, begging for an office."[32]

After Johnson's refusal, editorials in Dana's *Republican* became even more critical of the president. The paper attacked Johnson's veto of the Freedmen's Bureau Bill. It insinuated that Johnson was a demagogue. And it criticized Johnson for his complaint that the Congress would not accede to his demands regarding the readmission of Southern states. "A Republican President, chosen as the peculiar representative of devotion to the Union and hostility to treason, has broken with Congress because it would not submit to his orders and receive back without examination and without guarantees all the rebel States . . . with their Union citizens proscribed and oppressed as relentlessly as when the states still swore allegiance to the confederacy."[33] After Johnson vetoed a civil rights bill, the *Chicago Republican* claimed that Johnson was a turncoat, a man who had "utterly abandoned" the platform of the Republican party that had nominated him for the vice-presidency.[34]

On May 23, 1866, Charles A. Dana's name disappeared from the editorial page of the *Chicago Republican*. Though the stockholders of the *Republican* denied it, there were persistent rumors that "Dana had made the *Republican* one of the most radical papers in the country, and when the stockholders determined to 'Johnsonize' it, Dana promptly resigned."[35]

Some of the details of Dana's resignation became public four years later when, in March 1870, he sued the *Chicago Republican* in U.S. circuit court, claiming that the company had not fulfilled the terms of his severance agreement. In accordance with the terms of his original contract, Dana had received one-fifth of the company's capital stock in July 1865. The contract had also stated that "in case of necessity . . . all the stock [would become] liable to assessment."[36] The Republican Company had decided to assess the shareholders in January 1866, and to pay the assessment on his stock, Dana had borrowed $5,000 from each of two Chicago banks. In May, when Dana resigned, the *Republican* company had agreed to pay Dana's two notes and an additional $10,000 if he surrendered his stock and vacated his interest in the paper.[37] In short, the stockholders of the *Chicago Republican* had been dissatisfied enough with Dana's performance to be willing to pay him $20,000 to sever the agreement. When the Republican Company failed to comply with this arrangement, Dana sued. The suit was settled in his favor and he was awarded $10,388.[38]

As for Dana's reaction to the incident, a laconic entry in biographer James Harrison Wilson's diary on June 6, 1866, notes, "Mr. Dana paid me a visit — long conversation — left Republican because of Mack's [the publisher's] rascality and mismanagement."[39]

While Dana may have chosen not to address the question of why he left the *Chicago Republican*, he could not prevent newspapers across the United States from reprinting his letter to Johnson, causing him acute professional embarrassment. His critics charged that the episode explained Dana's sudden attacks on the president. To some, it also explained the end of his tenure at the *Republican*. The *Brooklyn Union* claimed that Dana's office seeking had destroyed his influence and usefulness as an editor in the West and had "put him under the ban with Republicans everywhere [sending] him headlong into political and official retirement from which he [will never] recover."[40]

Dana's abrupt departure from the *Republican* was the result of both an ideological dispute with the paper's stockholders and his avid and unseemly pursuit of public office. At the end of the Civil War, Dana was a Radical Republican whose views were far more progres-

sive than those of the stockholders of the *Chicago Republican*. Even
a quick perusal of the early issues of the newspaper suggests that Dana
opposed many of Andrew Johnson's policies from the start. Most other
Radical Republicans had become disenchanted with Johnson by December 4, 1865, when the Thirty-ninth Congress assembled.[41] Dana
was hardly alone in turning on the president, though his opposition
to Johnson became increasingly vicious after January 1866. For example, Dana claimed in a typical editorial comment that "the President is an obstinate, stupid man, governed by preconceived ideas, by
whiskey, and by women."[42]

Dana had thus put the stockholders of the *Chicago Republican*
in a bind. He had compromised himself by petitioning the president
for public office while he was the editor of the newspaper. The newspaper's trustees did not share Dana's Radical Republican views, but
Dana's contract gave him complete editorial control. The stockholders were, for both practical and ideological reasons, dissatisfied with
Dana's attacks on Johnson and wanted him out. In short, the collectorship incident was not the only factor in Dana's resignation from
the *Republican*. Dana had philosophical reasons for opposing Andrew Johnson, but it was his embarrassment over the collectorship
debacle that inflamed his criticism into virulent attacks. When he
turned on the president, it did not matter that he also had ideological
reasons for doing so. Charles Dana had two great passions throughout his life: journalism and politics. The debacle over the collectorship made him an object of ridicule in both. Initially, Dana had looked
into getting out of Chicago on his own terms; now he simply had
to get out.

The question remains about how Dana could have made such
an error in judgment — and indeed, why he wanted the collector's job
in the first place. Dana's interest in the collectorship revealed a significant aspect of the editor's personality. Capable of the highest idealism, he could also work up a great thirst for money and political
power. At Brook Farm, Dana had attacked wealth and privilege, and
he continued to do so in public for much of the rest of his career.
Yet in private, Dana had a lifelong, contrary fascination with rich
and powerful men. The job of collector of the Port of New York was
widely recognized as the highest-paying patronage position in New

York State. If Dana had been named collector, he would have achieved the financial success that had always eluded his father. Instead, his hunger for wealth and power nearly derailed his career.

The editor kept silent on these matters for nearly thirty years. Then, in 1896, in a talk before the New Haven Colony Historical Society, the seventy-seven-year-old Dana gave a tantalizingly indirect explanation "unrecorded in any history." In an address that was supposed to be about his own recollections of President Lincoln and his Civil War cabinet, Dana seemed to suggest that he had been promised the collectorship by Lincoln and that Johnson had reneged. Dana broached the issue by devoting a disproportionate amount of time to a seemingly obscure incident. He described in detail how, to obtain the House votes necessary to pass the Thirteenth Amendment abolishing slavery, Lincoln had authorized Dana to promise one New Jersey Democrat and two from New York whatever was necessary to obtain their support. Dana recalled:

> I sent for the men and saw them one by one. I found that they were afraid of their party. . . . Two of them wanted internal revenue collectors appointed. "You shall have it," I said. Another one wanted a very important appointment about the Custom House of New York. I knew the man well whom he wanted to have appointed. He was a Republican, though the Congressman was a Democrat. I had served with him in the Republican Party County Committee of New York.[43]

The unnamed Republican whom the Democratic Congressman wanted appointed seems to have been Dana himself.

Dana claimed that he promised the Democratic congressman the appointment on Lincoln's authority, and that Andrew Johnson later failed to honor the bargain. In the same New Haven talk, Dana added that the office of collector was easily worth $20,000 a year, and he recalled that Roscoe Conkling had telegraphed him from Washington, D.C., to leave Chicago and urge Johnson to uphold Lincoln's promise.

Why, thirty years after the fact, did Dana not mention the Republican job seeker's name? And why did he believe that setting the record straight was so important in the first place? The date of this incident, (January, 1866) the individuals involved, (Dana and Conkling) and the suggestion of grievous wrongdoing lead to the conclusion that the Republican to whom President Lincoln had promised the collectorship was none other than Dana himself. Technically, the construction of his speech was accurate. Dana did indeed "know the man well."

For thirty years, Dana's critics had needled him with the charge that he had begged for the collectorship in an undignified manner reminiscent of Horace Greeley's notorious lust for office. Chances are that Dana wanted to justify his appeal to Johnson, in however circuitous a fashion. Not as impervious to criticism as he liked to claim, Dana believed he had informed the world of the truth. He had, in some small way, vindicated himself.

Despite his failure at the *Chicago Republican*, Dana was able, with impressive self-confidence, to interest his wealthy Republican friends in speculating with him on another newspaper venture. Carefully, he laid the groundwork for a move east. As Dana built the financial backing he needed, he demonstrated a solid practicality that had been lacking in his impulsive actions at the *Republican*. It would be evident Dana had learned from experience.

1. "The Red Flag in New York," *Frank Leslie's Illustrated Magazine*, January 31, 1784. Courtesy of the Library of Congress.

2. Matthew Brady daguerreotype, the *New-York Daily Tribune* staff, early 1850s. *Seated, left to right:* George N. Snow, Bayard Taylor, Horace Greeley, George Ripley. *Standing, left to right:* Thomas McElrath, Charles A. Dana, John F. Cleveland. Courtesy of the Library of Congress.

3. George William Curtis, Charles Dana, and Thomas Hicks, early 1850s. Courtesy of the Print Collection, Miriam and Ira D. Wallach Division of Arts, Prints and Photographs, the New York Public Library, Astor, Lenox and Tilden Foundation.

4. Charles A. Dana, early 1850s. Courtesy of the Library of Congress.

7. Matthew Brady, "Ass't Sec. of War Charles A. Dana at Grant's Cold Harbor Headquarters," June 11 or 12, 1864. This photograph was taken at the same pine tree as General Grant's more famous portrait, probably about ten minutes later. Dana has moved the folding chair and is sitting on it. Courtesy of the Library of Congress.

5. *Opposite, above:* Timothy Sullivan, "A Council of War at Massaponox Church, 21st May, 1864." Ulysses S. Grant is seated with his legs crossed, directly in front of the two trees. Dana, having arrived at the scene moments before the photograph was taken, is seated to General Grant's immediate left. Courtesy of the Library of Congress.

6. *Opposite, below:* Matthew Brady, "Gen. Grant at His Cold Harbor Headquarters," June 11 or 12, 1864. Courtesy of the Library of Congress.

8. An 1873 view of Park Row, New York City, showing the Sun building and French's Hotel. Courtesy of The New-York Historical Society, N.Y.C.

9. Another view of Park Row, probably taken around 1910, showing from *left to right*, City Hall, the World, Sun, Tribune, and Times buildings. Notice how Pulitzer's domed World building symbolically towers over the tiny Sun headquarters. Courtesy of The New-York Historical Society, N.Y.C.

ANOTHER RESTORER OF ANTIQUITIES À LA CESNOLA.

C. A. Dana (having excavated an Old Fossil):—"I guess I can palm him off on the people for their Museum in 1884!"

10. "Another Restorer of Antiquities à la Cesnola," *Puck*, April 8, 1887. Courtesy of the General Research Division, the New York Public Library, Astor, Lenox and Tilden Foundation.

11. "A Little Private Mutual Admiration Scheme, Joss Ben [Butler] and His Only Priest, Sun-Sun," *Puck*, August 27, 1884. Courtesy of the Library of Congress.

12. "A Hopeless Undertaking," *Puck*, January 12, 1887. Courtesy of the Library of Congress.

13. "Slipped Up Again!" *Puck*, October 17, 1888. Courtesy of Alderman Library, the University of Virginia.

14. Charles A. Dana, 1895. *"[Mother] said . . . that it is true of all the Danas that they were a little bit outside. They tended to be brainy and not to get on. . . . There was a certain glamour around Charles A., and tremendous affection, and a feeling that he was . . . a splendid figure, and after that it was all a little bit shrinking."* Duncan Longcope (Dana's great-grandson), Cornhill Farm, Lee, Massachusetts, August 16, 1986. Courtesy of the Library of Congress.

15. Charles A. Dana with son Paul Dana and grandson Anders Dana, at Dosoris, 1891. *"Our grandfather [Paul Dana] was a Park Commissioner for a little while, and he used to take his children for rides on elephants. . . . I think he retired and spent a good deal of his life raising dogs. Although he ran the* Sun *briefly, I think they edged him out."* Duncan Longcope, August 16, 1986. Courtesy of Duncan Longcope.

16. Charles A. Dana with grandson Anders Dana, at Dosoris, 1891. *"Uncle Andy would have had a lot of things to say about [Charles A. Dana] . . . he was very good at remembering that kind of thing. He died a long while ago; he'd gotten a cancer and he shrank to nothing. [Though] his whole life and career ended in disaster or sadness, he had tremendous style, even standing waiting for a taxi. . . . In a shabby old raincoat, he had more style than most people who were going into his club."* Duncan Longcope, August 16, 1986. Courtesy of Duncan Longcope.

18. Charles A. Dana and grandchildren, at Dosoris, early 1890s. The editor is the shadowy figure in the background. *"My dear little Janet, that was a very nice letter which I received from you about a half hour ago. . . . I hope Anders and Duncan are blooming and happy. Has Anders got a bicycle too, and does he ride about the country and up and down the mountains on it? I can see him standing on the top of a high mountain, with his hair blowing in the wind, and waving a flag to the people down below."* Charles A. Dana to Janet Dana, May 18, 1895, private collection, Duncan Longcope. Courtesy of Duncan Longcope.

17. *Opposite, below:* Charles A. Dana with granddaughter Janet Dana Longcope, at Dosoris, 1891. *"This is Charles, walking with a little girl, my mother. That's the way my mother was. She had this wild glee, they're all that way. She was a lot of fun always."* Duncan Longcope, August 16, 1986. Courtesy of Duncan Longcope.

6

Turnabout

The Politics of "Independence"

"A few years from now . . . I shall be willing to accept whatever judgment the nation passes on my course of action; but now I must do as I think right."[1]
— Charles A. Dana, ca. 1869

By May 1866, Charles A. Dana had suffered his share of adversity. Forced to resign as editor of the *Chicago Republican* after barely ten months, he seemed to be out of luck as well as out of work. His dream of editing his own paper had again been dashed, this time by his own bad judgment. The embarrassing publicity that had followed disclosure of his pursuit of the New York collectorship, as well as his attacks on President Andrew Johnson, made appointment to public office unlikely. And if he entertained the hope that his talents might be better recognized by the next administration — presumably Republican, headed by his friend Ulysses S. Grant — that contest was still more than two years away.

Yet despite this less than promising outlook, Dana would, during the next three years, orchestrate a personal and professional turnabout of astonishing proportions. His purchase of the *New York Sun* in 1867 and the decisions he made during the first few years he owned the paper would demonstrate both his genius as a newspaper editor and his grasp of political and social conditions in postwar New York City. At last having the freedom to edit a newspaper in the manner he chose, Dana would bring all of his experiences to bear on the new enterprise. The newspaper he created would dominate New York journalism for the next fifteen years.

If Charles Dana's abrupt departure from the *Chicago Republican* caused him any sleepless nights of regret or self-doubt, he kept these worries to himself. Seemingly undaunted, he wrote to New York journalist and lawyer William Bartlett, "I am now free, and looking around to see where the world wants me to go to work. My inclinations take me to New York; but it is possible that I may still stay in Chicago. . . . There is a great chance to make a prosperous and powerful newspaper there. I shall be in New York after I get through here and shall like to see you."[2] In June 1866, according to biographer James Harrison Wilson, the editor "went East . . . for a conference with his friends, in consequence of which he decided to start a newspaper of his own in New York."[3] A letter Dana sent to Bartlett a few weeks after that initial meeting suggests his enthusiasm for the new project: "I get on well and hope to have everything settled in a fortnight. . . . All practical men consider it a great speculation. There is a great chance to make an evening paper here. . . . Why not try it!"[4]

Establishing a new newspaper would take Dana more than "a fortnight"; he spent the next eighteen months trying to raise the money. As Wilson explained, "There were already enough daily newspapers in New York City," and the "project proved harder to carry through than he expected."[5] Regardless, it was testimony to Dana's reputation that within a few months he had raised a subscription fund of $110,000. It was not entirely clear, however, what he would do with this money.

By the end of 1866, Dana seemed discouraged. In a letter to Roscoe Conkling, he asked the Republican senator what he thought of the idea of using the fund to buy two newspapers in Rochester, New York. "I suppose that if I want to do so, I can go to Rochester, and buy both the Democrat and the Express and unite them into a profitable concern, out of which I can get a decent living without very hard work. My subscription . . . will be raised to $200,000 within a month I think; but the work here will be harder than at Rochester, and the return less speedy. What do you think?"[6] Regardless of Conkling's reply, Dana stayed in New York City.

It took Dana nearly another year to complete his plans. He almost succeeded in establishing a newspaper to be called the *New York Evening Telegraph*. On September 27, 1867, he and seven other trustees, including Roscoe Conkling's brother, incorporated the New York Evening Telegraph Association.[7] *New York Herald* reporter Frederick Hudson asserted that "this fact became the talk of editors and reporters all over the country."[8] In New York, it was widely believed that Charles Dana would establish a Republican newspaper because his stockholders were prominent Republican politicians and lawyers.[9] At a Republican party dinner in October 1867, Dana boasted to *Springfield* [Massachusetts] *Republican* editor Samuel Bowles that he "would of course 'run' his newspaper in [New York Senator Edwin] Morgan's interest."[10] As it turned out, this confidence was a bit premature.

Despite solid financial backing, the *Evening Telegraph* amounted to nothing more than articles of incorporation. According to Hudson, "two or three members" of the Associated Press upset Dana's plans by refusing to give the *Evening Telegraph* access to the organization's daily report.[11] By the late 1860s, it was virtually impossible for a large metropolitan newspaper to succeed without the Associated Press report. Neither Hudson nor anyone else has identified these "two or three members," but there were several editors among New York's newspaper establishment who had cause to spite Dana by denying him access to the Associated Press. Horace Greeley, for one, may well have nursed a grudge against his former lieutenant. Amos Cummings, the first managing editor of Dana's *New York Sun*, later hinted that James Gordon Bennett of the *New York Herald* may also have had reason to fear competition from a new afternoon paper. As Cummings recalled, "Negotiations were begun with the Associated Press for the supply of news to the paper, but there [*sic*] failed, and Mr. Bennett established 'The Evening Telegram,' to anticipate 'The Evening Telegraph.' These untoward events were very discouraging to Mr. Dana and his associates, and the prospects of their enterprise looked, for a while, very gloomy."[12]

Then, Dana's luck unexpectedly changed. Moses Beach offered to sell him the *New York Sun* for $175,000. The *Sun* was one of the founding members of the Associated Press, and because an A.P. franchise belonged to a newspaper itself rather than to its owner, access to the organization's news continued even if the newspaper changed hands. Beach's package also included $50,000 worth of new presses, the good will of the *Sun's* advertisers, and a small job printing office. Dana immediately accepted the offer.[13]

The *Sun* was a terrific bargain. The successful morning daily already had a large readership among the city's "mechanics and small merchants." Dana told James Harrison Wilson of his purchase in a letter that also encouraged his friend and future biographer to think about investing in the *Sun*.

> It has a circulation of from fifty to sixty thousand a day, and all among the mechanics and small merchants of the city. We pay a large sum for it — $175,000 — but it gives us at once a large and profitable business. If you have a thousand dollars at leisure, you had better invest it in the stock of our company, which is increased to about $350,000, in order to pay for this new acquisition. Of this sum about $220,000 is invested in the Tammany Hall real estate, which is sure to be productive, independent of the business of the paper.[14]

The "Tammany Hall real estate" was a small red brick structure built in 1811 for the Tammany Society. Improbably, Dana and his Republican shareholders had just purchased Tammany Hall — the clubhouse of New York City Democrats' most powerful organization. Dana immediately moved the *Sun's* offices from their old location at Nassau and Fulton streets to the Tammany building, at Nassau and Frankfort.

The building that was the *Sun's* home for the twenty-nine years that Dana edited the paper occupied a central site on what New Yorkers called Printing House Row. Like most other industries in nineteenth-century New York City, newspaper production was concentrated in a small geographic area, in this case a narrow strip along Park Row between Fulton Street and the future site of the Brooklyn Bridge. Newspaper buildings were traditionally situated near the Post Office, City Hall, and the U.S. courthouse. The Post Office brought in "the exchanges," other newspapers from around the country, while the nearby municipal buildings provided the press with easy access to stories of vice, crime, and city politics.[15] The *Sun* building faced City Hall and fronted on City Hall Park. The proximity of other newspaper offices on Printing House Row allowed for easy relations among reporters, particularly at such convivial spots as Nash and Fuller's, known for its oyster broils, billiards, and gossip.

Charles Dana's purchase of the *New York Sun* astonished observers of the newspaper business: Dana, one of the country's most prominent Republicans, had bought a newspaper that reported in a sensational style for working-class readers who were overwhelmingly Democratic.[16] It seemed obvious that he would transform the *Sun* into a Republican journal and that Beach's sale would forever change the character of the venerable paper. Even the usually astute Frederick Hudson, a *New York Herald* reporter and author of a contemporaneous history of American journalism, mistakenly proclaimed, "[Thus] the first penny paper of the country, after a prosperous existence of over thirty years with its democratic tendencies, became an independent organ of the Republican party in the metropolis, and a thorn in the side of the *Tribune*."[17] Several of the *Sun*'s veteran writers, expecting Dana to refurbish the paper as a Republican daily, left the *Sun* to establish the *New York Star*, which they claimed would carry on the *Sun*'s tradition of support for the "masses," not the "millionaires." They promised that the *Star* would continue to report on trade union meetings, labor disputes, and other news of interest to the producing classes. The former *Sun* writers announced, "The Daily *Star* has taken the field vacated by the *Sun*, when the latter journal was sold to Messrs Dana and Co., to be transformed into a radical [Republican] journal."[18]

The editors of the *New York Star* were thus among those who mistakenly assumed that Dana would abandon the *Sun*'s traditional readership. The reality of what he did during the first year that he edited the newspaper was far more interesting. As *Sun* reporter Frank O'Brien admiringly concluded, "Only a genius" could, backed by an aristocracy of Republican stockholders, "make a hundred thousand mechanics and tradesmen, nearly all Democrats, like their paper better than ever before."[19]

The *Sun* had a long and colorful history even before Dana bought it. Founded in 1833 by Benjamin Day, the *Sun* was one of New York's oldest newspapers. It was also the city's first "penny paper." Like the imitators that would follow it, the *Sun* cost one cent a copy, while its more staid competition sold for six times that much. Nominally independent of politics, it was popular with the mostly Democratic working class. The old *Sun* made money from street sales and classified advertising, rather than from subscriptions and political subsidies. The penny press was notorious for its laissez-faire attitude toward advertisers, its claim of political independence, and its revolutionary definition of "news," which emphasized timeliness, human interest, and sensational accounts of vice and crime.[20]

Though entrepreneurs of the penny press such as Benjamin Day and James Gordon Bennett of the *New York Herald* claimed that their papers were politically independent, this assertion was not quite accurate. Like Bennett's *Herald*, the old *Sun* was "independent" in that it was not an official organ of a political party. It did, however, have a clear political ideology.

There were advantages in claiming political independence, the most obvious being appeal to a larger number of readers. Sociologist Michael Schudson has suggested that the penny press of the 1830s catered to middle-class entrepreneurs and professionals in search of information. In his interpretation, "The qualities contemporaries admired or detested in these papers — relative independence from party, low price, high circulation, emphasis on news, timeliness, sensation — [had] to do with the rise of an urban middle class."[21]

This view has been convincingly challenged by communication scholar Daniel Schiller.[22] Drawing on studies of the antebellum working class, the tradition of the labor press, and close analysis of the *National Police Gazette*, Schiller contends that the penny papers were read by craftsmen steeped in the artisan republicanism of Tom Paine, men and women who valued economic independence and pride in the trades. Far from being the voice of a rising middle class, the penny papers reflected the angry rhetoric of "downwardly mobile artisans." Readers of penny papers resented the breakdown of the apprentice system brought about by industrialization, and they feared becoming permanent wage earners.

The so-called independence of the penny press, with its disdain of political parties, its invocation of the public good, and its exposure of corruption, thus imitated the old labor papers in their appeal to the artisan class. According to Schiller, "This much vaunted independence was not the benign voice of middle-class progress sweeping away vestiges of premodern mentalities but the angry protest of journeymen filtering through the self-interest of the cheap journals."[23]

While emphasizing that the cheap dailies were fundamentally commercial in character, Schiller argues that their editors shrewdly used sensationalism and the exposure of corruption as a means of selling papers. The democratic promise of the penny press, "extension of public access to information and metamorphosis of the character of public information itself," was encapsulated in the *Sun*'s well-known motto, It Shines for All.[24]

Once Dana bought the *Sun*, he immediately changed its appearance. He did this in a way that would have been recognizable to anyone who had examined the pages of the *Chicago Republican*. Like the *Republican*, the *New York Sun* was a four-page "blanket sheet," printed on both sides of a single piece of newsprint measuring thirty-six by forty-six inches, which was folded in half. Dana reduced the number of columns on each page from eight to seven, giving the paper a sharp, clean look. He also emphasized the editorials by enlarging their type size. The *Sun*'s new format remained more or less constant until 1888, when competition from Joseph Pulitzer's eight-page *World* forced Dana to double the number of pages in his paper.

The front page of the *Sun* contained state, national, and international news in stories of widely varying lengths. Although international news was generally culled from Associated Press reports, the *Sun* had its own Washington, D.C., and Albany, N.Y., correspondents. Local items were organized into the "Jottings about Town" column, which featured news on everything from crimes and weddings to fashion and the latest heat wave. The longer articles, taking up one to two columns, were interspersed with the short, concise paragraphs for which the paper was noted.

The second page of the *Sun* featured the editorials, which were generally short. Dana believed his readers preferred a few paragraphs to a long-winded essay. As he wrote in 1875, "The American newspaper-reader demands of an editor that he shall not give him news and discussions in heavy chunks, but so condensed and clarified that he shall be relieved of the necessity of wading through a treatise to get at a fact, or spending time on a dilated essay to get a bite at an argument."[25]

Page 2 also contained letters to the editor and a regular feature, "Sunbeams," which reprinted items of interest collected from other newspapers. City news usually appeared on the third page, along with pieces on literary topics, business news, market reports, and results of sporting events like walking matches and the racetrack. Page 4 consisted of classified advertisements and, if there was space, reprints of speeches and lectures.

The style of reporting in Dana's *Sun* is markedly different from that found in today's newspapers. Rather than using the modern device of the inverted pyramid, in which details follow a lead sentence or paragraph, the *Sun*, like other nineteenth-century newspapers, organized information in a chronological pattern. A sea of detail preceded the essentials of the story, which were usually buried at the bottom of the column. For example, an article on the visit of a foreign dignitary might begin with a leisurely account of the guest's arrival, then drift on to the breakfast menu, the day's itinerary, and the names of those who were traveling in the party. Only in the last few paragraphs would the writer reveal the point of the visit.

Until the 1890s, the *Sun* used single-column headlines.[26] If an editor thought a news story was particularly interesting or important, he would draw attention to it with indented subheads, which highlighted the point of the story. The significance might otherwise be hard to find, given the popularity of the chronological format.

In contrast to the longer articles, the *Sun's* short, paragraph-length stories touched on an eclectic range of subjects, often with a humorous twist. These news items reflected Dana's view that a newspaper should be "clean, lively, and interesting."[27] When Dana hired Uriah H. Painter as the *Sun's* Washington correspondent on January 3, 1868, he told him: "We want nothing but real news. Most of what Mr. [John Russell] Young sends to the *Tribune* for instance, does not come within this definition. Please let me have the telegrams as early in the evenings as possible. Don't forget either to send us all public documents that are of any value."[28] One *Sun* writer later remembered that Dana's motto was, Make the paper interesting.[29]

In addition to the daily "Jottings about Town," Dana published another regular feature called "Life in the Metropolis — Dashes Here and There by the Sun's Reporters." Both features were columns of short paragraphs that reported on miscellaneous events, large and small, that had occurred in the city. For example, on July 13, 1882, the "Jottings" column included these five items:

The ocean in front of Manhattan Beach this evening will be illuminated by fireworks.

The body of Carl Ulrich, who was drowned on Monday, was found floating in the Hudson River, off Mount St. Vincent, yesterday.

The elevator men and cleaners employed under the custodian of the Post Office building have not been paid for June this year or for June, 1881.

The will of the late Henry A. Polhamus of New Rochelle was admitted to probate at White Plains yesterday. The real and personal estate is estimated at from $200,000 to $250,000, and is divided between the widow and the son and daughter.

The menu of the 7th dinner of the Thirteenth Club, which will be attacked at 8:13 precisely this evening (July 13) at the Knickerbocker Cottage, is printed on a coffin-shaped card with thirteen screwheads depicted around the rim. Lobster salad a la morituri te salutamus is the most perilous looking of the dishes enumerated. [30]

Not only did these short items "make the paper interesting," they also gave the *Sun* the "pastiche" quality that historian William Taylor has described as characteristic of commercial culture in the Gilded Age. [31] In its columns of rapid-fire paragraphs on unrelated topics, the *Sun* depicted metropolitan life as being full of miscellaneous happenings connected only by being part of the fabric of the city. Violent death, happy coincidence, and personal tragedy coexisted in the pages of the *Sun* as "jottings," "dashes," and "sunbeams," much as they did on the streets of the city. The only meaning that the *Sun* bestowed on such seemingly random events was that they were all of equal importance in the life of the metropolis.

Most of the *Sun*'s advertisements during the 1870s and 1880s were classified notices of "Help Wanted" or "Situation Wanted," referring to domestic, skilled, or semiskilled work. While a few theaters, dry goods retailers, and manufacturers of patent medicines advertised in the *Sun*, they were overshadowed by the classifieds. The smattering of city notices suggested that the paper had procured desirable advertising patronage from the Democratic machine. The *Sun* announced its own advertising and subscription rates on page 4, as well as the availability of its job printing office.

Charles Dana disliked advertising, which he considered to be a waste of valuable space. In his view, a newspaper should be able to support itself on subscriptions alone. Despite the fact that one-quarter of his paper was committed to advertising, he continued to express the hope that one day the *Sun* would "politely decline to have any of our space used by advertisers."[32]

There was more than a touch of arrogance in Dana's hostility to advertisers. Both his disdain for advertising and his stubborn pride are evident in an episode recalled by J. Henry Harper, heir to the New York book publishing firm of Harper and Brothers.

> When Charles A. Dana had in mind the acquisition of the *New York Sun* he came to my grandfather and suggested that he should be a party to its purchase. They had a long conversation together and my grandfather finally told him that he already had too many irons in the fire and did not feel justified in accepting his complimentary offer, but he added, "I shall be pleased, however, to give you advertising when you begin the publication of the *Sun*." Dana replied, "That would be of no importance to me. I propose to make a newspaper in which advertisers will be only too anxious to appear."[33]

Dana's dream of a newspaper supported by subscription revenue alone would never become reality. He did, however, limit the number of advertisements in the *Sun* until the late 1880s.

Dana's most pressing problem in 1868 was not how to banish advertisements from the pages of the *Sun*, but how to reconcile the Radical Republican views of his stockholders with the Democratic interests of his working-class readers. For the *Sun* to survive, Dana had to maintain the allegiance of these readers.

The postwar Democratic party was in disarray, tarred, some would say, by the brush of treason. Many of New York's foreign-born laborers had had no sympathy for the abolitionist crusade of the antebellum years. Nearly all opposed racial equality, some for economic reasons. Most feared competition from a free black labor force that would be willing to work for subminimum wages. Such feelings had erupted during the war, particularly in the violent and racist anti-draft riots of 1863.[34] Democratic leaders within the city fueled racist fears and rose to power on peace platforms that Republicans considered traitorous.[35]

After the war, Democrats scrambled to distance themselves from wartime issues and to build a national party that would reflect the new political reality. Opposed to what they considered to be the vindictive policies of the Radical Republicans, Democrats were eager to "restore" rather than to "reconstruct" the South, preferably under its white, antebellum leadership. Committed to speedy restoration of the Union, they drew upon the Jacksonian ideal of decentralized government in urging the return of political authority to the South's "natural" leaders.

New York City Democrats eager to reinvigorate the commercial alliance with the South called for a quick end to military occupation and congressional Reconstruction of the former Confederate states. If this call failed to rally the city's voters, Democratic leaders knew they could do so with the ugly trumpeting of racism and white supremacy.[36] While on state and local issues the lines between the two parties tended to blur, on national questions the litmus test of Republican loyalty was a hard line toward the South. Only the Radical Republicans defended the rights of the freedmen to enjoy full civil liberties.

On January 27, 1868, Charles Dana published the prospectus of the *Sun*'s new management. It was a remarkable document that began with a remarkable statement. The editor proclaimed that the *Sun* would both maintain journalistic independence and support Republican presidential hopeful Ulysses S. Grant—all within a context of Democratic slogans and rhetoric:

> In changing its proprietorship, the *Sun* will . . . continue to be an independent newspaper, wearing the livery of no party, and discussing public questions and the acts of public men on their merits alone. It will be guided, as it has been hitherto, by uncompromising loyalty to the Union, and will resist every attempt to weaken the bonds that unite the American people into one nation.

The Sun will support General Grant as its candidate for the Presidency. It will advocate retrenchment and economy in the public expenditures, and the reduction of the present crushing burdens of taxation. It will advocate the speedy restoration of the South, as needful to revive business and secure fair wages for labor."[37]

In this prospectus Dana used the familiar notion of "independence" as a strategy to keep both his readers and his stockholders happy. Every decision he made during the first year he edited the *Sun* was governed by this dual obligation. Unlike his journalistic mentor, Horace Greeley, Dana was a realist. Seldom, if ever, did he let ideals stand in the way of more practical concerns. As the new editor of the *Sun*, he played down his own political views and claimed that the paper would "belong to no party and wear the livery of no faction." With luck, this political "independence" would work to keep sales high and allow him to make long-term changes in the newspaper.[38]

Dana undoubtedly had some sort of quid pro quo with his Republican stockholders. Most likely he had agreed to help elect Ulysses S. Grant president in exchange for financial support. But if Dana's backers believed he would transform the *Sun* into a Republican newspaper, his prospectus should have given them pause. Outside of the promise to support Grant for president and the nod to preservation of the Union, the new declaration of principles included phrases, such as "speedy restoration of the South," that made it sound suspiciously Democratic.

If Dana was forced to walk a fine line, so was the *Sun*'s staff. As editor in chief, Dana laid down the rules in no uncertain terms. On February 1, 1868, he wrote to Washington correspondent Uriah H. Painter: "I want to avoid the appearance of too much partiality for the Republicans in your dispatches, as in every other part of the paper. When a Democrat makes a [great?] speech, please say so, just as well as you say the same of a Republican when he is entitled to it."[39] Again on March 31, he warned Painter, "Please be careful in speaking about Mr. Evarts. He is a stockholder in the Sun, and we must not say anything unpleasant about him."[40]

Dana was as solicitous of the Democrats as he was of his stockholders. His strategy was unusual: the *Sun* blurred party differences (and probably confused its readers) by urging Northern Democrats to be more like Radical Republicans. The paper called upon Democrats to clear their party of the "ancient Federalism" that encrusted it, and to return to the "liberal ideas, radical doctrines, and reformatory measures" of its founders. It was calculating in its invocation of Democratic icons Thomas Jefferson and Andrew Jackson. The *Sun* used the rhetoric of the antebellum producing classes when it pointed out that in addition to being national heroes, these men were "the champions of the masses in their struggles against the combination of wealth." Dana carefully identified the *Sun* with those heroes of the Republic who had championed universal suffrage and dealt their "heaviest blows" against "imperious moneyed corporations."[41]

There was further evidence that Dana sought to upset traditional partisan loyalties in the *Sun's* suggestion in 1868 that the Democrats should nominate Chief Justice of the United States Salmon P. Chase for president. Chase, a former Free Soiler, had run against Lincoln for the 1860 Republican nomination and had later served as his secretary of the treasury. When Dana supported Chase's nomination for president, he was presiding over the impeachment trial of Andrew Johnson. While Chase was anathema to Democratic regulars, Dana argued that Chase would restore "many able and influential leaders of the old Barnburner faction who left the party on account of the slavery question, but have not differed from it on other subjects."[42]

The *Sun* supported civil rights for African-Americans during its first year, a courageous step in a city where the freedmen had few friends. The paper was highly critical of those Democrats who opposed congressional Reconstruction of the South simply because they did not want to give blacks the vote. In the first issue of the *Sun*, Dana stated, "We are not among those who originally desired the universal and unqualified enfranchisement of the Southern Negroes. We preferred to see the test of intelligence applied to them as it ought to be applied to all electors. But whether right or wrong, that question has been settled and cannot safely or wisely be reopened."[43]

When the problems of Reconstruction became entangled in the effort to impeach Andrew Johnson, Dana faced another dilemma. The editor and his Republican stockholders favored congressional Reconstruction, but most Democrats supported Johnson's more conservative plan.[44] Any position Dana took on the impeachment trial ran the risk of alienating either his stockholders or his readers.

The *Sun*'s coverage of the crisis was thorough. Publisher and business manager I. W. England ordered Washington correspondent Uriah Painter: "We want a capital special account of the close of the Impeachment for Wednesday's paper. . . . The *Rendering of the Verdict* will undoubtedly be one of the most impressive, as it will be one of the most important events in our history. If you do not have time to do it for us, please engage some brilliant assistant so that we shall not be behind in this matter."[45]

Editorially, Dana had little to say about the impeachment crisis, and he distanced the *Sun* from the proceedings in the Senate. Strange as this silence seemed on the part of a man who had been forced to leave the *Chicago Republican* because of his attacks on Johnson, Dana's dual obligations made him magnanimous. He was also convinced that Grant would be elected president in November. The *Sun*'s editorial page trumpeted the idea that the country would soon be rid of Johnson one way or another.

On May 18, 1868, the *Sun* announced Johnson's acquittal, congratulated the Senate for its nonpartisanship, and applauded those Republicans who had voted with their consciences instead of with their party. In the spirit of bipartisanship, the paper called the votes of the seven Republican dissenters "the highest instance of impartiality and honesty in all political history," adding, "It does not, therefore, become the triumphant minority to hurl charges of partisan partiality and proscription at the majority."[46]

Dana predicted a Republican landslide in November. To assist in the campaign, the *Sun* published excerpts from a campaign biography of Ulysses S. Grant written jointly by Dana and James Harrison Wilson. Though Dana added his name and prestige to the book, Wilson wrote all but three chapters.[47] Dana read over Wilson's portion, however, and revealed what was perhaps his true opinion of the work in a comment that Wilson proudly recorded in his pocket diary. "Dana writes in complimentary terms of the history—says nothing like the rapidity with which it was written was ever known before."[48] The selections from the *Life of Grant* that Dana printed in the *Sun* beginning in July 1868 adhered to the nineteenth-century convention of contrasting the general's native abilities as a soldier and man of action with the more artificial skills of politicians and office seekers. "[Grant] has planned campaigns, proclaimed truces, received the capitulation of cities, and negotiated the terms of surrender of an armed Confederacy, but he has never waited in the presence chamber of Kings, nor wearied the patience of Ambassadors with vapid diplomatic dispatches."[49]

When the Democrats nominated Horatio Seymour, New York's wartime governor, for the presidency on a platform calling for universal amnesty and an end to "Negro supremacy," the *Sun* accused the party of "advocating a revolutionary and violent overthrow of all that has been accomplished since the war came to an end."[50] What's more, Dana urged Seymour to withdraw from the race, in a tongue-in-cheek editorial that was a vintage blend of contradictions and impossibilities: "[We] suggest the withdrawal of Governor Seymour. We do not advise the Democrats to turn Republicans, but only recommend that they change front in their opposition to General Grant, a sterling Democrat of the old Jeffersonian and Jacksonian school, and go in with his present supporters, and thus make him in name what he is in fact — a Democratic-Republican candidate."[51]

Professional Democratic politicians viewed Dana's idea with horror. As Samuel Tilden and August Belmont privately observed: "The proposition is regarded as absurd, and is received by our masses with astonishment, derision, and indignation."[52] Dana, however, used his rejection of Seymour as evidence of the *Sun's* high-mindedness, and he disingenuously claimed to have the best interests of the Democratic party at heart.

After Grant won an easy victory, Dana published an editorial describing what he expected from the new Republican administration. The editorial hinted at the tensions in Dana's agreement with his Republican stockholders, and it anticipated the rupture of this unstable alliance. Dana predicted that Grant would reconstruct and pacify the South and reintegrate it into the national economy through commerce and industry rather than military rule. "Let them cease to hurl the contemptible epithets of 'carpetbagger' and 'scalawag' at immigrants from the North and from Europe, who would bring them capital, labor, and skill to restore their waste places."[53] He anticipated that the "spirit of repudiation" would be exorcised by the new confi-

dence of capital and labor in the North, and he called for retrenchment and reduction in the size of the national government. This final
suggestion in particular did not bode well for the *Sun*'s future relations with the Radical Republicans, who contended that massive federal presence was necessary to reconstruct the South and guarantee
the rights of the freedmen.

Dana reversed the *Sun*'s opinion of Ulysses S. Grant shortly after
the president's inauguration in March 1869. This about-face would
be one of the most controversial events of Dana's thirty years at the
newspaper. Unbelievably, it appeared that the editor had once again
been stymied in his pursuit of the office of collector of the Port of
New York. The sequence of events seemed identical to his embarrassment at the *Chicago Republican*. To Dana's critics, the facts were
obvious: Dana had again applied for the post of collector and when
Grant turned him down, Dana turned on Grant.[54]

As appealing as this explanation was, the truth was more complex. In Chicago, Dana had applied to President Andrew Johnson
for the New York collectorship as a means of leaving the *Chicago Republican*. Four years later, the editor may have intended to be both
collector of the Port of New York *and* editor of the *New York Sun*.
Or perhaps his vanity led him to pursue the office simply so he could
publicly turn an offer down.

The new controversy over the New York collectorship began with
a promise that John Rawlins, General Grant's closest aide, made to
Dana late in 1868. According to James Harrison Wilson, who appeared
to enjoy having his own bit part in the drama, he and Rawlins had
met to discuss cabinet appointments. They agreed on Dana's merit.

> [Dana] had rendered both Grant and the government most im-
> portant service. . . . He was a vital, able man; and . . . having
> a metropolitan newspaper fast rising into popularity and influ-
> ence, he could be of great benefit to the new administration. In
> consideration of the fact that he could not with justice to his own
> interests leave his newspaper, we concluded that the most suit-
> able place for him was that of Collector of Customs at New York.
> Rawlins, who was a prudent man, took the matter under further
> advisement, and at our next meeting, not only expressed his con-
> currence in the conclusion we had reached, but requested me to

inform Dana that he was to have that place, and this was with-out qualification or condition.[55]

While Wilson later claimed that Dana had not been an appli-cant for the office and that "the action which I had taken with Gen-eral Rawlins was entirely on my own responsibility," it is unlikely he had taken such steps without the knowledge and approval of the edi-tor. Furthermore, Wilson obviously believed that Dana would accept the job.[56] Through Rawlins, Grant notified Wilson, who told Dana that the president-elect intended to offer him the post.

Then, for unknown reasons Grant gave the collectorship to Moses Grinnell, a Republican of whom the *Sun* generously commented: "With [Grinnell's] well-known energy, integrity, and business capac-ity in the control of that establishment we may expect soon to see its abuses mercilessly corrected, its expenses reduced, its stealings stopped, and its returns to the treasury largely increased."[57]

Dana's reaction to this slight became public after George Bout-well, the new secretary of the treasury, offered him the lesser office of New York Customs appraiser. Boutwell, a friend of Dana's, referred to the office as one "for which probably you have neither taste nor inclination," but he nonetheless hoped that the editor "[would] not decline." The *Sun* printed Boutwell's offer, along with Dana's answer on April 19, 1869. Dana's reply read:

Having been educated to commercial pursuits, the office is not repugnant to my tastes; and as for serving the government at some sacrifice of my own interest and convenience, I trust that during the past few years, I have sufficiently proved my readiness to do it. But I already hold an office of responsibility as the conductor of an independent newspaper, and I am persuaded that to aban-don it or neglect it for the functions you offer me would be to leave a superior duty for one of lesser importance. Nor is it cer-tain that I cannot do more to help you in the pure and efficient administration of the Treasury Department by remaining here and denouncing and exposing political immorality than I could as Appraiser by the most zealous effort to insure the faithful and honest collection of the customs.[58]

Was Dana sincere in his claim that he no longer had much interest in public office? Most *Sun* employees thought so, and at least one expressed surprise that Dana should even be interested in the job. In a private letter to the *Sun's* Washington correspondent Uriah Painter, a Mr. Byington wrote that he did not think Dana would accept the post if it were offered. "Guess the Collector matter is a revamp of the old Chicago application. D. is too heavily invested here to remove I think."[59]

Perhaps Dana thought he could be both collector of the Port of New York *and* editor of the *Sun*. There can be no doubt that Dana would have liked an offer — even if only to turn it down. No one who knew of the thin-skinned editor's extraordinary sensitivity was surprised at his pique when he was not offered the job. Dana believed that Grant had failed to honor his promise.

Dana was a man of great vanity, as his enemies knew. When the president appointed George M. Robeson secretary of the navy three months later in July, 1869, the *Brooklyn Union* pointed out, "Mr. Robeson was appointed Secretary of the Navy for the same reason that Mr. Dana wasn't appointed Collector." As usual, Dana felt impelled to clarify the matter. The difference, according to the *Sun*, was that Robeson had given Ulysses Grant money, and Dana had not.

> As Mr. Robeson gave General Grant five hundred dollars in money, subscribed toward the purchase of his Philadelphia house, and Mr. Dana never gave him any money at all, but only supported him during the war — when his friends were not so many nor so rich as at present — worked for his elevation to the command of all our armies, and promoted his election to the Presidency, it must be admitted that the *Union* has solved with perfect success the problem of the reason for Robeson's appointment.[60]

Would Dana have criticized the Grant administration had the president offered him the New York collectorship? Yes, but perhaps with less vehemence. While Dana's enemies were not entirely wrong in their claim that the editor was motivated by spite, they missed an important point. In 1865 Charles Dana had turned on Andrew Johnson not only out of embarrassment over the New York collectorship but also for ideological reasons. The events of 1869 were different:

Dana's reversal on Grant was an act of personal pique to be sure, but it was also a sound business decision.

The election of 1868 brought about significant changes in the uneasy balance of power at the *New York Sun*. Until Grant's victory was secure, Dana had honored what was at least an informal agreement with the paper's Republican stockholders. In exchange for their financial backing, he had thrown the weight of the *Sun* behind Ulysses S. Grant. He had helped to elect Grant president, thus meeting his obligations. Dana had accomplished this feat without losing Democratic readers by claiming that the *Sun* was politically independent. Here the chaos of the postwar Democratic party had played into his hand.

Yet in a tight market in which consumers bought newspapers largely on the basis of partisan loyalty, Dana could not assume that the strategy of independence would work indefinitely. To stake a claim in the cut-throat New York newspaper industry, Dana needed to define and win a loyal audience. For a variety of reasons, personal as well as pragmatic, he would choose to keep that audience a Democratic one. In doing so, he would graft the language of producerism onto the *Sun*'s antebellum roots to create a new version of urban, Jacksonian democracy.

7

Two Cents' Worth
The Politics of Humor

Sparkling, lively, interesting, "the newspaperman's newspaper"—
that is how late nineteenth-century New Yorkers described the
New York Sun.[1] At the height of its popularity, approximately from
1870 to 1884, the *Sun* had a larger circulation than any other morning daily in the city. Noted for its urbanity, its concise reporting, and
its deft use of language, the *New York Sun* set standards for a generation of journalists.[2] Charles Dana combined three elements—
sympathy for the working class, independence from political party,
and a playful sense of humor—into a unique editorial voice that was
central to the *Sun's* success.

From the time Dana bought the paper, according to one *Sun*
reporter, "it may be truthfully said that Dana was the *Sun* and the
Sun was Dana. He was the sole arbiter of its policy and it was his
constant practice to supervise every editorial contribution that came
in while he was on duty."[3] This complete editorial control—which
nineteenth-century Americans called personal journalism—worked
so long as a newspaper remained profitable. The financial success of
the *Sun* during the 1870s allowed Dana to champion the producing
classes by remaining politically independent. Under Dana's direction,
the *Sun's* satirical barbs stung Democrats and Republicans alike. As
Frank Leslie's Illustrated noted in 1875, "[The *Sun's*] field has not been
disputed for a share of its profits, because Dana's peculiar strength
as a writer and a fighter makes capitalists and politicians afraid of

him. . . . Dana's personal strength is the *Sun's* safeguard against a
rival in two-cent journalism."[4]

Ever mindful of his preexisting working-class readership, Dana
announced in October 1868 that the *Sun* would be "an uncompromising advocate of the laboring masses."[5] The *Sun* provided extensive coverage of labor organizations, union meetings, and strikes.
On a typical day in 1868, it reported on strikes by the journeymen
bakers and the Singer machine iron molders, fund-raising attempts
by the Coach Makers' Union, and the activities of Typographical Union
No. Six, the union of the *Sun's* printers.[6] When the journeymen bakers struck for shorter hours and higher pay, the *Sun* called their actions "eminently just and proper" and printed the names of the master
bakers who had acceded to the demands of the union.[7] When the
journeymen bricklayers struck for the eight-hour day in the summer
of 1868, the *Sun* also sided with the workers. An editorial that appeared on June 25, 1868, used the labor theory of value to defend
not only the journeymen's demand for shorter hours but also their
right to organize.

> On the main question between the two parties our sympathies
> are decidedly with the men. . . . The price of labor, like that of
> any other commodity, can only be determined by those who have
> it to dispose of holding out for the best price they can obtain.
> . . . Just so, the bricklayers have fixed their price on what they
> have to sell, namely their strength and skill, and have a right to
> abide the result. . . . But that it is proper for them to combine
> in this step and stand by one another is too plain for argument.
> The labor of a single man is insufficient by itself to test the market.
> It is only when it is massed together with the labor of many that
> it has a fair chance; and whatever rules are necessary to give this
> combination an effective discipline are as justifiable as the regu-
> lations of an army.[8]

Dana used this same logic to call for the repeal of the Conspir-
acy Law, an ordinance that forbade union members to act together
in a manner injurious to trade. *Sun* editorials suggested that workingmen's combinations were no worse than stock market manipulations that "plunder[ed] the public." Of the two, in fact, the paper
asserted that the capitalists were the "greater criminals," arguing that

"if they want liberty to carry on their combinations, they cannot deny to laboring men the privileges of combining to resist them."[9]

Although the *Sun* was consistently sympathetic to the interests of the working class, the paper found no serious fault with capitalism. Dana's views on labor issues during the 1870s were similar not only to those he had held as managing editor of Horace Greeley's *Tribune* but also to those he had espoused at Brook Farm. Dana distrusted monopolies, but the only alternative he raised was greater competition. Propelled by a hazy ideal of labor as "the noblest duty of life," he argued that higher wages for labor would add to the prosperity of all.[10] Though progressive for its time, the *Sun* nevertheless trod a carefully moderate, even paternalistic course, evident in Dana's "note to workingmen" published in March 1869. "We believe that sincere respect can only be won by manly honesty, and while we take the workingmen's side, we claim also the privilege of being their critics and advisors. This course . . . will render our services doubly useful. It will point out to the workingmen the mistakes they are in danger of committing, and compel the rest of the world, seeing our impartiality, to respect the principles we advocate."[11]

The *Sun* reflected a Jacksonian emphasis on self-help and cooperation — the same values that Dana had espoused in the 1840s. Like the old Fourierist *Harbinger*, the *Sun* advocated cooperative associations of workingmen that would build housing, establish reading rooms, and provide lectures and self-help programs.[12] The paper frequently raised what it called the "theory of cooperation as the best substitute for strikes." In "An Example for Workingmen" published on October 5, 1871, the *Sun* described a successful cooperative printing association established by twenty-five journeymen printers after an unsuccessful strike for higher wages: "This rapid growth of a cooperative association, which started with a mere trifle of money, ought to be an encouraging example for other workingmen who may be discussing the expediency of striking for higher wages. Let some of the eight-hour theorists try cooperation."[13]

Charles Dana also defended the interests of his readers by printing frequent reminders that city services, such as parks and public baths, should be made available to the producing classes on days and at hours when they were free to benefit from them. This concern prompted one reader to thank Dana for the "spirited articles in your influential journal vindicating the rights of 'poor boys' to recreate on the grounds of Central Park."[14] In a similar vein, the *Sun* fought against Sabbath laws that threatened to close reading rooms on the only day that most working men and women were free to use them.[15]

Dana believed that his predominantly working-class readers were interested in more than stories of vice and crime. The *Sun* gave its readers a dizzying array of information on politics, literature, and stories of general human interest.[16] These stories were presented in seven columns of small and relatively hard-to-read print, and met what were considered to be the highest literary standards of the day. When a 1919 anniversary issue of the *Sun* looked back on Dana's achievements, it recalled that the editor had believed his readers would "enjoy a discourse upon the architecture of the tombs of the Pharaohs as much as [they] liked a description of the Tombs of Centre Street."[17]

The *Sun*'s high literary standards did not mean, however, that the paper was either stuffy or formal. Indeed, Dana believed that an editor was obliged to print all the news, whether or not it was acceptable to polite society. In his words:

> The newspaper must be founded upon human nature. It must correspond to the wants of the people. It must furnish the [news] which the people demand, or else it never can be successful. . . . By news I mean everything that occurs, everything which is of human interest. . . . There is a great disposition in some quarters to say that the newspapers ought to limit the amount of news they print; that certain kinds of news ought not to be published. . . . I have always felt that whatever the Divine Providence permitted to occur I was not too proud to print.[18]

Dana's views contrasted sharply with those of his peers in New York's literary establishment, who held that editors should sanitize the news before they published it. For example, in 1871 *Harper's Monthly* editor George William Curtis called upon newspaper editors to become "moral censors." Curtis (who had been a student of Dana's at Brook Farm) asserted that in "assuming the responsibility of publication," an editor "has not divested himself of his individual accountability."[19] A similar article in *Forum* charged the press with failing in its duty to teach and lead the masses. In a democracy, the article claimed, newspapers are "the direct sources of those floating opinions which have drifted into [the people's] minds, wherewith they judge all social and political problems."[20]

Such calls for editorial self-censorship were the views of elites who sensed the danger to their own authority posed by a rising tide of popular democracy. Many blamed newspapers for encouraging what they believed to be the ignorant rule of the political machine.[21] Men like Curtis believed that editors should provide social ballast and print only what was high-minded and moral. A typical article in the *North American Review* questioned the need to cater to the lowest tastes of the people and concluded with a condemnation of the marketplace in which sensational stories were bought and sold. It voiced the patrician critique of a world in which the pursuit of money had replaced traditional social values.

> To say that all this is necessary in order to report the news is absurd. . . . This is a confession that making money is the chief end of a newspaper, and this places it on a level with the grog shops and the houses of ill-fame. . . . If merely making money is what a newspaper is for, let it be frankly stated and understood. We shall then hear somewhat less about the great moral and religious influence of the press.[22]

The motto of the *New York Times*, All the News That's Fit to Print, would reflect the views of these social elites. By contrast, the *Sun's* slogan, It Shines for All, threatened to encourage the unruly democracy they most feared.[23]

To a large extent, the unique style of the *Sun* under Charles A. Dana grew out of what the editor called the paper's "independence." There is considerable difference of opinion about the exact meaning of the nineteenth-century term "independent press." The number of newspapers calling themselves independent increased from a quarter of those listed in the 1880 newspaper directories to a third of those listed in 1890.[24] But many of these papers had decided political leanings. Both the *New York Sun* and the *New York Herald*, for example, claimed to be "independent," but both had largely Democratic readerships and nearly always supported the Democratic party.

At its most narrow, independent journalism meant that editors did not run for public office.[25] At its broadest, independence meant the absence of formal ties between the press and political organizations. As *New York Tribune* editor Whitelaw Reid wrote in 1872, "Independent journalism! . . . That is the watchword of the future in the profession! An end of concealments because it would hurt the party, an end of one-sided expositions . . . of doctoring the reports of public opinion . . . of half truths . . . that is the end to which every perplexed journalist a new and beneficent Declaration of Independence affords."[26]

Significantly, the "independent" press of the 1870s was not nonpartisan. Most of Dana's contemporaries would have agreed with Whitelaw Reid's 1879 distinction. "I have been one of the apostles of independent journalism, but I never intended to keep entirely aloof from party. Really influential editors will seek to lead a party, not thrust it aside."[27] Dana shared this view, which explained his often adversarial relationship with the Democratic party. It also explained the newspaper's 1885 masthead, which proclaimed the *Sun* "an independent newspaper of Democratic principles, but not controlled by any set of politicians or manipulators."[28]

Dana prided himself on the *Sun's* lack of loyalty to any political organization.[29] Indeed, the editor was said to have boasted that no reader could go to bed certain of what would appear in the *Sun* the following morning.[30] Far from giving unquestioning support to the Democratic party, Dana was a gadfly. Ironically, Dana's style of independence was similar to that of both the Independent Republicans in 1872 and the Mugwumps in 1884 — politicians whom Dana despised.

What historian Geoffrey Blodgett has said of nineteenth-century political independents — that they were in the two-party system but not of it — can also be applied to the editor of the *Sun*. What raised the ire of party regulars was the independents' insistence on "instant factional influence at the highest levels of whatever party they chose to support, while they claimed total immunity from any sort of party discipline."[31] At a time of intense partisanship and equally balanced parties, party leaders feared that Dana's brand of independence would upset their political calculations. As a result, Dana's unpredictability had the overall effect of minimizing the *Sun's* influence within the Democratic party.[32] Dana's views, though widely read, were thus easily dismissed by political leaders.[33] After Dana's death, *Evening Sun* editor Amos Cummings wrote, "Mr. Dana, as I often told him, had no party behind him, and the missiles he shot lacked the weight and momentum that party organization gives."[34]

Although Dana claimed that the *Sun* was politically independent, it became consistently anti-Grant beginning shortly after the President's inauguration in March 1869. Beginning with his cabinet appointments, the new president had taken one false step after another. Grant's first mistake was his failure to consult the appropriate Republican leaders concerning cabinet nominations. His second was his attempt to name New York department store baron Alexander T. Stewart secretary of the treasury. Stewart was a Scottish immigrant and self-made man who had acquired a fortune in the import trade. Unfortunately for Grant, Stewart caught the attention of the president's powerful rival Charles Sumner. Piqued by Grant's failure to consult Republican leaders, Sumner "discovered" an obscure law that forbade anyone engaged in trade or commerce to be appointed treasury secretary.[35] After a futile attempt to get around the law, Grant had to withdraw the nomination. Even more embarrassing for the president was the resignation of his new secretary of the navy, Adolphe E. Borie. Borie was forced to leave office when it became known that he had contributed large sums of money to build a house for the president and his wife, Julia Dent Grant.

Grant's "want of discretion" in accepting Borie's gift launched a theme with which Dana tormented the president for the next eight years.[36] The *Sun*'s almost daily attacks on Grant as "the great gift-taker" drew considerable attention to the newspaper, most of it negative. Republican diarist George Templeton Strong referred to the *Sun* in 1870 as "the lowest sensational newspaper in the city," adding that "Dana knows better, is capable of better things, and ought to be ashamed of himself."[37] Sometimes Dana published lists of Grant's friends and relatives who had received appointments. At other times he simply inserted the name "President Useless S. Grant" at the head of an article, usually one that did not mention either Grant or the Presidency. When reporting on the gift of a watch to the president during a visit to a watch factory, the *Sun* noted, "He takes presents on all occasions and from everybody; and, as is well known, he has appointed men to the highest offices in consideration of the presents they have given him. . . . Perhaps he will make [the watch manufacturer] a member of his Cabinet, in the changes which are about to take place in that remarkable organization."[38]

Charles Dana became obsessed with slinging mud at the president. On April 3, 1869, he wrote to *Sun* Washington correspondent Uriah Painter, "Can you get me the lists of subscribers to the Grant house and money present? And also to that for General Sherman?"[39] Three months later he reminded Painter to send the names of subscribers to the Sherman fund, and "also a copy of the letter from USG to someone in this city, by which the subscription was started."[40] Dana readily used Painter to ferret out information for his own private crusades, but he made it clear to the Washington correspondent that personal attacks would appear only in the editorials, not in the news columns: "The general rule of the Sun is not to attack anybody. . . . What we want is facts. The comments, and especially the ill-natured ones, we wish to add ourselves. Besides, we have a preference for editing our own paper."[41]

Dana became a thorn in the side of the Grant administration. Republican officials found the *Sun*'s attacks on the president and his cabinet particularly deplorable because they had anticipated that Dana would run his paper in the interest of their party. According to the conventions that governed relations between nineteenth-century politicians and the press, Dana had irresponsibly violated the trust of the Republican stockholders who financed the *Sun*. This explains why Secretary of State Hamilton Fish called the editor a "blackguard" and a "liar."

Fish also had personal reasons for animosity toward Dana. The *Sun* tormented Fish and his son-in-law Sidney Webster, counsel for the Spanish government, with charges of nepotism and political impropriety. Dana, a staunch advocate of Cuban liberation from Spanish colonial rule, charged, "It is highly indelicate and improper for Mr. Fish to occupy the position of Secretary of State, pursuing a course extremely hostile to Cuba, while at the same time the Spanish government is pouring money into the pockets of his son-in-law — and, as it were, into the lap of his own family."[42]

Hamilton Fish's diary contains abundant evidence of the secretary's fury at Dana's attacks. Fish found it particularly galling that the Grant administration had given patronage jobs to "friends" of

Sun stockholders and to associates of its untrustworthy editor. Fish noted that on December 23, 1869, he had spoken with the president about "the course of the NY *Sun* and its abusive attacks on the Administration," and had suggested a means of retaliation.

> It is . . . time to draw a line, and let it be understood that those who control the "Sun" are not regarded as friends: and that these Gentlemen have their friends in the Custom House and Post Office, etc. in New York, and that if some of them were removed, it would soon be understood that the Administration does not intend to sustain its most bitter enemies. [Grant] replied that he would remove everyone appointed on the recommendation of any of the proprietors of the "Sun."[43]

There was no doubt in Fish's mind about what was motivating Dana's attacks: "The assault . . . is assumed to be from hostility to the President, and with the intent of forcing him to break up his present Cabinet and thus to gratify his disappointment and to injure at the same time the President who did not give him the appointment he coveted, and the Republican party which has not recognized him as its leader."[44]

Dana may indeed have had personal reasons for his assaults on the president and Fish, but his commitment to revolution in Cuba was genuine. The *Sun* blamed Grant and the "crushing apathy of the pseudo-philanthropic Republican Party" for their failure to assist in the Cuban drive for independence. "The only hope for the slaves of Cuba and for the friends of freedom throughout the world is the success of the Cuban revolution."[45] Dana had other motivations as well, including an ethnocentric and expansionist view of manifest destiny: "It is the natural law of nations as well as of nature, that larger bodies attract toward them smaller ones. . . . With the acquisitive eye which has ever been a striking feature in the history of the Anglo-Saxon race, we had spied out other lands, lying both at the North and the South, and marked them for future conquest or purchase."[46]

Dana's interest in Cuban revolution lasted until his death in 1897. He corresponded personally with leading Cuban revolutionists, including his "warm friend" José Martí, and met with them when they came to New York.[47] It was said that "a Latin-American accent was a sure card of admission" to Dana's office. In 1899 a square in Camagüey, Cuba, was renamed Charles A. Dana Plaza in tribute to his support of the New York Cuban junta.[48]

The *Sun* was making money, which perhaps helped to placate Grant's friends among the paper's stockholders. As one *Sun* employee facetiously noted to Washington correspondent Uriah Painter, "It *pays*, but *oh dear* what a Republican paper it has [become]!"[49]

During the 1870s, Dana called on both political parties to bury the divisive issues of the Civil War era. He warned Democrats of the folly of intimidating blacks, and he pointed out that if they continued to "wander and wail and wound . . . among the tombstones of the dead past," they would only allow the Republicans to make political hay out of saving the Union.[50] The *Sun* supported the immediate ratification of the Fifteenth Amendment, which enfranchised former slaves, arguing that it would "bring to a final settlement the last of those long standing questions which have remained to us as a legacy."[51] The *Sun* urged both parties to leave behind those questions that had "passed into history."[52]

At the same time, Dana failed to press for the continuation of the revolution in race relations that had begun with the Civil War, and in so doing he broke irrevocably with his own Radical Republican past. By announcing that the Republican party had achieved glory when "in all the breadth of our land it abolished slavery," Dana implied that the true mission of the party had been accomplished and there was little need for concern about the freedmen.[53] Though the editor continued to champion the white laborers of New York City in their fight against "wage slavery," he refused to draw any parallels or see any connection with the struggle of Southern blacks. Because of his need to keep the allegiance of the *Sun*'s white, working-class constituency as well as his dislike of Republican centralized government, the editor failed to speak out for justice for the freedmen.

While Dana took every opportunity to discredit Grant and the Republicans with charges of nepotism, he tended to ignore corruption among the sachems of New York's Democratic Tammany Hall. The *Sun*'s relationship with Tammany Hall was complex, fluid, and often contradictory. Dana had to live with the Democratic machine if he wanted to keep the *Sun*'s readership of immigrants, small merchants, and mechanics. As a result, he tacitly supported Tammany Hall while satirizing and ridiculing its leaders.

Though the *Sun* generally held its fire against Tammany, it was not a machine newspaper. The *Sun* often supported anti-Tammany Democratic candidates. For example, when Tammany swept all of the offices in the 1870 congressional race, the *Sun* commented, "A superficial observer might conclude that this machine is so powerful . . . that it would as one of its managers expressed it, elect a jackass to Congress if they chose to nominate him."[54] Compared with what the *Sun* was saying about the Republicans, this gibe was rather mild.

But Dana may have paid a price for this compromise. Republicans charged that the "Tweed Ring," headed by New York Democratic boss William Tweed, made payoffs to reporters—including at least one on the *Sun*—in exchange for favorable coverage. Historian Morris Werner has claimed that reporters on nearly every New York City newspaper were put on the city payroll at salaries of $2,000 to $2,500 a year.[55] Others have argued that the press's indifference to Tammany's corruption was purchased with city advertising or with the opportunity to publish official New York City proceedings. Even scholars sympathetic to the Boss's efforts to simplify and centralize the city's government have echoed these charges.[56]

An anonymous 1870 pamphlet, "The Biter Bit, or the Robert Macaire of Journalism," raised the charge that the *Sun* had been bought. The author of "The Biter Bit" was Col. James B. Mix of the *New York Tribune*. Among other things, "The Biter Bit" charged that the *Sun's* Albany correspondent, A. M. Soteldo, had accepted Ring money for writing editorials in favor of the proposed New York City Charter of 1870. Mix claimed that while the *Sun* had initially opposed the charter, the paper had reversed itself after Soteldo accepted the bribe.[57]

There was some truth to the charges of "The Biter Bit." Dana admitted in a signed editorial on January 6, 1871, that a *Sun* reporter had indeed accepted a bribe. Though he fired Soteldo, Dana denied that the *Sun* had changed its editorial policy toward the charter. He also accused *Tribune* editor Horace Greeley of spreading the lies.

James B. Mix, blackmailer, A. M. Soteldo, Jr., self-acknowledged scoundrel; [and] Horace Greeley, philanthropist . . . are responsible for an anonymous pamphlet of sixty-nine pages, the product of a malicious but feeble disposition to injure the *Sun*. Mr. Greeley is a Universalist, and believes that nobody will ever go to Hell, or he could not have been tempted to stand godfather to the anonymous libel of two scoundrels and one thief.[58]

Though Dana thus admitted the truth of the lesser charge, the accusation that such a bribe had reversed the paper's editorial policy is more difficult to assess. The Charter of 1870, often called the Tweed charter, was a landmark in the sustained effort of New York City to achieve municipal home rule. The charter was supported by a curious alliance of reformers who favored centralization in local government, businessmen who sought consolidation and order, and political opportunists out for self-enrichment. The charter simplified and centralized the city government by abolishing the County Board of Supervisors and the commission system, and by consolidating the police, fire, health, and excise boards into departments under the mayor's jurisdiction. In addition, the charter gave the mayor the power to appoint department heads and to remove city officials.

Good-government forces were happy with these provisions, which were intended to increase the accountability of the mayor. Yet these same reformers were appalled by provisions of the charter that would institutionalize the power of Boss William M. Tweed by concentrating authority in him as the superintendent of public works. While this marriage of reform and political opportunism did not sit well with some Democrats, most, including the reform-minded Citizens' Association, eventually came to favor it.[59]

The *New York Sun* had long been an advocate of municipal home rule, arguing in 1869 that it was folly for the state legislature at Albany to decide all matters of local interest to New York City. "[These] men have no more knowledge of our affairs than they have of those of Boston or Philadelphia. . . . A more flagrant violation of the true democratic principle of self-government can scarcely be imagined."[60] Yet at the same time, the *Sun* was mistrustful of the Tammany Democrats and their efforts to rewrite the charter "for their own profit."[61] In an editorial on March 29, 1870, the *Sun* came out conclusively for the charter as a means of strengthening local government. It was this editorial that "The Biter Bit" claimed had resulted from a bribe.

Dana flatly denied that the *Sun* had been influenced by the activities of its Albany correspondent.[62] There is no evidence either way about the truth of Dana's countercharge that Horace Greeley had been involved in publishing "The Biter Bit." Nor is there any evidence regarding Dana's even more peculiar accusation — made in his cables to *Sun* Washington correspondent Uriah Painter — that the Government Printing Office in Washington had printed the pamphlet.[63] In the editor's mind, any one of his enemies might have been responsible for publishing "The Biter Bit." If it was not Greeley, then perhaps it was Grant. Dana fired off letters to Painter: "A. M. Soteldo, Jr. has gone to Florida, as he tells his friends, as a special supervising agent of the Treasury. Is it so?" And, "You are certainly wrong. . . . [Soteldo] has an appointment as a travelling Treasury agent in Texas and Florida. Pay $8.00 a day and expenses. . . . I am quite sure this is so. Please see if you can't get me the proof of it." And most bizarre of all, "What is the evidence that Hamilton Fish revised the proofs of the Biter Bit pamphlet?"[64] Personal relationships often outweighed ideological consistency in determining Dana's political views. In his attempt to discover the source of "The Biter Bit," Dana was rounding up the usual suspects.

Ultimately, the bribe probably had little influence on the *Sun's* attitude toward the Charter of 1870. Not only did Dana favor the idea of municipal home rule, but he also believed that if municipal reorganization was to be achieved, he would have to put up with the "grotesqueness" of William M. Tweed. It was no coincidence that, shortly after the passage of the New York City charter, Dana launched his satirical attempt to erect a statue of the Tammany Boss.

The idea was to make Tweed look absurd, and it worked. A week after the *Sun* first proposed the idea, it asked sardonically, "Has Boss Tweed any friends? If he has they are a mean set. . . . As yet only four citizens have sent in their subscriptions. They were not large, but they were paid in cash, and there is reason for the belief that they were tokens of sincere admiration for Mr. Tweed."[65]

Other newspapers took up the *Sun's* call and made suggestions for the statue. The *Herald* proposed a "colossal hollow figure in brass of the 'Boss' as the big indian, seated in an arm chair, holding in his right hand the scroll of our new city Charter, and in his left hand the pipe of peace."[66] The *Sun* preferred a "nautical statue, exhibiting

Boss Tweed as a bold mariner, amid the wild fury of a hurricane."[67] In an illustration by Thomas Nast in *Harper's Weekly*, Edward J. Shandley, the head of the Tweed Testimonial Association, is trying to thrust upon Tweed a bust in the form of an ass's head.[68]

The Boss went along with the scheme until it became obvious that the publicity was making him look ridiculous. On March 16, he wrote to Shandley, "I was aware that a newspaper of our city had brought forward the proposition, but I considered it one of the jocose sensations for which that journal is so famous. . . . The only effect of the proposed statue is to present me to the public as assenting to the parade of a public and permanent testimonial to vanity and self glorification, which do not exist."[69] Taking note of Tweed's public objections, *Sun* headlines gleefully proclaimed, "A Great Man's Modesty. The Hon. William M. Tweed Declines the Sun's Statue. Characteristic Letter From the Great Philanthropist. He Thinks That Virtue Should Be Its Own Reward—The Most Remarkable Letter Ever Written by the Noble Benefactor of the People."[70]

Charles Dana's attempt to ridicule William Tweed was characteristic of political humor in newspapers of the Gilded Age. Historian Tom Leonard has pointed out that "Tammany had a very thin foundation of principled belief. Like the national Democratic party, and unlike most groups of Republicans, there were few symbols or remnants of ideology to draw constitutents together. . . . Ridicule, as it discounted their power, was a particularly serious threat to these Democrats."[71] Just as *Harper's Weekly* illustrator Thomas Nast exaggerated Tammany's power by depicting the Boss as a bloated figure of wealth and arrogance, Charles Dana diminished the political machine by making its Boss an object of ridicule.

While the *Sun* was consistent in calling upon Tammany to "turn honest, stop stealing . . . and give this city a cheap and just government," it was slow to join the chorus of attacks on the Tweed Ring.[72] One explanation for Dana's reluctance to bring down Tweed was his antipathy toward the crusading and elitist Ring investigation. The fight for Tweed's removal, led by the respectable Republicans of the *New York Times* and *Harper's Weekly*, was the kind of political crusade that Dana despised. When the nonpartisan Committee of Seventy was created at Cooper Union in September 1871, Dana praised Samuel Tilden and the Democrats' own efforts to remove the Boss as housecleaning, but condemned "hypocritical reformers" who for "partisan ends" were out for Tweed's blood. When the evidence against Tweed became overwhelming, however, Dana joined the other New York papers in condemning the Ring. The *Sun* congratulated itself on Tweed's removal, but without much justification.

Newspapers were the primary source of humor in the Gilded Age.[73] They popularized the writing of major literary figures such as Mark Twain, Joel Chandler Harris, and Eugene Field. The parodies that appeared in the pages of the *Sun* made a significant contribution to late nineteenth-century humor. The *Sun* attacked frauds and humbugs; it ridiculed pomposity and self-righteousness. Some of the paper's best-known targets were Grover Cleveland, Rutherford B. Hayes, Horace Greeley, and Henry Ward Beecher.

Sun reporter Charles Rosebault recalled in his memoirs that one of the frustrations of working for the "newspaperman's newspaper" was the anonymity of the unsigned editorial. According to Rosebault, the funnier a piece was, the more convinced *Sun* readers were that they saw Dana's hand in it. Although Dana personally dictated many editorial paragraphs, much of the writing was done by his assistants.[74] Dana had a remarkable ability to appreciate and use the work of very different editorial writers. When the trade weekly the *Journalist* published a feature article on Dana in 1888, it discussed his method of organizing the editorial page. Dana worked at the *Sun's* office every day but Sunday, and he alone determined the paper's editorial course.

> After hearing the suggestions of his staff of editorial writers and adding to them a few pertinent ones of his own, the work of writing is begun. . . . By four o'clock he has read in proof the editorials submitted by his assistants, and marked those which must go in the next morning's edition. Nothing goes in that has not met his approval. The editorial page of the *Sun* is just what Mr. Dana desires it to be. It represents his own ideas and no one else's, and when he leaves the office the page is closed.[75]

Of all the *Sun's* editorial writers, Francis P. Church is best remembered today — for an assignment he did not want. Church wrote the answer, published on Christmas Day 1897, to Virginia O'Hanlon's query, "Please tell me the truth; is there a Santa Claus?"[76]

Of the humorous techniques popular in the late nineteenth-century *Sun*, satire was the most important. David G. Croly of the *New York Graphic* observed in 1876 that at least one of the *Sun's* writers was a "born humorist," a writer who compared favorably with Mark Twain and Artemus Ward. According to Croly, "It is this infusion of wit, with a flavor of bitterness and wrath, which excites and attracts the mass of idle people."[77] Satire, or "the recognition of the discrepancy between the ideal and the norm of human conduct," can wear a variety of masks, from the benign to the malevolent.[78] Even at its mildest, the *Sun's* wit concealed a sting.

The *Sun* frequently sharpened an otherwise dull story with the counterpoint of an ironic headline. Often the humor was so subtle that an unwary reader might miss it altogether. One such example appeared on March 6, 1874, in the page 1 account of the activities of the women crusaders of the National Temperance Society in Columbus, Ohio. The story of how the crusaders urged grocery dealers to pledge that they would stop selling distilled spirits was archly titled "Another Busy Day in Columbus," with the subhead "Two Hundred Women Praying in Squads."[79] The derision of "another busy day," coupled with the quasimilitary term "squad," made the crusaders look silly. In case anyone missed the point, a two-sentence paragraph on the editorial page noted, "It is authoritatively announced that Senator Chandler of Michigan has joined Vice-president Wilson's Congressional Temperance Society. To this important step he was not led by the entreaties of praying women."[80]

Some of the *Sun's* humorous leitmotifs went on for months, or even years. The story of the "office cat," created by Willard Bartlett, appeared early in the Cleveland administration and ran on into the 1890s. It began when a flimsy copy of one of Cleveland's presidential messages fluttered off the desk of the telegraph editor and was lost. After the *Sun* failed to print the message, Bartlett, knowing that no one would believe the truth, suggested that the paper claim the office cat had eaten it. The idea amused Dana, who published an editorial noting "the universal interest which this accomplished animal has excited throughout the country." It described the cat's proclivity for consuming tariff discussions ("big speeches full of wind and statistics"), "long-winded prosy articles," and essays on civil service reform ("They are so pretty that he hates to kill them, but duty is duty").[81] The office cat made his presence known at the *Sun* office for the next ten years.

There were numerous examples of whimsy in Dana's *Sun*. Sometimes *Sun* editorials teased prominent figures by giving them silly initials or middle names. Dana insisted, for example, that *Philadelphia Ledger* editor George W. Childs's middle name was Washington. Furthermore, he credited Childs with being the author of all the "absurdly sentimental" verse that appeared in his newspaper.[82] Thousands of readers believed both (untrue) claims.

Another way of making someone look ridiculous was mocking admiration. The *Sun* often pretended to start subscription funds for monuments or other public testimonials. Sometimes the *Sun* printed harmful statements about those whom Dana disliked and then self-righteously professed not to believe them. The result was burlesque so subtle that some readers did not know whether to take the paper seriously.

The *Sun's* sense of humor gave its columns a particularly modern sound. Richard Boyd Hauck has suggested that grim humor occurs in American fiction when "straight reality is presented as being absurdly humorous."[83] Dana's careful confusion of satire and reality was most effective when it parodied the absurd, such as Horace Greeley's well-documented lust for public office or what Dana once referred to as Greeley's tendency to "rush into a fight with his armor unfastened."[84] When the *Sun* dubbed Horace Greeley "the philosopher of Spruce Street" or "the Woodchopper of Chappaqua" and nominated him for every conceivable office from state prison inspector to minister to China, New Yorkers could not agree whether the paper was being malicious.

The nominations of Horace Greeley were funny because they exaggerated Greeley's own unquenchable political ambition. When the *Tribune* expressed the plaintive wish that the *Sun* not promote its editor for any office he did not seek, the *Sun* cheerily replied that it would not renounce its right to advocate measures promoting the public good and chided Greeley for his unwillingness to make the sacrifice of taking an office he did not want.[85]

By the fall of 1872, it was difficult for New Yorkers to be anything other than cynical about politics. The Democratic party was tainted with still-lingering charges of disloyalty, as well as daily revelations of the rottenness of machine politics at the municipal level. The Republicans offered little alternative. Their fiery idealism of the war years had died down to embers, fanned by what most believed were a handful of extremists. Few Americans had any genuine interest in the freedmen, and most were eager to forget about such divisive issues altogether.

It was within this context that Charles Dana began his campaign for the nomination of Horace Greeley as the nation's Democratic candidate. As one *Sun* reporter who later wrote a history of the paper concluded, Dana was convinced that no Democrat stood a chance against Grant in 1872. That being the case, he could think of no better sacrificial lamb than Horace Greeley. "Dana was always possessed by an irresistible inclination to let the world know the profound depths of Greeley's innocence."[86] This suggestion has been repeated by most of Dana's confidants, including Amos J. Cummings, Dana's long-time managing editor. "Mr. Dana started Greeley's candidacy for the Presidency merely as a joke. I warned him that his efforts would be taken seriously, but up to the very morning of the day the Cincinnati Convention met, he insisted that Greeley had no chance of getting a nomination. Of course he had to support him, as he wanted to defeat Grant, but he must have known it was of no use."[87]

Dana was not the only former supporter to abandon Grant in 1872. A group of Republicans dismayed with what looked like Grant's inevitable renomination bolted the party at the same time. These Liberal Republicans, as they called themselves, were dissatisfied with both the corruption of the Grant administration and what they viewed as an oversized federal presence in the South. Most of the liberal dissenters had been Republicans since the party's organization in the 1850s. Dana knew many of the group's leaders (including George Ripley and George William Curtis) from either the *New York Tribune* or his days at Brook Farm. After the war, these men were torn between their objections to federal intervention in the South and their abhorrence of white supremacist attacks on black citizens.[88] By 1872, most had abandoned Radical Reconstruction and hoped to see a reconciliation between the two sections.

Liberal Republicans believed that the Southern legislatures were run by ignorant men who were excluding the region's "best men" from natural positions of leadership. The Liberal Republican insistence on government by the educated and propertied extended beyond their interest in Reconstruction. Their campaign to reform and sanitize urban politics aroused the suspicions of machine politicians and also of Charles Dana. Though the editor in fact agreed with the Liberal Republicans on most issues, he distrusted their crusading, elitist morality. Moreover, Dana was not about to join forces with former friends who, in his eyes, had acceded to his expulsion from the *New York Tribune.* If these factors were not enough to keep Dana out of the Liberal Republican movement, their choice of a standard-bearer did the job. Their nominee for president was none other than Dana's own ubiquitous candidate, *Tribune* editor Horace Greeley. Once Greeley was nominated, first by the Liberal Republicans and then by the Democrats, Dana — given his vehement opposition to Grant — had no choice but to support him as a sacrificial lamb. It was an odd sort of support.

The *Sun* compared "Useless S. Grant" with Greeley, whom it found to be "Great and Useful." Dana printed editorial leaders to this effect nearly every day after Greeley's nomination on July 11, 1872. This one was typical:

> For President
> The Workingmen's Candidate
> Horace Greeley,
> Printer,
> The Man who never Lived an idle, Useless,
> or Dishonest Day.[89]

The *Sun* also supported Greeley with poems such as "Old Greeley's a-Coming," a ditty which probably did little to convince anyone of Dana's sincerity:

> Old Horace is coming hoho, hoho,
> Let us give him a welcome, for all of us know
> That corruption and vice are rife in the land
> And he'll chop it all up, with an axe in his hand.[90]

Grant defeated Greeley in a landslide, and Democrats braced themselves for four more years of Republican rule. Greeley, exhausted by the rigors of the campaign and broken by the sudden death of his wife, died a few weeks after the election.

The *Sun*'s support of Horace Greeley in 1872, however peculiar, did show how far Dana had taken the paper toward the Democratic party since its endorsement of Grant four years earlier. Though the paper was still nominally independent, *Sun* editorials nearly always reflected a Democratic point of view. In fact, the only real point of contention remaining between Dana and the Democrats was whether the protective tariff, which Dana favored, was in the true interests of workingmen. Dana shared the view of his urban working-class readers that protectionism would keep wages high.

Four years later, Dana's commitment to the Democratic party was sealed by the 1876 landmark presidential contest between Rutherford B. Hayes and Samuel Tilden. No longer even attempting to claim political independence, the *Sun* rejoiced prematurely at Tilden's election. The paper predicted that Tilden, for whom it had nothing but praise, would bring peace and harmony to the relations between North and South and mark an end to "bayonet rule."[91] When the electoral commission decided the disputed results in favor of the Republican Hayes, Dana led the New York metropolitan press in the cries of fraud, usually referring to Hayes as "his fraudulency," or "the fraudulent President." The *Sun*, which so many New Yorkers had predicted would be the voice of Radical Republicanism, had undergone a complete transformation.

By 1874, the *Sun* had the highest circulation among all dailies in the city.[92] This success at the newsstands, along with the low cost of newsprint, meant that the *Sun*'s dividends were huge, ranging "almost continually upward from twenty-eight percent to fifty, with an annual average of thirty-six percent."[93] The formula for the *Sun*'s prosperity was easy to understand. Blessed with an established name and market, Dana was able to draw new readers to the paper with concise reporting of the news and breezy wit on the editorial page. Appreciating the need for a strong Democratic newspaper in the city, independent in the sense that it represented no faction, he was able to increase the *Sun*'s circulation every year.

A number of factors began to eat away at the *Sun*'s easy domination of the metropolitan newspaper market in the 1880s, not the least of which were the burgeoning reform movements led by the same liberals who had supported Horace Greeley in 1872. By the early 1880s Dana had elevated his opposition to their crusading morality into a full-scale war.

8

Mugwumps, Shams, and Reformers
The Politics of Conscience

By the 1870s, no newspaper editor in America knew better than Charles Dana what a difficult business it was to balance the concerns of a paper's stockholders against those of its readers — particularly if, as in the case of the *New York Sun*, the two had vastly different political interests. To Republican critics like Secretary of State Hamilton Fish, Dana was an unprincipled blackguard, a treacherous turncoat whose journalistic "independence" violated nineteenth-century political conventions. To its Democratic readers, the *Sun* was the "independent" voice of the workingman, free of obligation to any party or faction.

Dana may have turned on the Republican party, but Fish and his friends were wrong when they charged that the editor of the *New York Sun* did not believe in anything. There was a consistency in Dana's ideology that connected his efforts on behalf of Fourierism with his championing of the metropolitan working class in the Gilded Age. By 1883, Dana had amassed Democratic working-class readers in unprecedented numbers, achieving the position and influence that he had sought his entire life.

Although Dana was a man of principle, he was also a man of great vanity, and his ego nearly proved to be his undoing. In 1884, to the astonishment of observers, he spurned the Democratic candidate for president, largely because of what he regarded as a personal slight. Unfortunately for Dana, this self-indulgent act would have long-term consequences that drove away many of his readers permanently.

117

Charles Dana's political convictions did not translate well into party loyalty, and the *Sun*'s nominal independence allowed Dana to shift partisan allegiance when it suited him. This independence from party should not, however, obscure the consistent voice of the paper. There was a regularity of temperament, if not of ideology, in the *Sun* for the thirty years that Dana edited the paper. This regularity stemmed from the editor's sense of himself as an outsider, which accounted for both his view of city life and his affinity with the immigrant working class of New York City.

Charles Dana believed in diversity and toleration of cultural differences, two notions in short supply among the era's reformers and "good-government men."[1] For fifteen years, the *Sun*'s attacks on Mugwumps, shams, and reformers earned the affection of its readers. Dana's commitment to cultural diversity appeared soon after he bought the *Sun* — in the paper's suspicion of civil service reformers, in its defense of Tammany Hall, and in its treatment of the 1874 Tompkins Square riot.

Not only did the *Sun*'s defense of the Tompkins Square "rioters" reveal the editor's understanding of the political and economic forces that governed the lives of his readers; it also demonstrated Dana's willingness to encourage diversity of opinion on his own staff. One of the organizers of the Tompkins Square rally, Scottish-born socialist John Swinton, was an editorial writer for the *Sun*.[2] Of his relations with Charles Dana, Swinton later wrote that the editor "never interfered with my moral independence, or . . . found fault with me for pursuing a course outside of the *Sun* office that may not have been to his liking."[3] Dana was so certain of Swinton's loyalty that in 1878, when he took a prolonged tour of Europe, he appointed the socialist acting editor of the *Sun*.

Yet Dana's tolerance for unpopular groups and ideas suggested more than the editor's personal sympathy for outsiders. The *Sun* accepted the diversity of urban life and defended the right of each group to its own place and integrity within the metropolis. The fabric of late nineteenth-century New York City has been described as woven in a "pattern of intensely local social intercourse."[4] By the 1870s New York City had become the center of the nation's expanding communications network. At the same time, there were tremendous barriers to communications within the metropolis itself. These obstacles included rigid segregation of neighborhoods by class and ethnicity, street design that impeded travel, and public transportation that isolated some parts of the city from others.

Within this complex and burgeoning city, newspapers were unique in transcending local patterns of intercourse and passing information across lines of class and ethnicity. According to the first great student of American journalism, sociologist Robert Park, the urban press had a cohesive function, helping to re-create the conditions of village life in the metropolis.[5] Newspapers helped people escape their daily routines with stories of vice, crime, romance, and tales of the rich and socially successful. They explained urban life to the newcomer and provided a guide to survival in the city.[6]

The *Sun* cornered so large a share of the New York City newspaper market during the 1870s because of Dana's willingness to accept diversity within the socially fragmented city. It radiated a straightforward message: opportunities for productive work and economic advancement should exist for all groups, including immigrants and mechanics, small merchants and trade unionists. The *Sun* was intensely local in outlook, despite its professed loyalty toward larger, less clearly defined communities such as "the Union."

Dana edited the *Sun* for New York City's working people. Polite society spurned the paper because, as was frequently said, "it is read by horse car drivers." Dana neither condescended to his audience nor lowered the *Sun*'s literary standards. Some observers noted the contradiction between the high quality of writing in the *Sun* and the paper's lack of social position. Few of Manhattan's prestigious social clubs subscribed to the *Sun*. (Dana, for his part, belonged to no social clubs after 1862.)[7] H. T. Peck, writing in the *Bookman*, commented on Dana's ability as a man of culture to cross the "thin, impenetrable wall" and reach "the great unlettered public."[8] Edward P. Mitchell, who became editor in chief of the *Sun* a few years after Dana's death, also noted that Dana "neither cheapened the quality of his wares nor revised his professional standards to court a new constituency on a lower level."[9]

Throughout the 1870s, Dana offered his readers a guide to "reading" the city. His newspaper provided extensive coverage of local trade unions, immigrant associations, and sporting events. It explained how to become a naturalized citizen and where to inquire for an apprenticeship. The paper recommended political candidates, Republican as well as Democratic, and warned the unwary against being "induced" to take false naturalization papers on election day.

The *Sun* denounced those individuals who discriminated against the foreign-born because of their religious or social customs. Maintaining his lifelong opposition to nativism, Dana championed political leaders who fought religious prejudice. He was sympathetic to the Democratic party's attempts to prevent the pietistic Republicans from legislating their own form of morality through Sabbath and prohibition laws.[10] In his efforts to keep the state out of matters of individual conscience, Dana suggested that Tammany Hall, despite its abuses, was democracy's greatest defender. He noted in 1890, "It is not to be forgotten that a very large body of Democrats, even while not sharing the view of Tammany leaders in respect to municipal questions, have come to regard Tammany Hall as the only trustworthy conservator of real Democracy in New York City."[11] As proof, he cited Tammany's battle against proposed property qualifications for voting, its opposition to Know-Nothingism, and its resistance to elite control of the civil service. In short, the *Sun* urged tolerance as a means of reconciling different and often conflicting social groups in the city. Evidence of this broad-mindedness could be seen in the *Sun*'s treatment of the violent Orangemen's parade of 1871.

The Orangemen were members of a secret political organization, the Ulster Protestant Society, founded in 1795. Their name referred to Protestant King William III of Orange, who in seventeenth-century Britain had ousted Catholic James II. The Orangemen marked each July 12 anniversary of the Protestant victory with parades and other demonstrations.

The violence of 1871 had its roots in the parade of the year before. In New York City on July 12, 1870, the Orangemen had celebrated the traditional anniversary by parading up Eighth Avenue to Elm Park for a picnic and dance.[12] The route took them through Chelsea, a predominantly Irish Catholic West Side neighborhood. Provoked by the taunts of the orange-clad Ulster Protestant Society, a "rabble" of Irish Catholics showered the paraders with stones and curses. By the time the police finally broke up the melee, five people had been killed.

The bitter legacy of the 1870 riot, as well as pressure from the

Hibernian Society (Catholic rivals of the Protestant Orangemen), led Democratic Mayor Oakey Hall to forbid the parade in 1871. The reaction was an uproar among the New York press, which defended the right of the Orangemen to assemble and march.[13] The *Sun* accused Mayor Hall of "cowardice" and submission to "mob rule." The paper suggested that the mayor's decision to forbid the parade was tantamount to an admission that "the Democratic rulers of this city . . . are incompetent to maintain the dignity of the laws and to preserve public order."[14]

Bowing under the pressure, the Democratic governor of New York, John T. Hoffman, rescinded the mayor's order and promised to protect the paraders. As city officials had anticipated, the march set off a riot that was even more violent than the one of the previous year. While the Orangemen and their Catholic rivals exchanged gunshots, the police "clubbed right and left without distinction." By the end of the day, two policemen had been killed and twenty-four wounded. Of the rioters, thirty-one were dead and sixty-seven wounded.[15]

The *Sun*, which sold 192,300 copies the next day, provided its readers with a relatively complex and evenhanded interpretation of the events. Dana portrayed the episode as a civic parable illustrating the need for religious toleration. The paper defended the constitutional rights of the Orangemen to free speech and assembly, and it blamed city authorities for having yielded to the demands of the Catholic Hibernian Society in the first place:

> About 100 men paraded yesterday in the Orange ranks, to vindicate the right of citizens to assemble; and about 100 men were killed and wounded in putting down the mob who wished to deprive them of that right. . . . The Democracy of the nation ought to spew Tammany Hall out of their mouths. They have convulsed the country with their shameful terror about a riot, and have done their utmost to produce a riot, when, if they had possessed ordinary courage, there was no reason to fear one.[16]

Perhaps most importantly, the *Sun* condemned both Catholics and Protestants for fighting over issues that should have been left in the Old World. The newspaper congratulated the Catholic clergy for trying to preserve the peace, and it pointed out that most Catholics abhorred the "brutal wickedness" of the "grog shop and bar-room ruffians." Finally, the *Sun* praised the courage of the largely Catholic police force. By emphasizing religious tolerance and equal rights, Dana had accomplished a nearly impossible feat. His even-handed treatment of the riot drew new readers to the *Sun* while satisfying all sides of his deeply divided constituency.

In his ability to reach a wide variety of readers, Dana differed markedly from the most prominent group of late nineteenth-century intellectuals, the genteel educators and writers who made up New York's literary establishment. This liberal, highly educated patrician group included college presidents, editors, and historians. Nominally Republican, most contributed to the best journals and socialized at the prestigious Century Club (which did not subscribe to the *Sun*). These men, including Charles Eliot Norton, Andrew White, George William Curtis, E. L. Godkin, Henry Adams, and Carl Schurz, have been described by historian Geoffrey Blodgett as being deeply alienated from the party system.[17] Insistent on propriety and political reform, they were dismayed by the pace and direction of social change in America. From the pages of respectable liberal publications such as Godkin's *Nation*, or from columns such as Curtis's "Editor's Easy Chair" in *Harper's Monthly*, they denounced the corruption of local government and called for systematic civil service reform.

The group of patrician reformers was held together loosely by common experience. Most had been born into prominent New England families. They were intelligent, successful in a variety of careers, and moved frequently from job to job. Yet they were ultimately ineffective at reforming society along the lines they desired. Their failure, according to Blodgett, "sprang from the distinctive structural conditions of the society they tried to influence. They sought a national, cosmopolitan function in a social matrix which remained profoundly local in the roots of its organization."[18]

Charles A. Dana, though personally acquainted with most of these men, had no use whatsoever for their cause. He popularized the epithet that has stuck with them to this day: Mugwumps. When asked to define the meaning and origin of the term, Dana answered, "Mugwump is an ancient New England term, and smacks of the language of the red man. It used to signify, when gravely spoken, a man of importance, but more commonly a man who thinks himself of importance. . . . A synonym for the word . . . is the New York term Big Bug, or the Washington expression Swellhead."[19] While reform elements existed in both political parties, most Mugwumps were nominal Republicans. The Mugwump movement reached its zenith in 1884, when these Republicans bolted their party to support Democratic presidential candidate Grover Cleveland.

At first glance, Dana's scorn for these liberal reformers seems surprisingly harsh. Yet their temperaments and his were at chilly, polar opposites, as a biographical sketch of the quintessential Mugwump, George William Curtis, reveals.

Charles Dana and George W. Curtis shared common experiences, but not common roots. Like Dana, Curtis grew up in a small northeastern town.[20] Also like Dana, Curtis dropped out of college to join Brook Farm. He was, in fact, a student of Dana's at the Brook Farm School.

Curtis left Brook Farm in 1844. A few years later, he went to Europe, touring many of the countries that Dana was to visit during his months abroad in 1848–49. Like Dana, Curtis contributed articles to the *New York Tribune*, dabbled in poetry and literary ventures, strongly espoused abolition and the Republican party on the lyceum circuit, and, after the war, settled into a career in letters, in his case a lifelong association with *Harper's* publishing company.

Yet despite these surface similarities, the differences between Dana and Curtis were striking. While Dana's boyhood had been characterized by poverty and virtual abandonment, Curtis came from a large, loving, affluent family. Unlike Dana, Curtis had little social consciousness at a young age, and he was drawn to Brook Farm instead by the strong individualism of Emerson and the Transcendentalists. He did not want to see Brook Farm politicized by a conversion to Fourierism. While Dana spent his years in Europe wrestling with revolution and working-class radicalism, Curtis tasted liberally of the pleasures of the aristocratic Old World. While Dana wrote articles exhorting the virtues of Fourierism and a producers' republic, Curtis wrote a travel book that later became popular for its steamy description of Egyptian belly dancers.

Both men were strong and outspoken advocates of the Republican party in the 1850s, but Curtis was not comfortable with the politicians whose job it was to put the ideals into practice. After the Civil

War, his discomfort blossomed into an intense dislike of the pragmatists who consolidated the Republican party into a working political organization. Retreating from active politics, which he had never enjoyed, into the symbolic sanctum of the "Editor's Easy Chair" at *Harper's Monthly*, Curtis became increasingly querulous as he preached reform of the system. His views and those of his friends and associates among the New England gentry seemed out of step with the complexities of industrial America.

Mugwumps like Curtis had no use for Charles Dana, and the feeling was mutual. Dana, the son of a poor man, had an appreciation of the working class that Curtis could not understand. Dana knew what it was like to get his hands dirty. He had watched his father fail as a farmer, and he had been working for his uncle when the family dry goods firm of Staats and Dana collapsed. Dana had seen the anger and frustration of the poor and hungry behind the barricades in Paris and also on the streets of New York City. He could sympathize with what it meant to have the promise of a job and some self-respect from Tammany Hall, an organization that was at least the people's own. Most importantly, Dana appreciated that the controversy over reform of the civil service masked issues of ethnicity and class. As he jeered in the *New York Sun:*

> [The reformer] is a creature generated by Mugwumpism, and as *The Evening Post,* his dry nurse, describes him, "is essentially a solitary animal," with a morbid dread of being regarded as anything else except highly respectable. Above all things he avoids association with "the boys," and flies instinctively from any political candidate who makes himself so popular that he is called by a nickname. . . . He would as soon think of parting his hair elsewhere than in the middle as of voting for the "Bobs," "Mikes," and "Pats" of politics. . . . He is very anxious to cast a "clean ballot" all by himself, and wants it generally understood that he has none of the enthusiastic devotion to party manifested by the ungenteel public. He speaks of filthy places fit only for the vulgar, and for Tammany Hall especially he has unutterable loathing. The thought that the "common people" are in the majority and have as much right to vote as he has almost drives him into exile. He would have the polls fumigated and perfumed before he entered to deposit his dainty ballot.[21]

Though Charles Dana eventually made quite a fortune at the *New York Sun* — one 1884 estimate placed his income at $150,000 annually — [22] he never lost touch with the experience and desires of ordinary people. This sympathy accounted for both his allegiance to the Democratic party and his dislike of the genteel reformers. Dana was convinced that the Mugwumps were motivated by distrust of the people. Eager to break the Mugwump façade of smug propriety, the editor devoted himself to unmasking their sham and humbug. Many working-class newspapers ridiculed the rich and well-born.[23] But Dana went even further. Speaking from outside the circle of New York City's literary establishment, he challenged the authority of those guardians of virtue who would put ordinary men and women in the straitjacket of Protestant morality. Though this crusade hardly endeared Dana to the politically powerful, it helps to explain his phenomenal success with the working people of New York City.

During the 1870s and 1880s, the *New York Sun* was full of contempt for "highbrows," hypocrisy, and the pretense of virtue. Perhaps the most infamous of Dana's attacks on a custodian of public virtue was the paper's treatment of one of the greatest scandals of the nineteenth century: the adultery trial of Henry Ward Beecher.

Beecher, the pastor and spiritual leader of the influential Plymouth Church in Brooklyn Heights, was one of America's most prominent abolitionists and reformers. Throughout the 1850s, Beecher promoted the antislavery cause with a Barnum-like appreciation of the art of publicity. Once he "auctioned" a slave girl named Pinkie before the stunned congregation of Plymouth Church, then used the proceeds to buy her freedom. His name later became a byword in the term "Beecher's Bibles," a reference to the Sharps rifles used in 1854 by free-soil settlers in the territory of "Bleeding Kansas." By the end of the Civil War, Henry Ward Beecher had become a hero in the North. Not one to rest on his laurels, he devoted the postwar years to the crusade for temperance and women's suffrage.

Beecher's reputation was sullied in November 1872, when journalist Victoria Woodhull published a story in *Woodhull and Clafin's Weekly* that became an overnight sensation. Woodhull accused Beecher of committing adultery with the wife of his parishioner and colleague Theodore Tilton. Given Dana's antipathy toward the upholders of Christian morality, it was not surprising that the *Sun* was among the pastor's fiercest critics.[24] Charles Dana launched a barrage of charges against the world-famous Brooklyn cleric that continued until long after Beecher's death.

The *Sun's* charges of Beecher's guilt appalled many of the pastor's friends, and at least one of his business associates. When the *Sun* published a particularly brutal editorial on Beecher's immorality, Robert Bonner, editor of the *New York Ledger* (to which Beecher frequently contributed), wrote to Dana.

> I am *so* sorry that you have printed that editorial on Mr. Beecher this morning. I have not read anything in a year that grieved me as much. As . . . a regular contributor to the *Ledger*, he is so prominently identified with my paper that I feel a blow aimed at him almost as keenly as if it were aimed directly at myself. . . . *Nothing under the heavens could induce me to hit anyone so prominently identified with your paper in that way.*[25]

Bonner's pecuniary interest in Beecher's credibility was obvious. Reprimands such as his, far from dissuading Dana, only heated up the *Sun's* rhetoric and widened the schism between the editor of the *Sun* and the rest of New York City's literary establishment.

The *Sun* vigorously pursued Plymouth Church's internal investigation of Beecher. On July 27, 1874, it printed the full transcript of Tilton's testimony, and commented, "Either Mr. Beecher is an abandoned and adulterous monster, debauching the women and desolating the homes of his flock, or else Mr. Tilton is guilty of inventing and circulating a mass of cruel and indecent libels intended solely to blacken the reputation and destroy the usefulness of Brooklyn's most respected citizen."

Though the church committee ultimately exonerated Beecher, Charles Dana did not. The *Sun* pronounced Beecher guilty in February 1875, and it continued for years to remind its readers of the pastor's "hypocrisy." A typical column read, "Henry Ward Beecher is an adulterer, perjurer, and fraud; and his great genius and his Christian pretenses only make his sin the more horrible and revolting."[26] Not only did Dana continually call on Beecher to step down, he also used the celebrated incident to point out the indiscretions of other upholders of public morality. One editorial leader slyly queried, "Beecherism — is it spreading?"

Dana's attacks on "Beecherism" are significant as an example of the *Sun*'s crusade against sham and hypocrisy. They are also interesting for their echo of the rhetoric of Brook Farm. As a young writer for the Fourierist *Harbinger*, Dana had crusaded against sanctimonious revivalists who "fleeced" the people, exposing them as frauds and confidence men. He continued to do so as editor of the *Sun*. On May 7, 1876, for example, the *Sun* reported the arrest of Henry A. Solomon, one of evangelist Dwight L. Moody's most "faithful attendants." Solomon, who was head usher at Moody's revival meetings, was charged with embezzlement. While the *Sun* wryly faulted Moody for emphasizing "points of belief" rather than "practical wickedness," it also exposed the sham of the revivalist's crusade.

In a similar vein, socialist editor John Swinton once described Dana's response to a reader's letter that asked, "Will you please tell me how to become a Christian?" Dana had passed the query along to Swinton with the suggestion, "Why not give him a ripping answer? Give him the socialist side of Christianity."[27] Swinton cited the incident as an illustration of Dana's open-mindedness. Yet another way to interpret the episode is that Dana was upholding an ideal standard of Christianity of which liberal Protestants, as well as their "licentious" ministers, fell woefully short.

Though the connection between Dana's characterization of Henry Ward Beecher as a "guilty person who pretends to be a Christian"[28] and his defense of Tammany against the attacks of the Mugwumps may not be self-evident, the two were closely related. Both illustrated Dana's distaste for hypocrites and self-righteous moralizers. Moreover, Dana, a perennial outsider, had a genuine sympathy for the city's downtrodden — Catholics, dissenters, and ethnic minorities. Together these groups made up the constituency of Democratic Tammany Hall.

Tammany had a well-deserved reputation for getting things done. The organization's success in providing such essentials as paved streets and good water had led one historian to conclude that "strong party government, so often denounced by reformers as the death of the city, seemed to be the basic requirement for vigorous public action."[29]

This practical ability to deliver public services appealed to Dana. He also believed that the Mugwumps who harped on the evils of Tammany and its patronage system were hypocrites who wanted simply to put men of their own party into office. In an 1896 lecture, Dana gave his opinion of reformers who objected to the domination of a political organization by a boss.

> [They say] there shouldn't be any boss, but that the party should direct itself. Well, exactly what that means I have not been able to understand. An army without a general is of no use, and a ship without a captain doesn't get navigated safely. I notice, too, that the class of politicians who are most strenuous against bosses are those who are not able to control for themselves the boss who happens to be in power in their district or their state.[30]

The call to oust the bosses and reform the civil service became the Mugwump rallying cry in 1884. It is true that government office-holders had never seemed as corrupt as they did in the period following the Civil War. Mark Twain and Charles Dudley Warner gave a name to the era in their popular novel *The Gilded Age*, and they immortalized the boodlers whose crimes filled the pages of the daily press.[31] The most common proposal to cleanse the civil service was a system of competitive examinations, together with some form of tenure of office. This scheme appealed both to the reformers' faith in the expertise of trained professionals and to their celebration of "true public spirit" over party enthusiasm.[32]

Dana explained his objection to competitive examinations for civil servants in 1882. While he conceded that some sort of qualifying exam was necessary, given the "vast" number of public offices and applicants, he contemptuously dismissed the idea that administrators should be obliged to appoint the person deemed the "smartest or most learned." Dana argued that administrators ought to be allowed to choose their own assistants. He concluded that "while an examining board is convenient and even necessary, it should never be allowed to usurp the more serious function of selecting those who offer the best guarantees of character and are most suitable in the judgment of the responsible officer at the top."[33]

Dana invoked the Democratic notion of home rule by local authority when he suggested that the real solution to public corruption lay in the reduction of government size and scope, rather than in the "German system" of tenured officeholders who were not responsible to the people. He concluded that genuine reform would be achieved only "by the repeal of all superfluous laws, the abolition of every needless office, and the dismissal of every unnecessary officer."[34]

Under Dana's stewardship, the *Sun* became the largest metropolitan newspaper in New York City, with at least 145,000 loyal Democratic readers. Yet in 1884, Dana nearly threw it all away. The man who became Dana's nemesis was Grover Cleveland, governor of New York State and the Democratic party's reform candidate for president.

At first glance, it is almost unimaginable that Dana could have opposed this particular nominee of the Democratic party. Dana favored nearly all of the 1884 Democratic platform. It was the candidate that Dana could not stomach, and for the most trivial of reasons: Grover Cleveland had slighted the editor in 1882, during his tenure as New York's governor. Charles Dana could not forgive the insult.

In 1882, Dana had anticipated good relations with the governor-elect. The *Sun* had endorsed Cleveland, proclaiming that "the election of Mr. Cleveland looks toward an honest, conservative and thoroughgoing administration of state affairs. . . . Every interest of the state will be regarded with impartial attention, and . . . we shall have a Governor of the whole people, and not of a party."[35] Grover Cleveland promised to be the kind of Democratic reform governor that the *Sun* would heartily support.

Charles Dana seldom asked politicians for favors, but in 1882 he asked one of Grover Cleveland. He suggested that the governor appoint Franklin Bartlett to the position of New York adjutant general. Bartlett, counsel to the *Sun*, was the son of editorial writer William Bartlett. Cleveland not only spurned Dana's recommendation but, adding insult to injury, he appointed instead the nephew of one of the editor's most bitter enemies: Henry Ward Beecher. As Amos Cummings, the *Sun's* first city editor, explained: "The breach with Cleveland took place soon after Cleveland was elected Governor of New York. Mr. Dana had recommended for appointment as Adjutant of the State Franklin Bartlett, but Cleveland, disregarding the recommendation, appointed a nephew of Henry Ward Beecher. . . . This slight Mr. Dana never forgave."[36]

Two additional factors made the Democrat's candidacy even more galling to Dana. One was the editor's relationship with perennial Democratic candidate Samuel Tilden. The other was Dana's contempt for the Mugwumps, the Republican Independents who rallied to Cleveland's banner in droves.

Since 1876, when the *Sun* had labeled Rutherford B. Hayes the "fraudulent" president, Dana had upheld Samuel Tilden as the rightful occupant of the White House. The *Sun* predicted a Tilden boom every four years, and it hailed the former New York governor as the inheritor of Jacksonian Democracy. In private correspondence, Dana went even further, writing to Tilden (who had "retired" from politics in 1882) of the confusion and leaderlessness of the Democratic party, once referring to it as a "mob." In 1884, the editor even proposed to write a political history that would number the Sage of Greystone among the "three statesmen who have had the genius to rule through their intellects . . . Bismarck, Disraeli, and Tilden."[37]

Other papers noticed the *Sun*'s unflagging support for Tilden. The *Journalist*, a gossipy trade publication, observed that "it is a mercy of heaven that [Mr. Dana] is faithful and loyal to somebody, though in the instance of Sammy Tilden he is slightly ridiculous at times."[38] An 1881 illustration from *Puck* shows Dana, dressed as an archeologist, brushing dust from a stone figure he has pulled from a crypt at Greystone. The figure, labeled "S.J.T.—Buried 1876" holds a sunflower marked "clean record." In the background stands the White House, under the banner "Presidential Museum." The caption reads, "C. A. Dana (having excavated an old fossil): I guess I can palm him off on the people for their museum in 1884."[39]

At least one explanation for Dana's extravagant support of Samuel Tilden is not flattering to the editor. On August 4, 1880, Dana borrowed $45,000 from the prominent Democrat. While their correspondence did not mention the purpose of the loan, Dana probably used the money to increase his holdings in the *Sun*.[40] Like most nineteenth-century businessmen, Dana drew no sharp distinction between public and private spheres of activity. If the *Sun*'s championing of Tilden paid off in a friendly loan, so much the better.

The *Sun* tried to create a Tilden groundswell during the summer of 1884, but to no avail. Tilden himself had declined to run for the presidency, and Grover Cleveland won the nomination on a reform platform. To the astonishment of loyal Democratic readers, Dana put the prestige of the New York *Sun* behind Benjamin Butler, the candidate of the Greenback-Labor party.

Sun reporter Charles Rosebault, who saw evidence of Dana's "cynical humor" in his choice of Butler, quoted editor Edward Mitchell's characterization of the candidate as one of "doubtful repute standing on a platform of Greenback-Labor declarations which Dana would scarcely touch with tongs."[41] There was indeed evidence of humor in Dana's support for the Massachusetts governor, but it is misleading to read the choice as a "joke."

There was an emotional if not an intellectual logic to Dana's support of Benjamin Butler. Butler, in his impassioned opposition to the Yankee elite of Boston, had won the loyalty of an immigrant, working-class coalition that was strikingly similar to the readers of the *New York Sun*.[42] Historian John Sproat has suggested that Butlerism represented "all that the liberals considered unwholesome in American politics." As the *Nation* put it, Butlerism was "the embodiment in political organization of the desire for the transfer of power to the ignorant and poor, and the use of Government to carry out the poor and ignorant man's view of the nature of society."[43] It was not coincidental that Dana threw the weight of the *Sun* behind a man abhorrent to the blue bloods.

The fact remains, however, that Dana did not support Butler's Greenback-Labor program. The *Sun* had always hooted down the idea of greenbacks.[44] Just about the only plank in Butler's platform that Dana favored was the protective tariff, which became the peg upon which he hung his opposition to Grover Cleveland. Dana called Cleveland the "foe of labor" and reiterated daily the charge that Cleveland's free-trade stand was not in the interest of workers.

As the campaign heated up, the *Sun* launched an unprecedented series of personal attacks on the Democratic candidate. The revelation of Cleveland's affair with Buffalo, New York, widow Maria Halpin and his fathering of an illegitimate child made sensational copy. The *Sun* called Cleveland a "coarse debauchee," and suggested that if elected he would "bring his harlots to Washington and hire lodging for them convenient to the White House."[45] Two weeks before the election, the *Sun* described Cleveland as "low in his associations, leprous with immorality, perfidious, [with a] name loathsome in the nostrils of every virtuous woman and upright man."[46] The paper concluded that Cleveland's "immorality" made him totally unfit to be president.

The charge of adultery enabled Dana to link Cleveland with another of his favorite targets, Henry Ward Beecher, and Beecher's support of Cleveland played right into the editor's hand. The Brooklyn pastor proclaimed: "If every man in New York State tonight who had broken the seventh commandment voted for Cleveland, he would be elected by a 200,000 majority." Dana printed the speech every day for a month.[47]

Dana's attacks on Cleveland also stemmed from his disdain for the Mugwumps, those Independent Republicans whom Dana claimed had never lost sight of partisan ends. The *Sun* insisted that the Mugwumps's support for Democratic candidate Grover Cleveland was temporary and conditional. Even when Dana agreed with the reformers' ideas, he called them hypocrites, claiming that they pretended to spurn partisan politics while avidly seeking the fruits of electoral success.

Charles Dana evidently believed that he could defeat Cleveland. On October 21, 1884, he wrote to a friend, "The religious movement against Cleveland is more intense than ever, and it cannot fail to be very effective at the polls. I may, of course, exaggerate the prospect, but it seems to me that G. C. is sure to be beaten."[48]

Beaten perhaps, but not by Benjamin Butler. It was no secret that Dana's campaign to elect anyone but Cleveland amounted to tacit support of Republican James G. Blaine.[49] Dana in fact had few objections to Blaine other than that he was the candidate of the Republicans, "the party traditionally illiberal in its dealings with foreign-born citizens, and especially with the Irish."[50] (Blaine's well-known supporter, the Reverend Samuel D. Burchard, strengthened that "illiberal" reputation with his memorable reference to the Democrats as the party of "Rum, Romanism, and rebellion.") Three weeks before the election, Dana explained the *Sun*'s support for Greenback-Labor candidate Benjamin Butler in an editorial remarkable for both its candor and its cynicism.

We intend to vote for Gen. Butler without regard to his ideas concerning various minor questions that are matters of controversy, and without inquiring whether his views on these subjects are the same as ours.

The Republicans have nominated Mr. Blaine, a most unfit candidate, whom we have opposed for years, and still oppose. The Democrats have nominated Mr. Cleveland, a candidate, in our judgment, very much more unfit than Mr. Blaine. In truth, we hold that Mr. Cleveland's disqualifications are so exceedingly grave and revolting that, as between the two men, Mr. Blaine should be preferred on the principle of choosing the lesser evil of two. But while we cannot support a representative of the Republican party it is a duty to make against Mr. Cleveland's nomination the most decided protest that is possible. For this reason we intend to vote for Mr. Butler. . . . Whether there should be more or fewer greenbacks, and how the public debt shall be paid; are not points that seem to us to be any way involved in the present contest.[51]

It was hardly surprising that Dana's competition dismissed him as irresponsible. One *Sun* reporter later noted that Dana's bolt from the Democratic party "tried the allegiance of many loyal workers" on the *Sun,* some of whom sported buttons bearing Cleveland's portrait.[52]

Once the election was over, the *Journalist* expressed the prevailing view that Dana's influence in the campaign had been virtually nil. It reflected that, though Dana had "trumpeted the virtues of Butler day in and day out, supporting him in the news as well as the editorial columns of his paper . . . [yet] in this very city, where the *Sun* is published and where Butler has his strongest organization . . . Butler received the utterly ridiculous total of 3,000 votes."[53] Though the weekly acknowledged that many believed Dana had backed Butler as a joke, it concluded that "the joke now is certainly on Dana."

Charles Dana, a thirty-five-year veteran of the New York City newspaper industry, made two serious errors during the election of 1884. First, the editor underestimated the strength of his readers' partisan allegiance. Dana's reckless attempt to carry the *Sun's* readers with him in his bolt from Democratic party ranks was self-defeating

during an age in which party loyalty was the measure of steadfast-
ness and reliability.

Second, Dana failed to anticipate the competition of the *New
York World*, a traditionally Democratic paper which Joseph Pulitzer
had bought and revitalized in October 1883. The *Sun's* abandoning
of the Democratic candidate was an unanticipated boon for the
World. Dana's bolt made the *World* enormously important to the
Democratic party.

The *Sun* lost hundreds of readers daily. At the beginning of 1884,
it had an average daily circulation of 145,000. In a little less than two
years, it lost almost 63,000 readers.[54] Not surprisingly, there were rumors that Dana had been asked to resign. As the *Journalist* reported:

> The reports of Dana's resignation no doubt proceeded from the
> conversation that took place at the last meeting of the *Sun's* stock-
> holders. Some of them were disposed to kick about the condition
> of affairs, though the dividends were still quite satisfactory. There
> was an intimation given to these gentlemen that if they felt tired
> and wanted to sell their stock it would be taken at their own price.
> Then they were silent. But Dana is not the man to resign under
> fire anyway. He will prove to these stockholders before he leaves
> that they made a mistake in doubting him, and that it would
> have been better to hold their tongues.[55]

Though the *Journalist* dismissed talk of Dana's resignation as
premature, troubled waters lay ahead for the editor of the *New York
Sun*. In 1884, Charles Dana nearly sank his own boat by supporting
a minor third-party candidate for president. As a result, he faced the
formidable task of navigating his way to security while avoiding personal and professional disaster. The growing competition of Joseph
Pulitzer and the *New York World* threatened to make his course even
more perilous.

9

Eclipsed

The Rise of a Culture of Consumption

hen Charles A. Dana threw the weight of the *New York Sun* behind Greenback-Labor candidate Benjamin Butler in 1884, he had no reason to be concerned about permanent damage to his newspaper. The editor's reputation as a curmudgeon was well established. Though the *Sun* had been pro-Democratic since the end of the first Grant administration, it bore the party's reins loosely. From the beginning, the paper had scorned Democratic commitment to "free trade."[1] It had also ridiculed sentimental nostalgia for an agrarian past, while promoting urban and industrial expansion. In both municipal and national politics, the *Sun* had blazed its own course. Often critical of Tammany's candidates as well as those of the national party organization, Dana's *Sun* attached itself to nominees on the basis of confusing and unpredictable criteria. Of these, the most important were the editor's personal predilections and loyalties.

Moreover, Dana's support for Democratic presidential candidates was often lukewarm. In 1880, for example, the *Sun* had described Gen. Winfield Hancock, the party's nominee, as "a good man, weighing 250 pounds." The laconic conclusion, "Hancock is not Tilden," explained the paper's coolness.[2] This kind of support found little favor with the party's national leadership.

While the *Sun*'s peculiar brand of loyalty to the Democratic party had caused some fluctuations in circulation, overall it had contributed to the paper's growth. As Ida M. Tarbell pointed out, people read the *Sun* because they were interested in what Dana had to say, not necessarily because they agreed with him.[3] But if Dana expected his rejection of Democratic candidate Grover Cleveland to create little disturbance, he was wrong.

Dana was caught by surprise when the *Sun's* daily circulation plummeted from 145,000 to 82,300 between 1884 and 1886. Although historians of journalism have generally concluded that Dana's bolting of the Democratic party caused this startling drop in readership,[4] Dana's poor political judgment was not solely responsible for the sudden decline in sales. The revolutionary kind of newspaper that Joseph Pulitzer was creating in the *New York World* also helped to send the *Sun's* fortunes reeling.

It is ironic that Joseph Pulitzer, the man who became Charles Dana's nemesis, began his career in New York journalism with occasional work on the *Sun*. The Hungarian immigrant had previously made a name for himself in St. Louis on the *Westliche Post*, a German-language daily edited by Carl Schurz. In 1876, Pulitzer visited the *Sun* offices in New York City to urge Dana to consider publishing a German edition of the paper. He offered to translate the *Sun's* news and editorials and to add features of interest to German readers. Though Dana was intrigued by the idea, Isaac England, the *Sun's* publisher, was not. Impressed with Pulitzer's aggressiveness, Dana hired him as a special Washington correspondent to cover the electoral controversy of 1876. In 1878, Pulitzer worked for the *Sun* as a European correspondent.[5] That same year, he purchased the bankrupt *St. Louis Dispatch*, which he merged with the *St. Louis Post*. Still interested in breaking into New York journalism, Pulitzer found the opening he needed in 1883 when Jay Gould put the *New York World* on the market.

The *World* had been established in 1860 as a religious daily. After a troubled beginning, it was revived by Manton Marble, who ran it successfully as a Democratic party paper until 1876. That year Marble sold the *World* to Thomas A. Scott of the Pennsylvania Railroad. In 1879, Scott sold the paper to Jay Gould as part of a package including the Texas and Pacific Railroad. Gould's reputation, still tainted by the 1869 "Black Friday" gold manipulations, hurt the newspaper. The financier was eager to be rid of the *World*, and in Pulitzer he found his buyer. In October 1883, Pulitzer paid what many considered to be the exorbitant sum of $346,000 for a newspaper with an Associated Press franchise and a circulation of about fifteen thousand. That price was twice what Dana had paid for the *Sun* – a paper with four times the readers – fifteen years earlier.[6]

In October 1883, when Pulitzer bought the *World*, Dana's two-cent *Sun* had the highest circulation of all the dailies in New York City. Despite the sharp competition of the metropolitan press, Dana's welcome to Pulitzer was unusually warm. He commented on the new editor's "quick and fluent mind . . . originality and brightness." Wrapped up in his quadrennial efforts to win Samuel Tilden the Democratic presidential nomination, Dana ignored the new ownership of the *World* for its first six months. Meanwhile, Pulitzer launched a campaign to make the *World* New York's most popular newspaper.

Almost immediately, the Hungarian immigrant attracted attention by his willingness to exploit new technology. Pulitzer recognized that New York City's growing dependence on rapid transit provided an opportunity to grab the attention of the commuter at the newsstand. Alliterative headlines drew in new readers, and illustrations made the paper appealing even to the illiterate. Before Pulitzer's purchase of the *World*, newspapers had been staid, conservative-looking blanket sheets, neatly divided into columns headed by modest titles. Pulitzer caused an explosion of pictures, bold advertisements, and dramatic headlines to rip through the New York newspaper industry.[7]

Building on the tradition of sensationalism established by penny papers like the antebellum *Sun*, the *World* published titillating stories of sex, vice, crime, and disaster. Front-page headlines on a typical day included:

An Appalling Disaster:
Twenty-two men killed and many wounded in a collision

Child Elopers Married

Twenty Drowning Men:
A Crew Driven into the River
by the Flames of their Vessel

Swept Away by a Flood

A Septuagenarian's Body Stolen

Nursing a Cold Corpse[8]

Like twentieth-century supermarket tabloids, the *World* used sensationalism as bait, but the underlying message was prim enough to satisfy rigid Victorian mores. For example, under the lurid headline "Nursing a Cold Corpse" was a lackluster story about Republican congressional leaders who had declared that sectionalism was dead.

The visual impact of Pulitzer's *World* was remarkable. Yet equally effective in drawing in new readers were his crusades for social justice. Though other Democratic newspapers, including Dana's *Sun*, had long championed the working class, Pulitzer outflanked them by transforming the *World* into a paper that was — at a glance — unmistakably the people's. Brilliantly, Pulitzer endowed traditional Democratic views with a class-based appeal. When the editor called for reform and social justice, he appealed to widely held fears of concentrated power and authority. Pulitzer must have startled New Yorkers with his revolutionary-sounding agenda, which he published on May 17, 1884.

1. Tax luxuries.
2. Tax inheritances.
3. Tax large incomes.
4. Tax monopolies.
5. Tax the privileged corporations.
6. A tariff for revenue.
7. Reform the civil service.
8. Punish corrupt officers.
9. Punish vote buying.
10. Punish employers who coerce their employees in elections.[9]

Despite the response of the working class, which purchased the *World* in every-growing numbers, conservatives had little to fear; the *World*'s program for reform was well within the mainstream of Democratic ideology. Pulitzer's biographer, W. A. Swanberg, has suggested that at heart the editor was a liberal Democrat with a commitment to "the Jeffersonian concept of personal liberty, the limitation of federal powers, and a low tariff [for revenue only]."[10] Like Dana, Pulitzer defended both the right of labor to organize and the right of businessmen to run their own enterprises. In the tradition of reform-minded journalists like Jacob Riis, Pulitzer believed he could end the problems of the poor by turning the glare of publicity onto their suffering.[11]

Joseph Pulitzer was adept at mixing charity with self-promotion. The *World* gave Thanksgiving dinners to hundreds of newsboys, clothing and special holiday matinee tickets to needy children at Christmastime, and summer excursions to the city's working boys and girls. Although such charities helped to sell newspapers, that subtlety was lost on the happy beneficiaries. If competitors sneered at this benevolence as ingenious advertising, it made no difference to the *World*'s readers, who apparently found in Pulitzer's style and message heartening evidence that the newspaper really cared about them.

The rapid growth of the *New York World* came at the direct expense of the *New York Sun*. Charles Dana and Joseph Pulitzer competed for the same market in the mid-1880s. Both papers were read by the city's skilled and semiskilled laborers, factory workers, immigrants, and small merchants. But why did these readers prefer the *World* to the *Sun?*

The answer lies in the differing ways that Dana and Pulitzer viewed their readers. In 1884, Charles Dana regarded the *Sun*'s working-class readers as he always had: as producers. While Dana championed the interests of the working class, he defined those interests in the rhetoric of antebellum workingmen's associations, emphasizing cooperation and self-help. Pulitzer, on the other hand, understood that the *World*'s working-class readers spent their leisure hours window shopping, seeing vaudeville shows, and planning weekend excursions to Coney Island. In short, Joseph Pulitzer defined the *World*'s readers as consumers, with leisure time and dollars to spend.

Pulitzer was one of the creators of an American consumer culture. One of the hallmarks of what has come to be known as the "culture of consumption" is the way in which ordinary people began to define themselves in terms of what they consumed rather than what they produced. It has become common to observe that the culture of late nineteenth-century America was transformed from one that enshrined the values of work, thrift, and self-sacrifice to one that celebrated consumption, leisure, and pleasure.[12]

Metropolitan newspapers at the turn of the century were unique in their relationship to the emerging culture of consumption. As the most important medium of communication that city dwellers had for learning about the abundance of consumer goods, the daily press not only took on an expanded identity as a vehicle for advertisers;

it also helped to create a climate of excitement, spectacle, and self-indulgence.[13] This dual role was evident in the development of sporting news, the women's page, and the paid advice column, as well as in the growing cooperation between newspapers and department store managers.[14]

The *World* offered its readers a guide to the abundance of the metropolis. Joseph Pulitzer understood and exploited the connections between text, advertisements, and illustrations, and the *World*'s illustrations had an extraordinary effect on the developing techniques of advertising and mass marketing.[15] Its pages displayed a dazzling array of fashion, consumer goods, and urban amusements. The *World* would, for example, juxtapose helpful articles such as the "Rage for Décolleté" with sketches of the latest ready-to-wear and advertisements pointing out where these garments could be purchased.[16] Foreign-born readers, wanting to adapt to American ways, eagerly turned to the pages of the *World* for guidance.

Many of these readers were women. Pulitzer's *World* was the first newspaper to experiment with a women's page that included society items and gossip columns such as "Women of the World." A regular feature called "Home Talks on Etiquette"—a series of letters from city girl "Edith" to country friend "Bessie"—described appropriate behavior for city life. Despite the occasional awkwardness of "Edith's" prose ("Perhaps as the ball season is just beginning it might be a good idea for me to give you some points on the etiquette of balls . . ."), the column was nevertheless appealing to those readers in search of guidance.[17] When Carrie Meeber, the Midwestern-born heroine of Theodore Dreiser's *Sister Carrie,* was invited by wealthy friends to dine at Sherry's, she knew what to expect. Like thousands of others, she had, in Dreiser's words, "read of it often in the *Morning* and *Evening World.* She had seen notices of dances, parties, balls, and suppers at Sherry's. . . . The common run of conventional, perfunctory notices of the doings of society, which she could scarcely refrain from scanning each day, had given her a distinct ideal of the gorgeousness and luxury of this wonderful temple of gastronomy."[18] In short, the *New York World* depicted—and advertised—a city rich with excitement and commercial amusements. The paper's explosive growth was testimony to the success of this new outlook.

The *New York World* radiated an energy and enthusiasm that

shook newspaper readers out of their settled habits and made an immediate hit at the newsstand.[19] The paper promoted itself by making daily announcements of its growing circulation, which within three months of Pulitzer's purchase had doubled to thirty-nine thousand readers. At first the additional sales came from a new market of the foreign-born who had never before purchased English-language papers.[20] But before long Pulitzer's aggressive promotions began to threaten the established dailies. It was testimony to Pulitzer's growing strength that, within a year of his purchase of the *World*, the other morning newspapers retaliated with a price war of astonishing proportions.

Early in 1884, the New York City newspaper establishment took the counteroffensive against the two-cent *World:* three of the city's biggest papers lowered their prices. The price of the *New York Times* dropped from four to two cents, the *Tribune* from four cents to three, and the *Herald* from three cents to two. When the *Times, Tribune,* and *Herald* cut their prices, the newsdealers' profits were also reduced. Many retaliated by selling the papers at the old prices. Dana kept the price of the *Sun* at two cents, but he continued to lose money. As a story in the *New York Times* pointed out, the *Sun's* profits came from its large circulation rather than from its advertising receipts, which were quite small. Estimating that Dana had to sell sixty thousand to seventy-five thousand papers daily if he was to break even, the *Times* concluded that when the *Sun* lost a third of its readers, it lost "very much more" than a third of its annual profits.[21]

Ultimately, the efforts of the *Times, Tribune,* and *Herald* backfired. The price reductions barely grazed Pulitzer's circulation, and they did nothing to stop the declining sales of the established dailies.[22] With the costs of publication remaining constant, the drop in price meant that each newspaper company had to win more readers in order to break even. This did not happen.

During the summer of 1884, when Dana began his series of attacks on Grover Cleveland, Pulitzer's competition really began to hurt the *Sun*. Sales started to fall off precipitously, even by the *Sun's* own count. After the presidential election in November, it was obvious that the fortunes of the paper had taken a sudden plunge. The *Journalist* commented that although the *Sun* was still a good paper, "the best of all, perhaps," the competition it had faced over the last year was

TABLE 1
New York Newspaper Circulation, 1874–1897

Year	Herald	Sun	Times	Tribune	World
1874	70,000	120,000	30,000	19,000	12,000
1875	65,000	119,792	42,000	43,833	10,000
1876	60,000	135,000	40,000	39,000	8,000
1877	65,000	100,000 90,000[S]	35,000	30,000	15,000
1878	65,000	100,000 95,000[S]	31,000	26,000	15,000
1879[*]	<100,000	>100,000	<50,000	<50,000	<15,000
1880[†]	100,000	147,444	34,000	38,000	18,000
1881	110,000	124,328 126,249[S]	34,000	40,000	18,000
1882	110,000	124,328 126,249[S]	34,000	40,000	18,000
1883	135,000	143,200 141,810[S]	34,000	40,000 35,000[S]	25,000
1884	135,000	145,030 152,106[S]	45,000	50,000 55,000[S]	59,000 60,324[S]
1885	–	119,123 138,715[S]	40,000	70,000 75,000[S]	104,955 145,031[S]
1886	–	82,300 124,045[S]	40,000	80,000 85,000[S]	149,439 209,993[S]
1887	–	80,000 120,000[S]	40,000	70,000 85,000[S]	189,283 244,850[S]
1888	100,000	80,000 120,000[S]	40,000	70,000 75,000[S]	228,465 257,267[S]
1889	100,000 110,000[S]	80,000 120,000[S]	40,000	65,000 75,000[S]	180,000 260,263[S]
1890	90,000 100,000[S]	80,000 120,000[S]	40,000 50,000[S]	80,000 85,000[S]	185,672 266,551[S]
1891	90,000 100,000[S]	80,000 120,000[S]	40,000 50,000[S]	80,000 85,000[S]	169,506 258,775[S]
1892	90,000 100,000[S]	80,000 110,000[S]	30,000 40,000[S]	75,000 85,000[S]	192,201 259,572[S]
1893–94	80,000 100,000[S]	120,000 150,000[S]	40,000 50,000[S]	73,000 76,000[S]	170,547 282,686[S]
1895	80,000 100,000[S]	120,000 150,000[S]	75,000 80,000[S]	73,000 76,000[S]	484,075[‡] 324,904[S]

TABLE 1 *(continued)*

Year	Herald	Sun	Times	Tribune	World
1896	80,000	120,000	75,000	73,000	484,075[‡]
	100,000[S]	150,000[S]	80,000[S]	76,000[S]	324,904[S]
1897	80,000	120,000	75,000	60,000	370,000
	100,000[S]	150,000[S]	80,000[S]	100,000[S]	568,000[S]

Sources: Geo. P. Rowell's American Newspaper Directory and N. W. Ayer's American Newspaper Annual.

[S]   Sunday circulation. All other figures cite daily circulation.
[*]   The last year of publication of Geo. P. Rowell's American Newspaper Directory.
[†]   Rowell's absorbed by N. W. Ayer's American Newspaper Annual.
[‡]   Includes both morning and evening World.

"unprecedented."[23] Competition from the *World*, as well as from the newly discounted *Times* and *Herald*, caused the *Sun* to fall from first in daily circulation to third by the end of 1885.

Table 1, based on data collected from N. W. Ayer's *Annual*, shows the phenomenal growth of the *World* and the relative decline of the *Sun* and *Herald*, which, as New York's major Democratic newspapers, competed for the *World*'s readers. Ayer's method of collecting data was responsible for the apparent lag between Pulitzer's purchase of the *World* and its impact on the New York newspaper market. The circulation figures printed in the *Annual* were gathered for the twelve months ending in March of each year. Thus significant fluctuations occurring in the last nine months of 1884 would be published in the 1885 *Annual*, and so on. Ayer's *Annual* printed no figures in cases where information was "unsatisfactory" or reports were "conflicting." The lack of data for the *Herald* during the mid-1880s suggests that Ayer found the *Herald*'s circulation claims to be unreliable.

Despite its flaws, Ayer's *Annual* lays to rest the idea that politics — specifically Dana's support of Butler in 1884 — was solely responsible for the *Sun*'s loss of circulation. Although the paper certainly lost readers in 1884, the drop continued for the next two years. Ayer's figures indicate that the primary source of Dana's problem was Joseph Pulitzer, not Grover Cleveland or Benjamin Butler.

Pulitzer achieved his dramatic rise in circulation by expanding the *World*'s market into the *Sun*'s Democratic working-class reader-ship. The correspondence between the *World*'s New York staff and their frequently absent editor in chief showed that Pulitzer considered Dana his greatest rival in the city. After the completion of the *World*'s well-known drive to erect the base of the Statue of Liberty, one of Pulitzer's assistants congratulated the editor on the coup the paper had scored and added, "You will see by the enclosed [circulation fig-ures] that the *Sun* is still falling. Last Saturday . . . they could not get above 98,000."[24] Enclosed in the letter were eight weeks' worth of circulation figures clipped from the *Sun*.

In the fifteen years that Dana had owned the *Sun*, he had never been threatened by anything like the competition of Pulitzer's *World*. The *Sun* had grown steadily under Dana's management. Although sales had occasionally fluctuated, particularly with presidential elec-tions, the trend was upward.[25] By 1885, however, Pulitzer's aggres-sive competition for Dana's readers threatened to ruin the *Sun*. Dana responded to the assault with characteristic venom.

Despite Dana's public persona of breezy confidence, the editor viewed an attack on the *Sun* as an attack on himself. He responded to the phenomenal growth of the *World* with an ugly anti-Semitism. Dana lashed out at Pulitzer in desperation, referring to his rival as "Judas Pulitzer," or the "Renegade Jew." Though Jewish by birth, Pulitzer had converted to Christianity and belonged to St. George's Episcopal Church. Dana's attacks on Pulitzer as the "Jew who does not want to be a Jew" were particularly offensive from one who had unfailingly championed religious toleration and diversity. As the *Sun* editorialized with mock solicitousness:

> The Jews of New York have no reason to be ashamed of Judas Pulitzer if he has denied his race and religion . . . the shame rests exclusively upon himself. The insuperable obstacle in the way of his social progress is not the fact that he is a Jew, but in certain offensive personal qualities. . . . His face is repulsive, not because the physiogamy is Hebraic, but because it is Pulitzeresque. . . . Cunning, malice, falsehood, treachery, dishonesty, greed and venal self-abasement have stamped their unmistakable traits. . . . No art can eradicate them.[26]

As Pulitzer's biographer, W. A. Swanberg, has concluded, "Dana could have hit on no tactic more brutal or mortifying."[27]

In 1885, Dana was beset by rumors that the *Sun's* stockholders, unhappy with his management of the paper, were going to ask him to resign.[28] Dana did not own a controlling share of the *Sun's* stock. Though he was the paper's largest stockholder, he held fewer than one-third of the shares.[29] Dana's fear that the *Sun* might slip from his grasp brought back nightmarish memories both of his forced resignation from the *New York Tribune* and of his abrupt dismissal from the *Chicago Republican.* The editor's growing obsession with gaining complete control of the newspaper was evident in his financial ventures of the 1880s.

Dana first tried to buttress his position at the *Sun* with increased stock holdings. In April 1886, he borrowed $18,000 from Samuel Tilden to buy eight shares of *Sun* stock from the estate of former publisher Isaac England. Later in the month, he asked Tilden for an additional $21,000 with which to purchase six more shares. Although Tilden agreed to advance Dana the money, he asked, "Are you not raising the average cost of your stock more than is expedient by buying at such large premiums?"[30] Dana's answer revealed his sense of urgency: "I am much impressed by the considerations you mention, and am well aware that under ordinary circumstances the purchase would not be one to make with eagerness. But my family already hold[s] so large an amount of this stock that it is very important that they should have the substantial control of it, in the event of my death; and every addition to their holdings brings us much nearer to that point."[31]

Tilden reiterated his willingness to make the loan, adding that he had been unaware of Dana's "collateral motive." He wrote, "I infer from your letter that although this purchase will not give you a majority, you consider the greater influence derived from a larger holding a sufficient object to induce you to take this parcel at a high price."[32] About two weeks later, Dana informed Tilden in an interesting slip of the pen that though the England family had kept ten shares, he had managed to "regain" seven.[33]

Before Pulitzer's purchase of the *World*, Dana had taken pride in the *Sun's* willingness to publish its circulation figures. Yet by July

1886, sales had dropped to eighty-four thousand daily, and Dana stopped publishing the numbers. E. L. Godkin, Dana's long-time adversary at the *Nation,* noted immediately that the *Sun* was no longer printing its weekly circulation. The *Nation's* editor described the *Sun's* decline as "without exception the most extraordinary thing ever known in the history of newspapers."[34]

In December 1886, Dana took the unprecedented step of mortgaging the Sun Association building to raise capital — probably to buy new presses (details of the *Sun's* mortgage are available in the New York County Clerk's office.)[35] On December 6, the trustees of the Sun Printing and Publishing Association agreed to a $175,000 mortgage, certifying that the loan was intended for a new plant and equipment.[36] There were also rumors that Dana had mortgaged his home for $60,000.[37] The *Sun's* competition jumped upon the mortgage as evidence that the paper was tumbling toward ruin. The *New York World* printed the mortgage in its entirety and thereafter referred to the paper as "the *Sun,* mortgaged."[38]

Though the outlook for the *Sun* appeared dire by the mid-1880s, Dana was not about to surrender. In 1886, the editor decided to abandon the *Sun's* traditional four-page length in order to compete with the eight-page *World.*[39] Dana started experimenting with the *Sun's* length in April 1886, and longer papers became the norm after the Sun Printing and Publishing Association purchased new presses. In 1888, Dana boasted, "The *Sun* has six, eight, twelve, and sixteen pages [on Sunday], as occasion requires, and is ahead of all competition in everything that makes a newspaper."[40]

The change in the *Sun's* length created new problems, however, because it required additional news and editorial material. Critics claimed that at eight pages the *Sun* lost its characteristic conciseness and instead became "puffed up" with serialized fiction and sporting news.[41] Although the paper imitated the *World* by the expanded use of illustrations, some readers found the result to be clumsy and haphazard. An illustrated article on New York's opera stars prompted the *New York Times* to comment that although one would expect a certain orderly relationship of illustration and subject matter, "in the case of the *Sun's* portraits . . . the wild hazard of the shovel and the inscrutable contingencies of the pitchfork seem to have been in firm control."[42]

Dana's belief that pictures added little of value to a newspaper explained the careless placement of illustrations in the *Sun*. As late as 1894, after newspaper illustrations had become commonplace even in the *Sun*, Dana insisted that they were nothing but a "passing fashion." He stated, "I don't believe so many pictures are going to be required for the next century."[43] Dana's lack of interest in illustrations, like his disdain for advertising, reflected the cultural orientation of his paper. The way in which Charles Dana viewed his readers — as Jacksonian-style producers — accounted not only for the political content of the *Sun* but also for the use he made of the technology available to him. That Dana paid a high price for this cultural conservatism would be evident in the 1890s during the controversy over the installation of the linotype machine.

Dana's gamble in mortgaging the *Sun* building paid off, however; the *Sun*'s new length and more modern look stopped the decline in daily circulation. No longer willing to watch Pulitzer steal his working class readers, Dana would reorient his newspaper in the 1890s to appeal to a different audience. Aided by the changing configuration of the Democratic party, Dana would reverse the *Sun*'s slide toward bankruptcy by silencing the voice of the *Sun* as the "uncompromising advocate" of the workingman.

Charles A. Dana made a considerable amount of money as editor of the *New York Sun*, but until the mid-1880s he did not share the outlook or concerns of the wealthy. Yet Dana's attitudes changed after Pulitzer siphoned off so many of the *Sun*'s readers. Deserted by the working men and women who now read the *New York World* in ever-increasing numbers, Dana began to espouse views more in keeping with those of his own elite social class. The editor adopted a philosophy similar to that of New York's Democratic "Swallowtails," those prominent merchants, bankers, and lawyers who directed the city's economy.[44] Although the Swallowtail Democrats favored lowered tariffs, civil service reform, and the political fortunes of Grover Cleveland (all of which the *Sun* continued to oppose), they shared Dana's growing conservatism on fiscal matters and labor issues. As Dana began to defend the interests of the conservative Swallowtail Democrats, he also began to sell more newspapers. Daily sales grew from the 80,000 record low set in 1888 to around 120,000 in 1893. Though not equaling the daily sales of Joseph Pulitzer's *World* — which by 1890 were upwards of 185,000 — Dana and the *Sun* nonetheless achieved a remarkable recovery.

There were a number of continuities in the *Sun* despite its drift toward conservatism. For example, Dana was unflagging in his opposition to Grover Cleveland. Cleveland, who had been defeated by Benjamin Harrison in 1888, was again nominated by the Democratic party in 1892. Dana professed astonishment at the tenacity of "Mugwump's disease," which the *Sun* described as "that strange and distressing mental malady which makes its victims see in the obese and by no means prepossessing figure of [Grover Cleveland] the quintessence of physical, intellectual, and moral perfection."[45]

Dana grudgingly supported the Democratic ticket in 1892, all the while making clear his personal opposition to both the candidate and his views on free trade. Dana's rationale for backing Cleveland, considered flimsy by Democrats as well as Republicans, was that the reelection of Republican Benjamin Harrison would ensure passage of the Force Bill, a Republican measure intended to protect the black vote by guaranteeing honest elections in the South.[46] The Democrats, motivated by both racism and support of states' rights, had inserted a plank in their platform condemning the Force Bill. In what was hardly the *Sun*'s finest hour, the paper proclaimed, "No Force Bill! No Negro domination! Better vote for the liberty and the white government of the Southern States, even if the candidate were the Devil himself, rather than consent to the election of respectable Benjamin Harrison with a Force Bill in his pocket!"[47]

The questionable nature of Dana's support for the Democratic ticket probably led many Democrats to agree with the sentiments expressed in the *Montgomery [Alabama] Advertiser.* "The devil might as well be quoted as a Christian as to quote the *New York Sun* as a Democratic paper."[48] Or, as the *New York Times* put it, "there are two or three fools in town who still suppose that the *Sun* is supporting Mr. Cleveland."[49] Of course, New York City Democrats who lost patience with Dana's peculiar brand of party loyalty found a ready haven in Pulitzer's *World.*

In the 1890s, Dana continued to charge that those Democrats who backed "non-partisan" reform candidates were politically naïve. When the "good government men" organized five reform clubs in New York City in the 1890s, Dana contemptuously labeled them "googoos."[50] To Dana, these clubs, which were intended to recruit more "gentlemen" in politics, were simply new Mugwump bottles containing the same old partisan wine.

Dana also maintained his scorn for the self-appointed guardians of morality who had a resurgence in the 1890s. In a manner reminiscent of the *Sun's* crusade against Henry Ward Beecher fifteen years earlier, the paper accused the new generation of reformers of cloaking hypocritical self-interest with virtue. For example, when Dr. Charles A. Parkhurst, pastor of New York's Methodist Square Church, fired what he called "the first gun of the campaign" against Tammany Hall, the liquor interests, and the allegedly corrupt police force, Dana responded by calling him a slanderer and hypocrite and demanding that he substantiate his charges.[51] Parkhurst and his Society for the Prevention of Crime were perfect targets for Dana, who took every opportunity to ridicule their self-righteousness. The *Sun* also sneered at the anti-Tammany Lexow Investigating Committee, a New York State legislative committee that was charged with investigating the New York City police department, as "experts from the sugar bushes of Herkimer, the lumber camps of Franklin, the hopyards of Oneida county, and from other localities somewhat remote from the metropolis."[52] Contemptuous of the committee's anti-urban bias, Dana never wavered in his opposition to the attempts of the upper-class Protestant elite to impose their own values on the people of New York City.

The most remarkable change in the pages of the *Sun* during the late 1880s was its growing conservatism with regard to labor questions — a development that occurred after working-class readers deserted the paper. In the 1870s, Dana's *Sun* had a well-deserved reputation as a friend of the working man. By the late 1880s, however, the paper had begun to defend the interests of capital.

In March 1886, Dana's *Sun* sided against the workers in the Knights of Labor strike against Jay Gould's Southwestern railroad. Likewise it opposed the eight-hour day, calling it the "supremest folly that can be conceived of."[53] Of the seven "murderous and frantic scoundrels" who were accused of murder in the 1886 Haymarket Square bombing, the *Sun* cried, "Let them hang. . . . The law they defied will be justified in their execution, and a prompt, stern, and necessary warning will be afforded to a class of exotic criminals for whom there is no room in this land."[54] When the *Sun* announced in

April 1888 that it would lead the fight against "the combined foes of Democracy," there was little doubt that the paper was referring to its newly discovered enemies, the "Socialists" and "Anarchists."[55]

Significantly, the *Sun*'s new sympathy with capital appeared at the same time that Pulitzer's *World* was becoming the self-proclaimed friend of the worker, making what Pulitzer's biographer has called a "total commitment" to the interests of labor.[56] The *World* sided with the striking railroad workers against Jay Gould, defended the use of boycotts, and urged New Yorkers to make donations to strike funds. It reported on the meetings of the Central Labor Union. It covered issues of interest to workers, including convict labor laws and the movement for the eight-hour day. In short, the *New York World* took many of the same positions on labor that Dana's *Sun* had taken in the 1870s.

Despite the *Sun*'s strengthened alliance with business interests, the newspaper never completely lost its "producer" orientation while Dana was alive. For example, the *Sun* remained steadfastly loyal to the union of its own typesetters, New York Typographical Union No. 6. Under Dana, the *Sun* had always paid its typesetters the union scale, even at a time, according to the union, when "the proprietor had the power to dictate his own terms."[57] When the Knights of Labor organized a boycott of the *Sun* in 1887 because of the paper's opposition to a strike of the longshoremen, Typographical Union No. 6 denounced the boycott "as a blow . . . at tried friends of labor unions."[58] The union sent a copy of its resolution to each of the city's morning papers and noted in its own publication, the *Union Printer,* that the *Sun* "was probably the strongest trade union office in the country. Its compositors, pressmen, stereotypers, and folders all belong to some body of organized labor." A few weeks later, the *Union Printer* quoted Dana as saying that union men were well worth the higher wages "because they were the most skillful as well as the most trustworthy."[59]

Dana's continued friendliness to the workers in Typographical Union No. 6 was not inconsistent with his growing hostility to labor in general, given the extent to which most of his actions were determined by personal loyalty. The *Sun*'s "Chapel," or union local, had been faithful to the interests of the paper's editor; he defended it in turn. This loyalty contributed to his refusal to install the linotype machine in the *Sun* offices. Significantly, Dana liked the look of a hand-set page. As he explained in a speech at Cornell University in

1894, "I have never taken to [the Mergenthaler linotype] very much, because it didn't seem to me to turn out a page as handsome, in a typographical point of view, as a page set up by hand. The difference of expense is something considerable, however. I have been told by one large newspaper publisher who employs that machine that he gets his typesetting done for one-half the cost of typesetting done by hand."[60] Dana added that Whitelaw Reid of the *Tribune* believed the linotype had cut his labor costs by more than half. His audience would have understood the reference to Reid's installation of the machines, which had led to a prolonged strike by the Typographical Union.[61]

The defection of working-class readers from the *Sun* to Pulitzer's *World* contributed to Dana's growing opposition to labor in the 1890s. Equally important, however, were the larger social and political currents that swept through the Democratic party, leaving no place for the Swallowtails who shared Dana's newfound conservatism. As a defender of what he believed to be true Democratic values against a tidal wave of reform, Charles Dana became comfortably conservative. By the 1890s, this conservatism undermined the satirical bite that had been the *Sun's* trademark. Although changes in the *Sun's* style developed so gradually that they are almost imperceptible from year to year, a comparison of the *Sun* of the early 1880s with that of the 1890s reveals an important distinction. As the *Sun* was becoming more conservative, it was also becoming less humorous. A significant turnover in editorial personnel was partially responsible. William O. Bartlett, the originator of much of the paper's memorable wit, died in 1881. Charles Dana himself contributed less to editorial writing in the *Sun* in the 1890s. Frequently traveling abroad, he left the paper in the hands of his son, Paul Dana.

Yet changes in personnel were not solely responsible for the gradual disappearance of humorous material from the paper. Two of the best-known satirists of the Gilded Age, Mark Twain and Thomas Nast, also suffered from pessimism and professional malaise during the 1890s. The increasingly bleak vision of Mark Twain during the 1890s has been well documented.[62] *Harper's* brilliant illustrator, Thomas Nast, provides an even more striking example of a humorist who underwent a professional crisis in the 1880s.[63]

Although an analysis of changes in American humor is beyond the scope of this book, the experiences of Dana, Twain, and Nast suggest a hypothesis. Perhaps their characteristic humor was bound up with a kind of individualism that was less possible in the increasingly corporate nineties.[64] With the postwar expansion of industrial capitalism, individuals seemed to become increasingly powerless and insignificant, while events appeared to be determined by factors far removed from the local community.

Twain and Nast shared Dana's rugged iconoclasm. Powerful individuals with strong opinions, they needed complete editorial independence. In the mid-1890s, Twain became ensnared in what turned out to be the futile endeavor of perfecting a mechanical typesetter — a diversion that drained both his creative and financial resources. In the broadest sense, Dana and Nast also ran aground on the shoals of mechanization. Developments in journalism, spurred in part by new typesetting and printing technologies, greatly increased the relative importance of the business office and lessened that of the creative processes of writing and illustrating. As publishing became more business-oriented, the opinions of iconoclastic individuals could become a liability. In the case of Nast, it was the death of Fletcher Harper in 1882 that brought about new management and a new editorial policy. Under John Harper, the illustrator was expected to perform as part of the corporate machine. According to Nast's biographer, Albert Bigelow Paine, the illustrator was restive under the new restraints: "He had been an autocrat and a leader so long — so firmly sustained and so surely vindicated — that he had no doubt of his ability to continue his success on the old lines. He yielded with poor grace to this new order of things which was to make him but a part of a vast complex mechanism, the whole kept in motion and whirled and driven by a restless tide of events."[65]

Unlike Twain and Nast, Charles Dana did not give in to despair, but his growing conservatism — which dissolved the tension from which his satire sprang — had the same effect. When the *Sun* lost its sense of humor, it lost its editorial distinction. Pushed aside by the currents of social and political change that swept through American society at the turn of the century, Charles Dana's *New York Sun* was increasingly out of step with the Democratic party. By the mid-1890s, the national party organization was caught up in a wave of rural discontent that crested in 1896 with the nomination of presidential candidate William Jennings Bryan. Once this occurred, Dana abandoned the party altogether.

Even at the time of his greatest sympathy with the downtrodden, Dana had been moved more by the problems of the urban worker than by those of the farmer. Beginning with his writing for the Fourierist journal the *Harbinger* in the 1840s, Dana had argued that the wrongs of industrial society could be mitigated through economic reorganization. Though Dana shared traditional Democratic fears of the danger of concentrated power and authority, he had never been caught up in the party's undertow of sentimental yearning for an agrarian past. Even as a Brook Farmer, Dana had a distinctively Whiggish faith in the benefits of industrial development. His lifelong commitment to protecting American industries with high tariffs also reflected his identification with the urban worker. Historians who have studied the social dimension of nineteenth-century political issues such as the tariff and the currency have emphasized the cultural chasm between the interests of the Eastern worker and the Midwestern farmer.[66] On such questions, the *Sun*'s sympathy with city dwellers was well known.

The *Sun* was contemptuous of the Farmers' Alliance movement springing up throughout the South and Midwest. When the organization adopted its notorious "Ocala Platform" in 1890 calling for a subtreasury, an income tax, and state control of the means of transportation and communication, Dana called it "weak and impracticable class legislation." He added, "The Democratic party does not recognize the existence of classes, and will certainly do nothing to help the farmers at the expense of the rest of the country."[67] The *Southern Alliance Farmer* answered: "In the first place, Mr. Dana knows nothing of the Alliance save what he reads in the partisan press. He lives in the city of New York, and we doubt if he ever spoke to a genuine farmer in his life, much less mingled with this honored class, that he could study their needs and inform himself of their political views. . . . Abuse from such lips is the highest encomium that our organization can receive."[68]

Dana's conviction that the Democratic party would never stand for "class legislation" was shattered by the 1896 nomination of William Jennings Bryan. In a landmark editorial published on August 6,

Dana reversed nearly thirty years of tradition at the *Sun* and openly supported the Republican candidate, William McKinley. Calling the editorial a personal response to queries from friends, Dana charged that the platform of the Chicago convention was a rejection of all the Democrats' ideas and traditions. Pointing to the proposed currency inflation, income tax, and presidential control of the judiciary, Dana claimed that "veiled in the language of moderation, the wild light of anarchy shines through." After he sorrowfully noted the differences that had pitted East against West, Dana concluded, "The duty and the necessity to compass the final overthrow of that platform by assisting in the defeat of William J. Bryan are more imperative and solemn."[69]

Dana's flight from the Democratic party in 1896 was the product both of sweeping changes in American society and of the evolution of his own ideas, especially his loss of identification with New York City's working class. The massive shift in the allegiance of working-class readers from the *Sun* to the *World* meant that Dana had to appeal to a new audience. New York journalism, always volatile, had been altered dramatically by Pulitzer's brand of mass appeal. Dana was perceptive enough to recognize that he had neither the inclination nor the capacity to compete with the *World* on its own terms. Thus when Dana repudiated the Democratic party in 1896, his economic and political convictions finally merged. Given the alternative of Bryanism, the *Sun* became a Republican newspaper.

10

The Independent Press

When Charles Dana started out in the newspaper business in the 1840s, most editors were financially dependent on the politicians whose interests they served. For example, when Horace Greeley established the *New York Tribune* in 1841, he planned to run the newspaper as an inexpensive Whig daily devoted to advancing the political fortunes of Thurlow Weed's Albany machine. Twenty-seven years later, when a group of Republicans helped Charles Dana raise money to buy the *New York Sun*, they did so because they believed that he would use the paper to promote the interests of Ulysses S. Grant and the Republican party.

To the chagrin of his Republican friends, Charles Dana did not transform the *Sun* into a Republican daily, but instead made the *Sun* a truly independent newspaper. Dana claimed that the *Sun* would "[wear] the livery of no party," and indeed it became the bane of Republicans as well as Democrats. As an independent editor, Dana was able to mock the corruption of the Grant administration, jeer at the hypocrisy of Henry Ward Beecher, and undermine Tammany Hall with ridicule. Hamilton Fish's vitriolic diary entries of 1869 suggest just how furious Grant and his administration were at Dana's attacks. In short, Dana's understanding of independence colored the *Sun*'s use of political humor, influenced the business organization of the paper, and governed the editor's relationship with advertisers. It also made the *Sun* New York's most widely read newspaper for fifteen years.

Charles Dana spent the greater part of his life trying to free himself from dependence upon other men and institutions. At the *New York Tribune,* he believed that he was being held back by Horace

Greeley's spinelessness and vanity; at the *Chicago Republican,* he thought that he was being hamstrung by politically unsympathetic stockholders. And even though not all of his colleagues at either paper would have agreed with Dana's analysis that other people had been responsible for his problems, it was still clear that the editor did not make a good subordinate.

Dana came closest to the goal of being his own master as editor of the *New York Sun.* According to reporter Charles Rosebault, Dana believed that the *Sun* was his paper, "the organ to express his will, his wishes, his views." This complete editorial control was what nineteenth-century Americans called "personal journalism." As proof of Dana's absolute authority over the content of the paper, Rosebault pointed to the editor's readiness to adopt editorial policies that resulted in great pecuniary loss; in reference to the Cleveland-Blaine election of 1884, Rosebault concluded that "millions of dollars were sacrificed by the exuberant indulgence of his will."[1] In 1876, Dana dismissed as "twaddle" the idea that the day for personal journalism had passed. He asserted, "Whenever in the newspaper profession a man rises up who is original, strong and bold enough to make his opinions a matter of consequence to the public, there will be personal journalism; and whenever newspapers are conducted only by commonplace individuals whose views are of no interest to the world and of no consequence to anybody, there will be nothing but impersonal journalism."[2]

Despite Dana's strong words, by the 1890s there was considerable agreement that "the day . . . of the editorial is past."[3] The *Journalist* attributed this change to a desire to give readers the "facts" and let them make up their own minds. In an 1889 article, the trade weekly concluded that "while such journals as the *Post* and the *Sun* would look empty indeed without their virile comment," nonetheless a time was rapidly approaching "when the reporter shall take a place superior in importance on the staff of the daily newspaper to the editorial writer."[4] In 1887, Joseph Pulitzer's *Evening World* did away with editorials altogether. Some scholars have attributed this late nineteenth-century decline in editorial opinion to a new scientific orientation in American culture, brought about in part by the influence of Darwin and Spencer.[5] Yet just as important were changes in the material underpinnings of the newspaper industry that made the corporation far more important than any single individual.

Despite Dana's comments that personal journalism would survive as long as there were those with opinions of consequence to others, the editor could not halt the trend toward corporatism, advertising, and impersonality. By the early 1870s, newspapers had become big businesses worth several million dollars — larger than all but a few manufacturing concerns.[6] The exploding production of the Gilded Age brought about an insatiable demand for new markets, which led to the growth of the advertising industry.[7] Newspapers attracted advertisers by boasting of high circulations and by investing in the plant and equipment that allowed for production on a larger scale.

By the turn of the century, dramatic improvements in the speed and quality of presses made it possible for the biggest papers to have daily circulations of between 350,000 and 400,000. The metropolitan press underwent a technological and managerial revolution in the 1880s and 1890s that coincided with the breakdown of "producer" values. Both of these transitions were indicative of the broader changes in American culture that led to the creation of a consumer society.

One industry-wide result of this managerial revolution was an unprecedented division of labor on the individual newspaper. At mid-century, a typographer might dream of emulating Horace Greeley, James Gordon Bennett, or Henry J. Raymond in becoming a writer or editor. By the turn of the century, however, a strict division of labor sealed off hope of upward mobility into the white-collar profession of journalism. Social stratification was just one sign of the pervasive corporatism that was changing the newspaper industry. What had at one time been the province of, as Dana put it, "strong" individuals with "bold" and "original" opinions, was being encroached upon by accountants, advertising salesmen, and production experts. Little wonder, then, that "virile comment" was increasingly relegated to signed columns, where it played second fiddle to the far less controversial "factual" reporting of the news.

Charles Dana's producerism and his view of independence were closely connected to both the contents of the *Sun* and the business strategies he pursued. His producer values not only contributed to his disdain for illustrations and advertisements; they also explained

his refusal to use the linotype machine and his maintenance of a management style that rejected corporatism and the lack of independence
it entailed. For most of his career, Charles Dana had been sensitive
to the interests of his readers — a sympathy crucial to the success of
the *New York Sun*. Yet the *Sun*'s circulation fell throughout the 1880s
precisely because Dana lost touch with the experiences and desires
of working people. By contrast, Joseph Pulitzer's *New York World*,
with its more vivid display of excitement, leisure, and consumer goods,
met with greater success among New York City's mostly immigrant
working class.

Pulitzer's *New York World* was the first distinctly modern newspaper; it initiated the advertising and self-promotional techniques
that became common in the twentieth century. Not only did Pulitzer's
New York World reach the first true mass audience, but the paper
was also modern in that its economic well-being depended upon the
steady infusion of advertising dollars. By comparison, Dana's desire
to edit a newspaper that was independent of advertisers was decid-
edly old-fashioned.

Indeed, Charles Dana's *New York Sun* creates a dilemma for
historians who trace the rise of the modern newspaper. This hegemonic explanation of the history of American journalism favors certain newspapers that anticipated the commercial journalism of our
own time, like the New York *World*, and ignores other equally significant ones.

Dana's *Sun* was in fact responsible for a number of innovations
in American journalism — brevity and conciseness in reporting, separation of advertisements from news and editorial material, and a
fresh definition of "the news." And although Dana's style of editorial independence ultimately disappeared, his view of the appropriate
relationship between newspapers and advertisers has striking implications for the practice of journalism today. By the 1890s, American
newspaper editors prided themselves on their freedom from political parties. What these editors — and the scholars who have studied
them — usually failed to note, however, was that the press had simply
traded in one form of dependence for another. Media institutions
that are dependent on the good will of advertisers are no more "free"
than those organizations that are dependent on the patronage of
politicians.[8]

Charles Dana initially hoped to edit a newspaper that would support itself by revenue from circulation alone, independent of both political and commercial interests. This ideal was impossible for a large metropolitan newspaper at the start of the twentieth century. As socialist Upton Sinclair wrote in 1919, American newspapers were capitalist institutions, and as such they lived by the capitalist system.

> A modern newspaper is an enormously expensive institution. . . .
> You cannot afford to pay for [the Associated Press] service . . . un-
> less you have a large circulation, and for that you need compli-
> cated and costly presses, a big building, a highly trained staff.
> . . . A capitalist newspaper may espouse this cause or that, it may
> make this pretense or that, but sooner or later you realize that
> a capitalist newspaper lives by the capitalist system, it fights for
> that system, and in the nature of the case cannot do otherwise."[9]

On the eve of the twentieth century, no major American news-paper could claim that it was independent of advertisers. Indeed, most were highly dependent on the good will of the businesses that bought their advertising space. As Upton Sinclair asked in 1919, "Is there a newspaper in America which will print news unfavorable to a depart-ment store?"[10] Thirty years later, the *New Yorker*'s "Wayward Press-man," A. J. Liebling, warned that big advertisers and economies of scale were leading the commercial press down the road "toward the one-newspaper town." Liebling's prescient warning, that when media institutions become monopolies they have little incentive for excel-lence in news gathering, bears repeating at a time when news organiza-tions are making deep cuts in staff, budgets, and overseas bureaus. "The function of the press in society is to inform, but its role is to make money. The monopoly publisher's reaction, on being told that he ought to spend money on reporting distant events, is therefore ex-actly that of the proprietor of a large, fat cow, who is told that he ought to enter her in a horse race."[11]

One striking example of the *Sun*'s independence of both politi-cians and advertisers can be found in Charles Dana's defense of the Tompkins Square "rioters" in 1874. Neither the city's political estab-lishment nor its business community had any interest in defending the unemployed workers or in criticizing the police for their violence.

Dana could afford to antagonize both business and civic leaders precisely because he was not dependent upon them for economic support. The *Sun*'s financial backing came from the thousands of readers who bought the newspaper. Charles Dana was attentive to the views of his predominantly working-class readers, and he edited the *Sun* with their interests in mind. That the *Sun*'s circulation continued to outpace that of the other New York dailies by wide margins for the next ten years is testimony to the editor's clear understanding of what those concerns were. Although Dana's unique style of independent journalism ultimately lost out to an industrywide dependence on advertisers, the *Sun*'s freedom from economic and political interests should give pause to those who believe that modern-day America has a truly free press.

Dana's defense of the Tompkins Square protesters suggests that, despite his idiosyncrasies, the editor had a remarkably clear social vision. In his lifelong sympathy with the concerns of working men and women, his support of religious tolerance and cultural diversity, and his belief that justice should be applied equally to all classes, the intellectual foundations of his thought remained constant. As a Fourierist at Brook Farm, Dana had argued that workers and the reformers who had their interests at heart should reorganize society along cooperative lines. As powerful editor of the *New York Sun*, Charles Dana continued to be guided by this vision of American life and culture, despite the rapidly changing social relations of the city that surrounded him. Initially, Dana found a wide audience among the working people of New York City. Yet his producer-oriented vision was not receptive either to change or to the consumerism that developed with industrial capitalism. With the new waves of reform and agrarian unrest mounting at the end of the decade, Dana finally embraced the conservatism that historian Vernon Parrington thought he saw in Dana during the years immediately following the Civil War. By the 1890s, Dana, comfortably ensconced in his own elite social class, defended a tradition that was no longer radical.

Many of Charles Dana's contemporaries believed that he was the greatest and most inventive editor of his day. Dana's emphasis on getting *all* the news, publishing stories of human interest, and making the paper interesting gave the *Sun* its distinctive character.[12] Charles Dana's desire to be independent of both political and commercial interests, his broadly democratic vision of producerism, and his modern understanding of newsworthiness came together in the *Sun* as an exuberant style of journalism that New Yorkers found enormously appealing. Indeed, one of Dana's most significant contributions to the journalism of the Gilded Age was his conviction that people wanted and deserved information that was readily available, for a small price. It was a promise that was implicit in the motto that appeared throughout the editorial columns of his newspaper.

The Sun, it shines for all.
Price two cents.

Epilogue

Charles A. Dana died on October 17, 1897, at the age of seventy-nine. He was buried in the graveyard of St. Paul's Episcopal Church in Glen Cove, Long Island. Of all Dana's achievements, he had asked to be remembered for only one. The *Sun*'s announcement of his death was brief. It appeared the next day on page two, at the top of the editorial columns. It read exactly as he had instructed.

CHARLES ANDERSON DANA, Editor of
THE SUN, died yesterday afternoon.

Notes
Bibliography
Index

Notes

Preface

1. Gorton Carruth and Eugene Ehrlich, *The Harper Book of American Quotations* (New York: Harper and Row, 1988), 300.

2. *New York Sun*, Aug. 25, 1871.

3. *New York Journal*, Oct. 18, 1897; *New York Herald*, Oct. 18, 1897.

4. There are no modern biographies of Dana. The best existing study is Candace Stone's *Dana and the Sun* (New York: Dodd, Mead and Co., 1938). See also James Harrison Wilson, *The Life of Charles A. Dana* (New York: Harper and Brothers, 1907); Edward P. Mitchell, *Memoirs of an Editor* (New York: Scribner's 1924); Frank M. O'Brien, *The Story of the Sun* (New York: D. Appleton and Co., 1928); and Charles J. Rosebault, *When Dana Was the Sun* (New York: R. M. McBride and Co., 1931).

5. Carruth and Ehrlich's *Harper Book of American Quotations*, 300, attributes this definition to Dana, but Frank M. O'Brien credits *Sun* city editor John Bogart with having first uttered the quip. O'Brien, 156.

6. Charles A. Dana to Marianne Orvis, Dec. 31, 1895, Henry S. Borneman Papers, microfilm edition, Illinois Historical Survey, University of Illinois. I am indebted to Carl Guarneri of Saint Mary's College of California for this reference.

7. It is this problem that accounts for the popularity of the *New York Times* in historical monographs; the *Times*, though indexed, was of far less distinction than the *New York Sun*.

8. Michael Schudson has called this the "natural history" explanation of newspaper history. Schudson, *Discovering the News: A Social History of American Newspapers* (New York: Basic Books, 1978), 39–43. This Darwinist argument was first elucidated in 1925 by sociologist Robert Park. Robert E. Park, Ernest W. Burgess, and Roderick D. McKenzie, *The City: Suggestions for Investigation of Human Behavior in the Urban Environment* (Chicago: Univ. of Chicago Press, 1925), 80–98.

9. See James W. Carey, "The Problem of Journalism History," *Journalism History* 1 (Spring 1974): 3–5.

10. Vernon L. Parrington, *Main Currents in American Thought*, vol. 3, *The Beginnings of Critical Realism in America* (New York: Harcourt, Brace and Company,

1930), 43. Parrington based his negative assessment of Dana on the memoirs of *Sun* reporters who worked for the paper during the 1880s and 1890s. These writers were generally conservative and had little interest in Dana's more progressive social ideas. Parrington also drew upon the analysis of Brook Farm historian Lindsay Swift, who was highly critical of Dana's departure from the ideals of Brook Farm. Swift, *Brook Farm: Its Members, Scholars and Visitors* (New York: The Macmillan Company, 1900).

11. Parrington, 44. For example, although Philip S. Foner quotes the *Sun* at several points in his study of the railroad strikes of 1877, he misidentifies the *Sun's* editor as John Swinton, and he fails to mention the readership of the paper. Philip S. Foner, *The Great Labor Uprising of 1877* (New York: Monad Press, 1977), 7. Mention of Charles Dana is also conspicuously absent from Iver Bernstein's otherwise fine discussion of the Tweed regime and the politics of labor in New York City between 1865 and 1872. Bernstein, *The New York City Draft Riots: Their Significance for American Society and Politics in the Age of the Civil War* (New York: Oxford Univ. Press, 1990), 195–264.

1. Zenith: The *New York Sun* and the Ideology of Producerism

1. For discussions of the Tompkins Square incident and its implications, see Herbert G. Gutman, "The Tompkins Square 'Riot' in New York City on January 13, 1874: A Re-examination of Its Causes and Its Aftermath," *Labor History* 6 (Winter 1965): 48–55, and Thomas Bender, *New York Intellect: A History of Intellectual Life in New York City, from 1750 to the Beginnings of Our Own Time* (New York: Alfred A. Knopf, 1987), 187–88. For the impact of the "riot" on *Sun* reporter John Swinton, see Marc Ross, "John Swinton, Journalist and Reformer; The Active Years, 1858–1887" (Ph.D. diss., New York Univ., 1969), 82–95.

2. Gutman, 55.

3. *New York World*, Jan. 14, 1874; *New York Tribune*, Jan. 14, 1874.

4. Bernstein, 17–42.

5. John Higham, *Strangers in the Land: Patterns of American Nativism, 1860–1925* (New York: Atheneum, 1968), 30.

6. *New York Independent*, Jan. 14, 1874; *New York Herald*, Jan. 14, 1874, quoted in Gutman, 56. By 1874, middle-class New Yorkers had become increasingly separated from the city's working class by both spatially segregated neighborhoods and "the most clearly defined social structure in American history." Stuart M. Blumin, *The Emergence of the Middle Class: Social Experience in the American City, 1760–1900* (Cambridge: Cambridge Univ. Press, 1989), 258.

7. *New York World*, Jan. 14, 1874.

8. The other newspaper that defended the "rioters" was the *New York Daily Graphic*, an illustrated paper that had been established one year earlier, in 1873.

9. *New York Sun*, Jan. 14, 1874.

10. Ibid., Jan. 16, 1874.

11. Ibid.

12. Ibid., Jan. 17, 1874.

13. Bender, 188.

14. *New York Sun*, Jan. 10, 1874. See also table 1, chap. 9.

15. For the persistence of the republican tradition in American thought during the Gilded Age, see Dorothy Ross, "The Liberal Tradition Revisited and the Republican Tradition Addressed," in *New Directions in American Intellectual History*, ed. John Higham and Paul K. Conkin (Baltimore: Johns Hopkins Univ. Press, 1979), 116-31.

16. *New York Sun*, Jan. 14, 1874.

17. Ibid., Jan. 16, 1874.

18. Gareth Stedman Jones's distinction between the language of Chartism and the Marxist understanding of class consciousness has useful implications for the study of artisan republicanism. See Gareth Stedman Jones, "Rethinking Chartism," in *Languages of Class: Studies in English Workingclass History 1832-1982* (London: Cambridge Univ. Press, 1983), 90-178.

19. See Sean Wilentz, *Chants Democratic: New York City and the Rise of the American Working Class 1788-1850* (New York: Oxford Univ. Press, 1983) for an overview of the ideology of artisan republicanism.

20. Michael Denning, *Mechanic Accents: Dime Novels and Working Class Culture in America* (New York: Verso Press, 1987) 45-6.

21. For a brief but thoughtful analysis of the uneasy alliance between liberal reformers and Parisian craftworkers in 1848, see David Harvey, "Paris, 1850-1870," in *Consciousness and the Urban Experience: Studies in the History and Theory of Capitalist Urbanization* (Baltimore: Johns Hopkins Univ. Press, 1985), 64-65.

22. The right to productive labor at fair wages had been central to both the ideology of the antebellum workingmen's movement and the Free Soil tradition of the Republican party at midcentury. For a seminal discussion of the theme of "free labor" in the ideology of the antebellum North, see Eric Foner, *Free Soil, Free Labor, Free Men: The Ideology of the Republican Party Before the Civil War* (New York: Oxford Univ. Press, 1970), 11-39.

23. See Wilentz, chap. 10, "The Labor Crisis of 1850," 363-89.

24. For a provocative discussion of the role of Tammany Hall in mediating between wage earners and elites in the postwar period, see Bernstein, 195-236.

25. Jean H. Baker, *Affairs of Party: The Political Culture of Northern Democrats in the Mid-Nineteenth Century* (Ithaca: Cornell Univ. Press, 1983), 317-52.

26. For example, on Sept. 19, 1874, August Belmont wrote to Manton Marble, "Tilden ought to cultivate Dana. He is certainly a valuable champion and, being a good deal of a free-lance, it is doubly necessary to secure his sword." Quoted in David Black, *The King of Fifth Avenue: The Fortunes of August Belmont* (New York: Dial, 1981), 437. Three years later, on Aug. 7, 1877, Belmont's son, Perry, wrote to Democratic Senator Thomas F. Bayard, "It is a pity there is not a more pronounced newspaper which can be called a Democratic organ, or mouthpiece for the Democrats in New York, for the *Sun* is edited by Dana." Quoted in Irving Katz, *August Belmont: A Political Biography* (New York: Columbia Univ. Press, 1968), 242.

27. Many studies emphasize the continuity between antebellum reform movements and postwar crusades for temperance and civil service reform. See Geoffrey Blodgett, "The Mugwump Reputation, 1870 to the Present," *Journal of American History* 66 (Mar. 1980): 867–87; Richard J. Jensen, *The Winning of the Midwest: Social and Political Conflict, 1888–1896* (Chicago: Univ. of Chicago Press, 1971); and Robert Kelley, *The Transatlantic Persuasion: The Liberal Democratic Mind in the Age of Gladstone* (New York: Alfred A. Knopf, 1969).

2. "Heaven on Earth": Brook Farm and the Harmony of Interest Between Labor and Capital

1. Harvard awarded Dana an honorary bachelor of arts degree in 1861, as of the class of 1843. Harvard University *Quinquennial Catalogue: 1636–1930* (Cambridge, Mass.: Harvard Univ. Press, 1930), 241.

2. Dana to Hannah Ripley, Jan. 24 [1845?], John Stillman Brown Family Papers, microfilm edition, Kansas State Historical Society, reel 1 (hereafter cited as Brown Family Papers).

3. Charles A. Dana, *A Lecture on Association in Its Connection with Religion* (Boston: B. H. Greene, 1844), 26.

4. For the best account of Dana's boyhood, see Wilson, 1–11.

5. Dana to Robert Bonner, Sept. 14, 1881, Robert Bonner Collection, New York Public Library (hereafter cited as Bonner Collection).

6. Wilson, 11.

7. Ibid., 6.

8. David F. Allmendinger, *Paupers and Scholars: The Transformation of Student Life in Nineteenth Century New England* (New York: St. Martin's, 1975), 8–27.

9. Ronald Story, *The Forging of an Aristocracy: Harvard and the Boston Upper Class* (Middletown: Wesleyan Univ. Press, 1980), 86.

10. Wilson, 11.

11. Allmendinger, 92.

12. Wilson, 12–32.

13. Ibid., 15.

14. Allmendinger, 46–47.

15. Story, 86.

16. Theodore Parker, "A Sermon of Merchants," Nov. 22, 1846, quoted in Story, 107.

17. Quoted in Charles Crowe, *George Ripley: Transcendentalist and Utopian Socialist* (Athens: Univ. of Georgia Press, 1967), 63.

18. Anne C. Rose, *Transcendentalism as a Social Movement, 1830–1850* (New Haven: Yale Univ. Press, 1981), vii–xi; and Crowe, 66–96.

19. Dana to Austin Flint, Nov. 20, 1840, quoted in Wilson, 26–27.

20. An excellent discussion of the differences between orthodox Calvinism, Unitarianism, and Transcendentalism can be found in William R. Hutchison, *The Tran-*

scendentalist Ministers: Church Reform in the New England Renaissance (New Haven: Yale Univ. Press, 1959).

21. For Ripley's views as a Unitarian minister and as a member of the Transcendentalist Club, see Crowe, chaps. 4–6.

22. George Ripley to Ralph Waldo Emerson, Nov. 9, 1840, quoted in Crowe, 140.

23. Sophia Ripley to John S. Dwight, Aug. 1, 1840, quoted in Crowe, 143.

24. Charles A. Dana to Maria Dana, Sept. 17, 1841, quoted in Wilson, 31–32.

25. Quoted in Wilson, 21–22.

26. Swift, 17–20.

27. Dana's letters from Brook Farm to George Ripley's cousin Hannah reveal his nearly obsessive concern with money and indebtedness. For example, "I am, to confess the truth rather blue this morning. . . . my perpetual torment, my debts, stands before me as ugly and burdensome as the night mare [*sic*]." Dana to Hannah Ripley, Sept. 22, 1842, Brown Family Papers.

28. Crowe, 150.

29. Margaret Fuller, quoted in Crowe, 154. For other discussions of the Brook Farm School, see Swift; Katherine Burton, *Paradise Planners: The Story of Brook Farm* (New York: Longmans, Green and Co., 1939); George P. Bradford, "Reminiscences of Brook Farm," *Century Magazine* 45 (Nov. 1892): 141–48; and Arthur Sumner, "A Boy's Recollections of Brook Farm," *New England Magazine* 10 (May 1894): 309–13.

30. *Harbinger*, Apr. 18, 1846, 304.

31. Swift, 72–73.

32. Ibid., 152.

33. Sumner, 311.

34. Quoted in Crowe, 159.

35. Horace Greeley to Dana, Aug. 29, 1842, James Harrison Wilson Collection, Library of Congress (hereafter cited as Wilson Collection). For other correspondence between Greeley and Dana, see the Horace Greeley Collection at the Library of Congress and the Bryant-Godwin Collection, Manuscript Division, New York Public Library (hereafter cited as Bryant-Godwin Collection).

36. Bradford, 142. See also Swift, 147.

37. For a good summary of Fourierism, see Ronald G. Walters, *American Reformers: 1815–1860* (New York: Hill and Wang, 1978), 61–75.

38. For a complete discussion of American Fourierism and its relation to American values, see Carl Guarneri, "Utopian Socialism and American Ideas," (Ph.D. diss., Johns Hopkins Univ., 1979).

39. See, for example, Swift, and Zoltan Haraszti, *The Idyll of Brook Farm* (Boston: Boston Public Library, 1937).

40. Crowe, 168.

41. Ibid.

42. *Harbinger*, Aug. 8, 1846, 142.

43. Wilentz, 107–42.

44. *Harbinger*, Aug. 30, 1845, 187.

45. Ibid., July 21, 1845, 31.

46. Dana, *A Lecture on Association*, 31.

47. *Harbinger*, Aug. 8, 1846, 142.

48. Dana, *A Lecture on Association*, 25.

49. Dana to Parke Godwin, Oct. 30, 1844, Bryant-Godwin Collection.

50. In 1842, the Brook Farmers refused to admit a nineteen-year-old woman and her illegitimate child to the community, despite the strong protest of editor Horace Greeley and abolitionist Lydia Child. Though it was concluded that the woman was of "sound moral character," the consensus was that the group should not risk offending public opinion. See Burton, 102–3, and Horace Greeley to Dana, Dec. 13, 1842, Greeley Collection, Library of Congress.

51. *Harbinger*, Nov. 8, 1845, 350.

52. Dana, *A Lecture on Association*, 37.

53. *Harbinger*, Sept. 5, 1846, 204. See also Sept. 27, 1845, 252–53.

54. For example, on Mar. 22, 1846, Marianne Dwight wrote: "The wedding party went off very well — very pleasantly indeed. I think about a dozen of our best people preferred to stay away. Others of us felt and thought, that altho' the privacy of the wedding and other circumstances were unpleasant, or perhaps worse than that, this public announcement was, at least, a right step; it was best to go, and in kindness and justice make it as agreeable as we could. . . . Fanny M. [MacDaniel?] has put me in possession of the whole, as she understands it, and gives me liberty to tell *you*, — but I will not write it. . . . I am glad, as it was to be, that they are married,— for they seem very happy." Marianne Dwight, *Letters from Brook Farm, 1844–1847* (New York: Vassar College, 1928), 159.

55. George Ripley to John S. Dwight, quoted in Haraszti, 28.

56. It appears that Dana considered a proposal of marriage to Mary Lovering late in 1844. Either she refused, or he, anticipating rejection, decided not to make the offer. At any rate, he poured out his feelings on the subject in a letter to his friend Hannah Ripley: "I feel now much as if all were really over, and as if I were quite widowed. . . . Oh, Hannah, what a wife I have imagined! Such patience, such tenderness, such depth and fervor of heart . . . but above all, such . . . devotion to the great cause in which with God's help, my heart's last days shall be spent. And now it is all gone.— all those beautiful dreams, they can never come again." Dana to Hannah Ripley, Dec. 21 [1844?], Brown Family Papers.

57. Dana to John S. Dwight, March 1846, Charles Dana Miscellaneous Manuscripts, Boston Public Library (hereafter cited as Dana MSS, Boston).

58. Dana to Hannah Ripley, Sept. 5, 1847, Brown Family Papers. I am indebted to Carl Guarneri of St. Mary's College both for first telling me of the existence of these letters and for discussing with me the mysteries of Charles Dana's marriage.

59. Crowe, 185–88.

60. *Harbinger*, Oct. 3, 1846, 268.

61. See, for example, the optimistic letter from Dana to John S. Dwight, Jan. 26, 1847, Alfred W. Anthony Collection, New York Public Library (hereafter cited as Anthony Collection). Dana's toast at the annual celebration of Fourier's birth in New

York demonstrated the same bright hopes for the future. See *Harbinger*, Apr. 20, 1847.

62. *Harbinger*, Apr. 29, 1848, 200.

63. *Harbinger*, Mar. 25, 1848, 161; Apr. 8, 1848, 180–81.

64. Horace Greeley to Thomas McElrath, June 1848, quoted in *New York Sun*, Aug. 4, 1934.

65. *Harbinger*, July 15, 1848, 85.

66. Ibid., 101.

67. *New York Tribune*, July 14, 1848.

68. Ibid.

69. Ibid.

70. For a fascinating discussion of the "transatlantic" character of Fourierism, as well as several astute insights into Dana, see Carl J. Guarneri, "Utopian Socialism as a Transatlantic Movement," paper presented to the Charles Warren Seminar for Boston Area Historians of American History, Harvard Univ., Apr. 7, 1982.

71. See *Harbinger*, Sept. 2, 1848; Sept. 16, 1848; Oct. 3, 1848; Oct. 5, 1848. For Dana's comments on Considerant's newspaper, see *Harbinger*, Aug. 5, 1848.

72. For example, in an article published in the *Harbinger*, Dana rejected Fourier's theory that capital deserved a share of labor's profits in the form of rent or interest, calling this arrangement the most powerful means of "indirect slavery" in the civilized world. *Harbinger*, Oct. 21, 1848.

73. *New York Tribune*, Aug. 21, 1848. Dana's newspaper articles on Proudhon were reprinted in 1896 in Charles A. Dana, *Proudhon and His "Bank of the People"* (New York: Benj. R. Tucker, 1896).

74. *New York Tribune*, Aug. 29, 1848.

75. William Harlan Hale, "When Karl Marx Worked for Horace Greeley," *American Heritage* 8 (Apr. 1957): 20–25, 110–11.

76. John Higham, *From Boundlessness to Consolidation: The Transformation of American Culture 1840–1860* (Ann Arbor: William L. Clements Library Associates, 1969), 17.

77. See David Harvey's description of the "strange assortment of bourgeois allies" who joined the craftworkers of Paris in their fight against capitalist control of production and distribution: "Paris, 1850–1870," in *Consciousness and Urban Experience*, 65.

78. *New York Tribune*, Feb. 13, 1849.

79. Ibid.

80. Ibid.

81. Dana to Hannah Ripley, Sept. 6, 1849, Brown Family Papers.

3. Apprenticeship: The *New York Tribune* and the Tradition of Free Labor

1. James Parton, quoted in Eric S. Lunde, *Horace Greeley* (Boston: Twayne Publishers, 1981), 20. Probably more has been written about Horace Greeley and the

New York Tribune than about any other editor or newspaper. See also Richard Kluger, *The Paper: The Life and Death of the New York Herald-Tribune* (New York: Knopf, 1986); Glyndon Van Deusen, *Horace Greeley: Nineteenth-Century Crusader* (New York: Hill and Wang, 1964); and Jeter Allen Isely, *Horace Greeley and the Republican Party: 1853–1861* (Princeton: Princeton Univ. Press, 1947).

2. For the *Tribune*'s in-house circulation estimates, see the Corporate Minute Books of the Tribune Association, Whitney Communication Corporation, New York, N.Y. (hereafter cited as Corporate Minutes, Tribune Association).

3. Quoted in Kluger, 70.

4. Van Deusen, 5–8.

5. For a discussion of Greeley's early newspaper ventures, see Van Deusen, chaps. 4 and 5.

6. Horace Greeley to Henry J. Raymond, June 20, 1840, Henry J. Raymond Collection, New York Public Library.

7. Proprietors' meeting, Jan. 1, 1849, Corporate Minutes, Tribune Association.

8. For an annual breakdown of the shareholders, see Corporate Minutes, Tribune Association.

9. There is evidence of Dana's continuing interest in Fourierism as late as 1851 in a letter of introduction that Dana wrote to Louis Blanc on behalf of Parke Godwin, Dec. 29, 1851, Bryant-Godwin Collection.

10. Eric Foner, chaps. 1 and 2.

11. See Arthur Bestor, "Patent-Office Models of the Good Society: Some Relationships Between Social Reform and Westward Expansion," *American Historical Review* 58 (Apr. 1953): 505–26.

12. Karl Marx to Joseph Weydemeyer, Mar. 5, 1852, Karl Marx and Friedrich Engels, *Collected Works* (New York: International Publishers, 1975), 39:62. According to Marx, the popularity of Carey's views showed that "in the United States bourgeois society is still far too immature for the class struggle to be made perceptible and comprehensible. . . . It is *par trop* naive to suggest that, if the *total product of labor* rises, the 3 classes among whom it is to be shared will share *equally* in that growth. If profit were to rise by 20%, the workers would have to strike to obtain a 2% rise in wages."

13. A. D. H. Kaplan, *Henry Charles Carey* (Baltimore: Johns Hopkins Univ. Press, 1931), 36–38; George Winston Smith, *Henry C. Carey and American Sectional Conflict* (Albuquerque: Univ. of New Mexico, 1951).

14. Stone, 15.

15. For a discussion of a generational response to what many viewed as the rise of the Slave Power, see George M. Frederickson, *The Inner Civil War: Northern Intellectuals and the Crisis of the Union* (New York: Harper and Row, 1965).

16. Mayo D. Hazeltine, "Charles Anderson Dana," *North American Review* 185 (July 1907): 510.

17. Beman Brockway, *Fifty Years in Journalism* (New York: Daily Times Printing and Publishing House, 1891), 141.

18. Proprietors' meetings, Sept. 7, 1849; Dec. 31, 1850; Jan. 4, 1851; Jan. 11, 1851; July 1, 1851; and Dec. 31, 1851, Corporate Minutes, Tribune Association.

19. Proprietors' meeting, May 1, 1852, ibid.

20. Dana to James S. Pike, Apr. 8, 1851, James S. Pike Collection, microfilm edition, Calais Free Library, Calais, Me. (hereafter cited as Pike Collection).

21. Ibid.

22. See Morton Borden, "Some Notes on Horace Greeley, Charles Dana and Karl Marx," *Journalism Quarterly* 34 (1957): 457–65; and "Five Letters of Charles A. Dana to Karl Marx," *Journalism Quarterly* 36 (1959): 314–16.

23. Karl Marx to Friedrich Engels, July 31, 1851, quoted in Marx and Engels, 38:398. In Feb. 1852, Jenny Marx wrote to Joseph Weydemeyer, asking him to inform Dana of their impoverished circumstances. "At this distance Karl could not possibly give Dana any real idea . . . since the situation was quite different when Dana knew us in Cologne and such a comfortably situated American has no idea how . . . ten shillings, coming at the right moment, can often rescue one from a horrifying situation." Jenny Marx to Joseph Weydemeyer, Feb. 13, 1852, quoted in Marx and Engels 39:35.

24. Ibid., 594ff.

25. *New York Tribune*, Apr. 7, 1853, quoted in Marx and Engels 39:594.

26. Karl Marx to Friedrich Engels, Jan. 5, 1854, quoted in Marx and Engels 39:407.

27. Ibid., Dec. 2, 1853, 404.

28. See Thomas Bender's discussion of *Putnam's Monthly* as a publication that was "at once a national force and a New York magazine." Bender, 162–68.

29. Dana to Bayard Taylor, Aug. 2, 1853, Bayard Taylor Correspondence, access no. 1169, Department of Manuscripts and University Archives, Cornell University Library (hereafter cited as Taylor Correspondence).

30. Gerard Wolfe, *New York: A Guide to the Metropolis* (New York: New York Univ. Press, 1983), chap. 5.

31. Charles A. Dana to James S. Pike, July 17, 1854, Pike Collection; ibid., July 24, 1854.

32. Ibid., June 25, 1856.

33. Ibid., July 17, 1854; Sept. 25, 1854; June 24, 1856; Oct. 5, 1856; June 14, 1859.

34. Ibid., undated fragment.

35. Ibid., July 24, 1854.

36. Ibid., Sept. 25, 1854.

37. Ibid., June 24, 1853, and undated fragment.

38. Ibid., July 14, 1855.

39. In 1898, Elizabeth Cady Stanton recalled that in 1893 she had visited Charles A. Dana and his family at their summer home near Glen Cove, Long Island. After remarking that "one seldom meets so gifted a man as the late editor of the *Sun*," she described his wife and her relatives, who "sympathized with him in all his most liberal opinions." Of Dana's extended family, she added, "I had the pleasure of sev-

eral long conversations with Miss Frances L. MacDaniel and her brother Osborne, whose wife is the sister of Mr. Dana, and who is now assisting Miss Prestona Mann in trying an experiment, similar to the one at Brook Farm, in the Adirondacks." Elizabeth Cady Stanton, *Eighty Years and More* (London: T. Fisher Unwin, 1898), 448–49. I am indebted to Carl Guarneri for this reference.

40. Dana to Henry C. Carey, Jan. 7, 1857, Henry Carey Gardiner Collection, Historical Society of Pennsylvania (hereafter cited as Gardiner Collection).

41. These included George Bancroft, William Gilmore Sims, Karl Marx, Theodore Parker, Horace Greeley, E. L. Youmans, and many others.

42. A good summary of Marx's contributions appears in Marx and Engels, 40: 60 n. 165.

43. Crowe, 236.

44. See, for example, Dana to Robert Balmanno, June 29, 1856, Dana MSS, Boston, and Charles A. Dana's letters to Richard Henry Dana in the Charles Dana Miscellaneous Manuscripts, Massachusetts Historical Society.

45. Dana to James S. Pike, May 29, 1850, Pike Collection.

46. Ibid., Feb. 9, 1852.

47. See Isely; Hendrick Booraem, *The Formation of the Republican Party in New York* (New York: New York Univ. Press, 1983).

48. Isely, 30.

49. Ibid., 87.

50. Proprietors' meetings, June 30, 1854, and Aug. 14, 1854, Corporate Minutes, Tribune Association.

51. Dana to James S. Pike, Sept. 1, 1854, Pike Collection.

52. Ibid., Nov. 22, 1854.

53. For accounts of Greeley's political strategy in the 1850s, see Isely; Van Deusen.

54. Horace Greeley to Dana, Apr. 2, 1856, Greeley Collection, Library of Congress. See also Horace Greeley, *On Lincoln, with Mr. Greeley's Letters to Charles A. Dana and a Lady Friend*, ed. Joel Benton (New York: Baker and Taylor Co., 1893). For other letters on this topic, see the Horace Greeley Collection at the New York Public Library.

55. Horace Greeley to Dana, Feb. 3, 1856, quoted in Benton, *Letters*, 110–11.

56. Ibid., Jan. 25, 1856, 103.

57. Ibid., Mar. 2, 1856, 123–24.

58. Horace Greeley to Schuyler Colfax, Apr. [n.d.] 1858, Greeley Collection, New York Public Library.

59. Rosebault, 53.

60. Isely, 177.

61. Proprietors' meeting, June 24, 1856, Corporate Minutes, Tribune Association.

62. Dana to James S. Pike, undated fragment, Pike Collection.

63. Ibid., Sept. 1, 1859. See also Dana to Henry C. Carey, Mar. 13, 1860, Gardiner Collection.

64. Dana to Henry C. Carey, Oct. 26, 1860, Gardiner Collection.

65. Trustee meeting, Sept. 24, 1860, Corporate Minutes, Tribune Association.

66. Ibid., Dec. 27, 1860.

67. Dana to Henry C. Carey, Nov. 29, 1855, Gardiner Collection.

68. For a discussion of Greeley's attitude toward peaceable secession, see Isely, 326–28.

69. Ibid., 330.

70. Ibid., 331.

71. *New York Tribune*, June 26, 1861.

72. Rosebault, 59; Isley, 332.

73. Dana to Thomas C. Carroll, Aug. 1, 1861, Charles Dana Miscellaneous Manuscripts, New-York Historical Society.

74. Horace Greeley to Sam Wilkeson, Feb. 3, 1862, James Wright Brown Collection of Horace Greeley's papers, New-York Historical Society.

75. In light of Dana's usual reticence about his feelings, his letters concerning this incident are extraordinary. See Dana to James S. Pike, Apr. 9, 1862, Pike Collection, and Dana to Henry C. Carey, Apr. 8, 1862, Gardiner Collection.

76. Dana to Pike, Apr. 9, 1862, Pike Collection.

77. The stockholders did, however, acknowledge "his many noble and endearing qualities," and they voted to continue his salary for an additional six months. Trustee meeting, Mar. 28, 1862, Corporate Minutes, Tribune Association.

78. Dana to James S. Pike, Apr. 8, 1862, Pike Collection.

79. Ibid., Apr. 9, 1862. Dana's departure from the *Tribune* also marked the end of that paper's arrangement with Karl Marx. According to historian William Harlan Hale, Marx agreed with Dana that the managing editor had been treated badly. In Marx's words, "It's that old ass [Greeley] . . . who is really responsible for everything." Quoted in Hale, 20.

80. S.H. Gay to Bayard Taylor, Apr. 7, 1862, Taylor Correspondence.

81. Dana to James S. Pike, Apr. 9, 1862, Pike Collection.

82. Dana to Henry C. Carey, Apr. 8, 1862, Gardiner Collection.

83. S.H. Gay to Bayard Taylor, Apr. 7, 1862, Taylor Collection.

84. Ibid.

85. Robert Bonner to Horace Greeley, Apr. 21, 1862, Greeley Collection, New York Public Library. The corporate minutes reveal that the unpleasantness between Dana and Greeley continued for another month or so. Greeley called a trustee meeting on May 19 to rescind the six-month continuation of Dana's salary because Dana, in trying to sell his stock, was allegedly "making war on the *Tribune*." A committee was appointed to investigate, and when the results were inconclusive, it was decided that "further consideration of the subject be postponed until some subsequent meeting." Evidently no such meeting took place. Proprietors' meeting, May 22, 1862, Corporate Minutes, Tribune Association.

86. Dana to Bayard Taylor, Dec. 30, 1862, Taylor Collection.

87. Dana to Robert Carter, Apr. 18, 1862, quoted in Wilson, 172.

4. Interlude: The Civil War

1. Wilson, 245.

2. See, for example, Salmon P. Chase to Dana, Nov. 10, 1860; William H. Seward to Dana, Jan. 27, 1859; and Edwin Stanton to Dana, Jan. 24, 1862, Charles Dana Collection, Library of Congress (hereafter cited as Dana Collection).

3. Wilson, 183.

4. Edwin Stanton to Dana, June 16, 1862, Dana Collection. A full but not entirely trustworthy account of Dana's experiences during the Civil War appears in Charles A. Dana, *Recollections of the Civil War* (New York: D. Appleton and Co., 1899). This book was ghost-written by Ida Tarbell and published after Dana's death. Of the completed version, he saw only the first chapter. Dana's recollections drew heavily upon his cables to Stanton, copies of which are available in the Dana Collection.

5. Dana, *Recollections*, 15.

6. William S. McFeely, *Grant: A Biography* (New York: Norton, 1981), 120.

7. Dana, *Recollections*, 16-17.

8. Dana to Edwin Stanton, Jan. 21, 1863, quoted in Dana, *Recollections*, 19.

9. Dana to James S. Pike, Mar. 13, 1863, Pike Collection.

10. Wilson, 201-2.

11. McFeely, 128.

12. Dana to Edwin Stanton, Apr. 25 and May 23, 1863, Dana Collection.

13. Wilson, 212.

14. Edwin Stanton to Dana, May 5, 1863, quoted in Wilson, 218.

15. Ibid., 223.

16. Dana to Edwin Stanton, June 19, 1863, Dana Collection.

17. Ibid., June 22, 1863.

18. Dana to James S. Pike, Aug. 18, 1863, Pike Collection.

19. Ibid., July 14, 1863.

20. Ibid.

21. Ibid.

22. Dana to Elihu Washburne, Aug. 29, 1863, Elihu Washburne Collection, Library of Congress.

23. Details of this account are drawn from McFeely, 133-35.

24. Dana, *Recollections*, 83.

25. Wilson, 232.

26. Quoted in McFeely, 135.

27. Dana to Edwin Stanton, July 13, 1863, quoted in Dana, *Recollections*, 73.

28. Dana to Edwin Stanton, Sept. 27, 1863, Dana Collection. See also dispatches from Sept. 19 and 20, 1863, and Oct. 5 and 12, 1863.

29. Ibid., Oct. 23, 1863.

30. Dana to James S. Pike, July 10, 1864, Pike Collection.

31. Dana, *Recollections*, 188-89.

32. Dana to Edwin Stanton, Apr. 10, 1865, Dana Collection.

33. Ibid., Apr. 12, 1865.

5. Experience: The *Chicago Republican* and Radical Republicanism

1. Quoted in David Lowe, *Lost Chicago* (New York: American Legacy Press, 1975), 149. Charles Dana was the first to call Chicago "that Windy City." He used the phrase in the *Sun* in 1890 in reference to Chicago Mayor Carter Henry Harrison's "nonsensical" claim that his city was the logical choice to host the Columbian Exposition of 1893. I am indebted to Martin Schram for this reference.

2. Wilson, 370.

3. Dana to James S. Pike, May 10, 1865, Pike Collection.

4. Philip Kinsley, *The Chicago Tribune, Its First Hundred Years* (Chicago: Tribune Company, 1946) 2:4.

5. Charles A. Dana to Richard Henry Dana, May 26, 1865, Richard Henry Dana Collection, Massachusetts Historical Society. Charles A. Dana was inordinately proud of his connection with the wealthy and prominent Danas of Massachusetts. In the same letter he wrote, "You notice that our friend General Dana has got into trouble by too great zeal. . . . By the way, is it true that Dana is not the name to which he was born, but one conferred by some legislature?"

6. Dana to Charles Nordhoff, June 16, 1865, Charles Dana Miscellaneous Manuscripts, New York Public Library.

7. Personal diary of James Harrison Wilson, Aug. 19, 1866, Wilson Collection.

8. Undated clipping from the *Chicago Tribune*, Dana MSS, New York Public Library.

9. A good summary of Dana's tenure at the *Chicago Republican* appears in Elmer Gertz, "Charles A. Dana and the *Chicago Republican*," *Journal of the Illinois State Historical Society* 45 (1952): 124–35.

10. *Chicago Republican*, Aug. 5, 1865. A complete file of the *Chicago Republican* is found in the Manuscript Division of the Newberry Library in Chicago.

11. Ibid., July 24, 1865.

12. Ibid., Nov. 1, 1865.

13. Kingsley, 8.

14. *Chicago Republican*, July 29, 1865.

15. Ibid., Nov. 9, 1865.

16. Ibid., Feb. 9, 1866.

17. Ibid., Dec. 17, 1865.

18. Ibid., Aug. 1, 1865.

19. William Taylor, "The Launching of a Commercial Culture: New York City, 1860–1930," typescript, Mar. 16, 1984, unpublished paper, 33.

20. *Chicago Republican*, Nov. 9, 1865.

21. Ibid., Nov. 19, 1865.

22. Ibid., Dec. 4, 1865.

23. Dana to James S. Pike, Nov. 10, 1865, Pike Collection.

24. "Our Annual," 1869 fragment, Dana MSS, New York Public Library.

25. Frederick Hudson, *Journalism in the United States, from 1690 to 1872* (New York: Harper and Brothers, 1873), 678.

26. Dana to James Harrison Wilson, Apr. 30, 1866, quoted in Wilson, 376.

27. Dana to Henry J. Raymond, Dec. 20, 1865, George Jones Collection, New York Public Library.

28. William Hartman, "Custom House Patronage Under Lincoln." *New-York Historical Society Quarterly* 41 (Oct. 1957): 440–57.

29. Quoted in Hartman, 450.

30. Dana to Andrew Johnson, Jan. 20, 1866, quoted in *New York Standard*, May 2, 1870.

31. Dana to William Bartlett, Jan. 27, 1866, Willard Bartlett Family Papers, Butler Library, Columbia University (hereafter cited as Bartlett Family Papers). From the dates mentioned in this letter, as well as the inordinate secrecy, it is clear that Dana was referring to his application for the collectorship.

32. Undated *Brooklyn Union*, Dana MSS, New York Public Library.

33. *Chicago Republican*, Mar. 15, 1866.

34. Ibid., Apr. 5, 1866.

35. *New York Independent*, June 14, 1866, quoted in Gertz, 134.

36. *Chicago Tribune*, undated clipping, Dana MSS, New York Public Library.

37. Ibid.

38. It is unclear whether this settlement also included payment of the two outstanding bank notes. Gertz, 135.

39. Personal diary of James Harrison Wilson, June 6, 1866, Wilson Collection.

40. Ibid.

41. Kenneth M. Stampp, *The Era of Reconstruction: 1865–1877* (New York: Vintage, 1965), esp. chap. 4, "The Triumph of the Radicals."

42. Quoted in Gertz, 133.

43. *Lincoln and His Cabinet; a Lecture Delivered on Tuesday, March 10, 1896, Before the New Haven Colony Historical Society* (New York: De Vinne Press, 1896).

6. Turnabout: The Politics of "Independence"

1. Quoted in O'Brien, 189.

2. Dana to William Bartlett, June 4, 1866, Bartlett Family Papers.

3. Wilson, 376.

4. Dana to William Bartlett, July 13, 1866, Bartlett Family Papers.

5. Wilson, 378.

6. Dana to William Bartlett, Nov. 28, 1866, Dana MSS, New-York Historical Society.

7. See the Act for Incorporation of the Evening Telegraph Association, Sept. 27, 1867, Dana MSS, New-York Historical Society. The eight trustees were Charles A. Dana,

Francis Palmer, Timothy Churchill, Marshall Blake, Frederick Conkling, Peter Mc-
Martin, William Blodgett, and John H. Sherwood.

8. Hudson, 678.

9. Undated typewritten transcript, Wilson Collection. Internal evidence suggests this was written by Amos Cummings, Dana's first managing editor at the *Sun*.

10. A. G. Browne to John A. Andrew, Oct. 22, 1867, John Andrew Collection,
Massachusetts Historical Society.

11. Hudson, 679.

12. Amos Cummings, undated transcript, Wilson Collection.

13. Ibid.

14. Dana to James Harrison Wilson, undated, quoted in Wilson, 378.

15. *The Sun's Guide to New York* (Jersey City: Jersey City Printing Company,
1892), 240–41.

16. The *Sun's* stockholders included William M. Evarts, Roscoe Conkling, Edwin D. Morgan, Alonzo B. Cornell, Thomas Murphy, George Opdyke, and Cyrus Field.

17. Hudson, 678.

18. *New York Star*, Jan. 16, 1868.

19. O'Brien, 151.

20. For the traditional explanation of the rise of the penny press — that it came
about in response to rapid technological improvements in transportation as well as
in printing and paper production — see Edwin Emery, *The Press and America*, 3d
ed. (New Jersey: Prentice-Hall, 1972), 160–61. This view has been challenged by new
interpretations that emphasize economic and cultural factors rather than technology.
The first and most influential of these is Schudson.

21. Schudson, 50.

22. Daniel Schiller, *Objectivity and the News* (Philadelphia: Univ. of Pennsylvania Press, 1981), chaps. 1 and 2.

23. Ibid., 49.

24. Ibid., 48.

25. Quoted in O'Brien, 171. See also the *Journalist*, Jan. 5, 1889, and *New York
Times*, Aug. 15, 1897, for discussions of Dana's editorial innovations.

26. Even Pulitzer used single-column headlines for a much longer time than
is usually acknowledged. George Juergens notes in *Joseph Pulitzer and the New York
World* (Princeton: Princeton Univ. Press, 1966), 27, that the first double-column headline appeared in the *World* in 1889.

27. Quoted in *New York Sun*, Aug. 8, 1919.

28. Dana to Uriah H. Painter, Jan. 3, 1868, Box 166-C, Uriah Painter Collection, Historical Society of Pennsylvania (hereafter cited as Painter Collection).

29. Rosebault, 160.

30. *New York Sun*, July 13, 1882.

31. Taylor.

32. *New York Sun*, Apr. 3, 1878.

33. J. Henry Harper, *I Remember* (New York: Harper and Brothers, 1934), 259.

34. For a fascinating look at the complexities of the 1863 draft riots, see Bernstein.

35. For a discussion of Democratic politics in New York City during the Civil War, see DeAlva Stanwood Alexander, *A Political History of the State of New York* (New York: Henry Holt and Co., 1909). See also Baker, 317-52.

36. For two excellent discussions of Reconstruction in New York, see Jerome Mushkat, *The Reconstruction of the New York Democracy, 1861–1874* (London: Associated Univ. Presses, 1981), and James C. Mohr, *The Radical Republicans and Reform in New York During Reconstruction* (Ithaca: Cornell Univ. Press, 1973). For an overview of Democratic party ideology during the same period, see Baker.

37. *New York Sun*, Jan. 27, 1868.

38. Ibid., July 9, 1868.

39. Dana to Uriah H. Painter, Feb. 1, 1868, Painter Collection.

40. Ibid., Mar. 31, 1868.

41. *New York Sun*, Apr. 14, 1868.

42. Ibid., Apr. 13, 1868.

43. Ibid., Jan. 27, 1868.

44. For a clear account of the various Democratic and Republican factions, see Stampp, chap. 5.

45. I. W. England to Uriah H. Painter, May 10, 1868, Painter Collection.

46. *New York Sun*, May 19, 1868.

47. Personal diary of James Harrison Wilson, Mar. 2, 1868, Wilson Collection. Wilson noted that he was to receive the first $2,500 in proceeds from the book and that all subsequent profit would be divided equally with Dana.

48. Personal diary of James Harrison Wilson, May 6, 1868, Wilson Collection.

49. New York Sun, July 27, 1868.

50. Ibid., Nov. 1, 1868.

51. Ibid., Sept. 30, 1868.

52. Samuel Tilden and August Belmont to W. F. Storey, undated, Samuel Tilden Collection, New York Public Library (hereafter cited as Tilden Collection).

53. *New York Sun*, Nov. 4, 1868.

54. See, for example, the *Journalist*, May 17, 1884. The influential trade weekly traced the editor's "relentless enmity" toward Grant to the president's refusal to appoint him collector.

55. Wilson, 406-7.

56. Ibid., 415.

57. *New York Sun*, Mar. 26, 1869.

58. Ibid., Apr. 17, 1869.

59. Byington to Uriah H. Painter, Dec. 18, 1868, Painter Collection.

60. *New York Sun*, July 6, 1869.

7. Two Cents' Worth: The Politics of Humor

1. Charles Barker Bradford quoted in the *Journalist*, Aug. 11, 1888; see also interview with David G. Croly in C. F. Wingate, *Views and Interviews on Journalism* (New York: F. B. Patterson, 1875).

2. W. A. Swanberg noted that the editor of the *World* "stole" many journalists from the *Sun*. Swanberg, *Pulitzer* (New York: Scribner's Sons, 1967), p. 147. Edward Page Mitchell, one of Dana's successors as editor in chief of the *Sun*, also recalled how, as a reporter in Lewiston, Maine, he had looked to the *Sun* for its "spirited expression . . . uncommon literary taste and humor." Mitchell, p. 109.

3. O'Brien, 393.

4. Quoted in Wingate, 103.

5. *New York Sun*, Oct. 19, 1868.

6. Ibid., July 27, 1868.

7. Ibid., June 6, 1868, and June 8, 1868.

8. Ibid., June 25, 1868.

9. Ibid., Nov. 7, 1868.

10. Ibid., Oct. 3, 1868.

11. Ibid., Mar. 17, 1869.

12. Ibid., July 13, 1868, and Dec. 3, 1868.

13. Ibid., Oct. 5, 1871.

14. Ibid., Mar. 22, 1871.

15. Ibid., Dec. 19, 1868.

16. Sociologist Robert Park credited Dana's paper with developing the genre of the human interest story. Park, Burgess, and McKenzie, 91–94.

17. *New York Sun*, Aug. 8, 1919.

18. Dana, "The Modern American Newspaper," lecture delivered on July 24, 1888; reprinted in Dana, *The Art of Newspaper Making* (New York: D. Appleton and Co., 1895), 11–12.

19. George William Curtis, "The Editor's Easy Chair," *Harper's Monthly Magazine* 43 (July 1871): 294–95.

20. W. S. Lilly, "The Ethics of Journalism," *Forum* 7 (July 1889): 503.

21. See Geoffrey Blodgett, "Reform Thought and the Genteel Tradition," in *The Gilded Age, A Reappraisal* ed. Wayne Morgan (Syracuse: Syracuse Univ. Press, 1963), 55–76.

22. M. J. Savage, "A Profane View of the Sanctum," *North American Review* 141 (July 1885): 152.

23. Dana's view of this "unruly democracy" encompassed class inclusivity as well. He frequently printed self-congratulatory editorial remarks such as "not only the working classes, but every class now reads the *Sun*. It shines for all!" *New York Sun*, Apr. 2, 1868.

24. Frank Luther Mott, *American Journalism: A History, 1690–1960*, 3d ed. (New York: Macmillan, 1962), 412. Z. L. White likewise concluded that "the newspapers that have gained the most rapidly in circulation since 1880 have been either those that have professed entire independence of political parties, or those upon whose necks the party yoke has set very lightly." Z. L. White, "A Decade of American Journalism," *Westminster Review* (Oct. 1887): 856.

25. Whitelaw Reid, "Schools of Journalism," *Scribner's Monthly* 4 (June 1872): 204.

26. Ibid.

27. *New York Tribune,* June 20, 1879.

28. *New York Sun,* Mar. 5, 1885.

29. Charles A. Dana, address to the Wisconsin Editors' Association; reprinted in the *Journalist,* July 28, 1888.

30. John Cockerill, *Cosmopolitan* (Oct. 1892), quoted in Stone, 113.

31. Blodgett, 882.

32. The *Journalist* frequently commented on the *Sun's* loss of political influence after 1884; see June 14 and Nov. 8, 1884.

33. *Journalist,* June 21, 1884.

34. Cummings transcript, Wilson Collection.

35. McFeely, 293. Interestingly, it was A. T. Stewart's "marble palace" at the corner of Broadway and Chambers Streets that became the *Sun's* home after 1915.

36. *New York Sun,* July 8, 1869; see also Oct. 3 and Nov. 24, 1870.

37. George Templeton Strong, *The Diary of George Templeton Strong,* ed. Allan Nevins and Milton Halsey Thomas (New York: Macmillan, 1952), 4:287.

38. *New York Sun,* Oct. 3, 1870.

39. Dana to Uriah H. Painter, Apr. 3, 1869, Painter Collection.

40. Ibid., July 21, 1869.

41. Ibid., June 29, [probably] 1869.

42. *New York Sun,* Jan. 13, 1870.

43. Diary of Hamilton Fish, Dec. 23, 1869, Hamilton Fish Collection, Library of Congress, reel no. 3, 280.

44. Hamilton Fish to J. C. Hamilton, Jan. 8, 1870, ibid. See also Fish to Archibald Russell, Jan. 23, 1870, and Fish to David Einstein, June 1, 1870.

45. *New York Sun,* Oct. 3, 1870.

46. Ibid., Apr. 6, 1869.

47. As recently as 1982, the revolutionary Cuban government was still honoring Dana's memory. A pamphlet, "José Martí Replies: Materials Referring to José Martí and the Radio Martí Project," describes Martí's twenty-year relationship with the *Sun* and quotes extensively from the Martí obituary written by Dana and published in the *Sun* on May 23, 1895. I am indebted to John S. Nichols, professor of journalism at Penn State University, for this reference.

48. Edward Mitchell made these remarks in the 1915 farewell dinner to the old Sun building. These and other comments were published in a memento pamphlet, a copy of which can be found at the New-York Historical Society.

49. Byington to Uriah H. Painter, Nov. 9, 1869, Painter Collection.

50. *New York Sun,* July 29, 1869.

51. Ibid., Mar. 5, 1869.

52. Ibid., Nov. 25, 1870.

53. Ibid., Dec. 12, 1870.

54. Ibid., Nov. 9, 1870.

55. Morris Werner, *Tammany Hall* (New York: Doubleday, 1928), 206–7. See also the account in Stone, 140.

56. Seymour J. Mandelbaum, *Boss Tweed's New York* (New York: Wiley, 1965), 17.

57. James B. Mix, *The Biter Bit, or the Robert Macaire of Journalism* (Washington, D.C., 1870).

58. *New York Sun*, Jan. 6, 1871.

59. See Mandelbaum, chap. 7, and Mushkat, chap. 5.

60. *New York Sun*, May 6, 1869.

61. Ibid., Feb. 11, 1870.

62. Ibid., Jan. 6, 1871.

63. See Isaac England to Uriah H. Painter, Jan. 10, 1871, Painter Collection.

64. Dana to Uriah H. Painter, Mar. 3, 1871; Mar. 13, 1871; Apr. 10, 1871, Painter Collection.

65. *New York Sun*, Dec. 12, 1870.

66. *New York Herald*, Jan. 21, 1871, quoted in Werner, 198.

67. *New York Sun*, Dec. 12, 1870.

68. Albert Bigelow Paine, *Th. Nast: His Period and His Pictures* (New York: The Macmillan Company, 1904), 159–60.

69. William M. Tweed to Edwin Shandley, Mar. 13, 1871, quoted in Werner, 201.

70. *New York Sun*, Mar. 13, 1871.

71. Thomas C. Leonard, *The Power of the Press: The Birth of American Political Reporting* (New York: Oxford Univ. Press, 1986), 107–8. For a useful discussion of the political power of visual thinking, see chapter 4, "Visual Thinking: The Tammany Tiger Loose," 97–131.

72. *New York Sun*, Sept. 17, 1871.

73. Walter Blair and Hamlin Hill, *America's Humor: From Poor Richard to Doonesbury* (New York: Oxford Univ. Press, 1978), 290, 369.

74. *Journalist*, May 1, 1886.

75. Ibid., May 5, 1888.

76. Mitchell, 108–15.

77. David G. Croly, quoted in Wingate, 333.

78. Basil Wiley, *The Seventeenth Century Background*, quoted in Kenneth S. Lynn, *The Comic Tradition in America* (New York: Doubleday, 1958), 193.

79. *New York Sun*, Mar. 6, 1874.

80. Ibid.

81. Many of the office cat stories are retold in the anniversary issue of the *New York Sun*, Sept. 2, 1933.

82. Stone, 130.

83. Richard Boyd Hauck, *A Cheerful Nihilism: Confidence and 'The Absurd' in American Humorous Fiction* (Bloomington: Indiana Univ. Press, 1971), xiii.

84. Quoted in Wingate, 55–56.

85. *New York Sun*, Mar. 11, 1869.

86. Rosebault, 200.

87. Cummings typescript, Wilson Collection.

88. See John G. Sproat, *The Best Men: Liberal Reformers in the Gilded Age* (New York: Oxford Univ. Press, 1968).

89. Dana printed this leader in the *Sun* for several weeks after July 12, 1872.

90. *New York Sun*, July 9, 1872.

91. Ibid., Nov. 8, 1876.

92. See Geo. P. Rowell, *American Newspaper Directory* (New York: Geo. P. Rowell and Son, 1874–79), and table 1 in chap. 9.

93. Mitchell, 228–29. Records of newspaper circulation were notoriously poor in the 1870s, but the fact that the *Sun* printed the weekly list of undeliverable letters at the New York Post Office — a privilege traditionally given to the city paper with the highest circulation — bears out this claim.

8. Mugwumps, Shams, and Reformers: The Politics of Conscience

1. A good overview of the range of reform opinion among late nineteenth-century New Yorkers can be found in David C. Hammack, *Power and Society: Greater New York at the Turn of the Century* (New York: Russell Sage Foundation, 1982).

2. See Marc Ross.

3. John Swinton, "Memoranda as to the Late Charles A. Dana," *Chautauquan* 26 (Mar. 1898): 612. See also the lengthy conversation with Swinton that is quoted in Robert Waters, *Career and Conversation of John Swinton* (Chicago: C. H. Kerr and Co., 1902), 36–37. A good short biography of Swinton is found in *Pearson's* (Feb. 1918), in which author Eugene V. Debs calls Swinton "one of the real heroes of American history."

4. Mandelbaum, 17.

5. Park, Burgess, and McKenzie, 84.

6. Schudson, chaps. 1–2.

7. Mitchell, 126. Dana belonged to the Century Club in the 1850s, but he resigned early in the 1860s. While the reasons are unknown, it is tempting to conclude that they were related to his "expulsion" from the New York *Tribune*.

8. H. T. Peck, "Mr. Dana on Journalism," *Bookman* 2 (Nov. 1895): 192.

9. Mitchell, 129.

10. See Baker and Jensen for discussions of the importance of the religious roots of partisanship.

11. *New York Sun*, May 6, 1890.

12. Joel Tyler Headly, *The Great Riots of New York: 1712–1873* (New York: E. B. Treat, 1873), 290–93.

13. Ibid., 294.

14. *New York Sun*, July 11, 1871.

15. Headly, 296–304.

16. *New York Sun*, July 13, 1871.

17. Geoffrey Blodgett, "Reform Thought and the Genteel Tradition," in Morgan, 55–76.

18. Ibid., 57.

19. *New York Sun,* Apr. 15, 1884.

20. Biographical data on Curtis come from Gordon Milne, *George William Curtis: The Genteel Tradition* (Bloomington: Univ. of Indiana Press, 1956).

21. *New York Sun,* Oct. 18, 1885. As early as July 12, 1869, Dana had remarked of Godkin's *Nation,* "[It] is unsurpassed in its malignity toward politicians who do not enjoy the sympathy of its select circle of men of culture and influence."

22. *Journalist,* Apr. 5, 1884.

23. Park, Burgess, and McKenzie, 94.

24. *New York Sun,* Apr. 1, 1874.

25. Robert Bonner to Dana, Apr. 1, 1874, Bonner Collection. See also Dana's answer of Apr. 1, 1874, denying that he had intended to treat Bonner unkindly or to injure the *Ledger.* Bonner answered Dana's letter on Apr. 2, 1874 with a reiteration of his point.

26. *New York Sun,* Apr. 16, 1878.

27. Swinton, 613.

28. *New York Sun,* Aug. 17, 1882.

29. Mandelbaum, 122.

30. Dana, *Lincoln and His Cabinet.*

31. Samuel L. Clemens and Charles Dudley Warner, *The Gilded Age; A Tale of Today* (Hartford: American Publishing Co., 1873).

32. Sproat.

33. Dana to Silas W. Burt, Jan. 13, 1882, Anthony Collection.

34. Ibid.

35. *New York Sun,* Oct. 31, 1882.

36. Cummings transcript, Wilson Collection.

37. Dana to Samuel Tilden, July 24, 1884, Tilden Collection. See also Dana to Tilden, Dec. 31, 1883, and July 18, 1884.

38. *Journalist,* July 19, 1884.

39. *Puck,* Apr. 5, 1882.

40. See Samuel Tilden to Dana, Jan. 4, 1882; July 29, 1882; and July 3, 1883, Tilden Collection.

41. Rosebault, 226.

42. For a thoughtful analysis of Butler's relationship to the Massachusetts elite, see Richard Harmond, "The 'Beast' in Boston: Benjamin F. Butler as Governor of Massachusetts," *Journal of American History* 55 (Sept. 1968): 266–80.

43. *Nation,* Apr. 9, 1884, quoted in Sproat, 49. Interestingly, Dana and Benjamin Butler corresponded during 1884, and there is nothing in the half-dozen or so surviving letters to suggest that the editor didn't take the candidate seriously. In January 1884, Butler approached Dana with two proposed resolutions on civil rights and the tariff, to which the editor responded favorably. Later that year, the two exchanged letters relating to campaign strategy. See Butler to Dana, Jan. 4, 1884; Aug. 6, 1884; and Aug. 17, 1884, Benjamin Butler Collection, Library of Congress.

44. *New York Sun,* Jan. 24, 1884.
45. Ibid., Aug. 7, 1884.
46. Ibid., Oct. 19, 1884.
47. Ibid., Oct. 23, 1884.
48. Dana to Thomas Carroll, Oct. 21, 1884, Dana MSS, New-York Historical Society.
49. Paine, 492.
50. *New York Sun,* June 26, 1884.
51. Ibid., Oct. 14, 1884.
52. Rosebault, 222–23.
53. *Journalist,* Nov. 15, 1884.
54. N. W. Ayer, *N. W. Ayer's American Newspaper Annual* (Philadelphia: N. W. Ayer and Son, 1880–97). See table 1 in chap. 9.
55. *Journalist,* Jan. 17, 1885.

9. Eclipsed: The Rise of a Culture of Consumption

1. See Irwin Unger, *The Greenback Era: A Social and Political History of American Finance, 1865–1879* (Princeton: Princeton Univ. Press, 1964) for a good analysis of Gilded Age economic issues.
2. *New York Sun,* Oct. 18, 1880.
3. Ida M. Tarbell, *All in a Day's Work, An Autobiography* (New York: The Macmillan Company, 1939), 175. Evidently Henry Adams was also interested in what Dana had to say. He referred to the editor's "blackguardism" in *The Education of Henry Adams* (Boston: Massachusetts Historical Society, 1918), 244.
4. Emery, 269; Stone, 380–85; Mitchell, 128.
5. Mitchell, 264; O'Brien, 191; Swanberg, 36.
6. Swanberg, 67–70.
7. For an excellent study of Pulitzer's first innovative years as editor of the *New York World,* see Juergens, 234–62.
8. *New York World,* Jan. 3, 1884.
9. Ibid., May 17, 1884.
10. Swanberg, 32.
11. Jacob Riis, *How the Other Half Lives: Studies among the Tenements of New York* (New York: Scribner's Sons, 1917); see also Schudson, 81–83.
12. Stuart Ewen, *Captains of Consciousness: Advertising and the Social Roots of the Consumer Culture* (New York: McGraw-Hill, 1976), 23–30. See also T. J. Jackson Lears, "From Salvation to Self-Realization: Advertising and the Therapeutic Roots of the Consumer Culture, 1880–1930," in ed. Richard Wightman Fox and T. J. Jackson Lears, *The Culture of Consumption: Critical Essays in American History, 1880–1980* (New York: Pantheon, 1983), 1–38.
13. Warren L. Susman, *Culture as History: The Transformation of American Society in the Twentieth Century* (New York: Pantheon, 1984), xix–xxx.

14. See Gunther Barth, *City People: The Rise of Modern City Culture in Nineteenth-Century America* (New York: Oxford Univ. Press, 1980), chaps. 3 and 4.

15. Juergens, 234–62. For a more general discussion of Pulitzer's use of advertising techniques, see Barth, 81–84, and Schudson, 91–106.

16. *New York World*, Jan. 6, 1884.

17. Ibid.

18. Theodore Dreiser, *Sister Carrie* (New York: New American Library Edition, 1980), 296–97.

19. Juergens, 366.

20. Swanberg, 78–79.

21. *New York Times*, Apr. 24, 1885.

22. *Journalist*, May 31, 1884.

23. Ibid., Dec. 13, 1884.

24. Unsigned letter to Pulitzer, June 23, 1885, Joseph Pulitzer Collection, Butler Library, Columbia University.

25. According to Candace Stone, who had access to circulation files that disappeared when the *Sun* went out of business, the only time that the circulation had dropped for more than a few days at a time was in 1875, at the height of Dana's attacks on Henry Ward Beecher. See Stone, 383–84.

26. *New York Sun*, Nov. 8, 1887, quoted in Swanberg, 141. Swanberg suggests that this editorial and others were intended to win Jewish readers over to the *Sun*, but this seems unlikely.

27. Swanberg, 140.

28. *Journalist*, Jan. 17, 1885.

29. Based on data found in Assent of Stockholders to Mortgage, Dec. 6, 1886, Office of Register of City and County of New York, Lieber 2020, 33.

30. Samuel J. Tilden to Dana, Apr. 21, 1886, Tilden Collection.

31. Dana to Tilden, Apr. 24, 1886, ibid.

32. Tilden to Dana, Apr. 26, 1886, ibid.

33. Dana to Tilden, June 4, 1886, ibid.

34. *Nation*, July 15, 1886.

35. By the mid-1880s, the Hoe company was building printing presses that could turn out newspapers of eight, ten, or twelve pages at the rate of 20,000 per hour. See *New York Tribune*, Jan. 21, 1894.

36. Though incomplete, the records also revealed several facts about the ownership of the paper. While the documents referred to increases in the number of trustees, it was striking how little the ownership had changed, being concentrated in the hands of men who actually wrote for the newspaper. Three of the *Sun*'s five original trustees, Charles A. Dana, Thomas Hitchcock, and John Sherwood, were still trustees in 1884. By that time the group had expanded to seven, and included Dana's son Paul and publisher Isaac England. See the annual reports of the stockholders' meetings in the New York County Clerk's Office.

37. The *New York Times* reported on Apr. 5, 1888, that this mortgage was held by the Equitable Company.

38. *New York World,* Jan. 11 and 13, 1888.

39. Since the *Sun's* business records no longer exist, it is impossible to establish exactly when this decision was made. However it must have occurred sometime between Apr. 1886 when the editor began to experiment with six-page papers and Dec. 1886, when the organization mortgaged the building to buy new presses.

40. *New York Sun,* Apr. 2, 1888.

41. *Journalist,* Apr. 24, 1886. See also May, 22, 1886. As impressionistic as these statements were, they had considerable impact, given the nature of the *Journalist's* readership among editors and reporters.

42. *New York Times,* Jan. 6, 1886.

43. *New York Tribune,* Jan. 21, 1894.

44. For a good discussion of New York's Swallowtail Democrats, see Hammack, 110–11, and 132–35.

45. *New York Sun,* Nov. 26, 1890.

46. The Republican *New York Tribune* called the Force Bill "a subordinate and comparatively unimportant question" that the *Sun* used to push "into the background all the issues which the Mugwump contingent had howled conspicuous." *New York Tribune,* Sept. 20, 1893.

47. *New York Sun,* July 24, 1892.

48. *Montgomery Advertiser,* Oct. 20, 1890, quoted in *New York Times,* Oct. 22, 1890.

49. *New York Times,* Oct. 29, 1892.

50. Sproat, 59.

51. *New York Sun,* Feb. 17, 1892.

52. Ibid., Feb. 3, 1894.

53. Ibid., Apr. 30, 1886.

54. Ibid., Aug. 21, 1886.

55. Ibid., Apr. 2, 1888.

56. Juergens, 312.

57. *Union Printer,* Apr. 23, 1887, Microfilm Division, New York Public Library.

58. Regular minutes, June 2, 1887, Typographical Union No. 6, Manuscript Division, New York Public Library.

59. *Union Printer,* Apr. 23 and May 21, 1887.

60. *New York Tribune,* Jan. 21, 1894.

61. Dana's successor at the *Sun,* William Laffan, did not share his loyalty to Typographical Union No. 6. In 1899, Laffan installed typesetting machines that threatened to reduce both hours and wages. Laffan locked out the union workers after a strike was threatened and hired strike breakers in what became one of the industry's worst strikes. *New York Times,* Aug. 6, 1899.

62. See Hauck; Blair and Hill; and Henry Nash Smith, *Mark Twain's Fable of Progress; Political and Economic Ideas in 'A Connecticut Yankee'* (New Brunswick, N.J.: Rutgers Univ. Press, 1969).

63. Paine, 454.

64. Alan Trachtenberg, *The Incorporation of America: Culture and Society in the Gilded Age* (New York: Hill and Wang, 1982), 3–4.

65. Paine, 455.

66. For a discussion of the cultural dimension of the tariff and currency questions, see Jensen.

67. *New York Sun*, Dec. 11, 1890.

68. *Southern Alliance Farmer*, quoted in *New York Times*, Apr. 2, 1891.

69. *New York Sun*, Aug. 6, 1896.

10. The Independent Press

1. Rosebault, 6.

2. Dana, quoted in Wingate, 55.

3. John Cockerill, "Some Phases of Contemporary Journalism," *Cosmopolitan* 13 (Oct. 1892): 697.

4. *Journalist*, Jan. 5, 1889; Sept. 22, 1888.

5. Schudson, 76.

6. Thomas C. Cochran, "Media as Business: A Brief History," *Journal of Communication* 25 (Autumn 1975): 155–65.

7. Trachtenberg, 38–69.

8. For an analysis of the way in which corporate priorities influence the news media of our own time, see Martin Lee and Norman Solomon, *Unreliable Sources: A Guide to Detecting Bias in the News Media* (New York: Carol Publishing Group, 1990), 59–101. See also Erik Barnouw, *The Sponsor: Notes on a Modern Potentate* (New York: Oxford Univ. Press, 1978), for an influential discussion of the advertiser's role in the electronic media.

9. Upton Sinclair, *The Brass Check: A Study of American Journalism*, reprint, (New York: Arno and the New York Times, 1970), 222–24.

10. Ibid., 226.

11. A. J. Liebling, *The Press* (New York: Pantheon, 1961), 6.

12. For a discussion of "newsworthiness" in late twentieth-century journalism, see Herbert J. Gans, *Deciding What's News* (New York: Pantheon, 1979), 146–81. See also Gaye Tuchman, *Making News: A Study in the Construction of Reality* (New York: Free Press, 1978).

Bibliography

Manuscripts

Library of Congress

Charles Dana Collection, which includes nineteen miscellaneous letters along
with typewritten and manuscript copies of Civil War dispatches to Secretary of War Edwin M. Stanton.

Horace Greeley Collection, particularly Greeley's 1842 letters to Brook Farm
and his correspondence from Washington, D.C., during the winter of
1855–56.

Selected letters from the collections of Benjamin F. Butler, Salmon P. Chase,
Hamilton Fish, Manton Marble, Elihu Washburne, and James Harrison Wilson.

New York Public Library

Alfred W. Anthony autograph collection, which contains fifteen letters from
Dana to various prominent New Yorkers.

Robert Bonner Collection.

Bryant-Godwin Collection, particularly ten letters from Dana to Parke Godwin written during the 1840s.

Charles Dana Miscellaneous Manuscripts, which include newspaper clippings and ten personal letters written between 1850 and 1892.

Horace Greeley Collection.

International Typographical Union of North America, Union No. 6, New
York, Records 1870–96; executive committee minutes and minutes of
regular meetings.

Selected letters from the collections of George William Curtis, George Jones, Henry J. Raymond, and George Ripley.

Samuel Tilden Collection, particularly forty-five letters dating from 1872 through 1884 that pertain to Democratic party affairs and Dana's personal loan. This collection also contains numerous scattered references to both Dana and the *New York Sun*.

Uncataloged morgue of the *New York Sun*, which contains clippings dating from 1910 through the 1950s.

New-York Historical Society

Charles Dana Miscellaneous Manuscripts, which contain twenty-four letters to Thomas B. Carroll, ten letters to Col. A. H. Markland, and several miscellaneous papers.

Edward Page Mitchell Miscellaneous Manuscripts.

Selected letters from the Stanford White Collection and the James Wright Brown Collection of Horace Greeley's papers.

Butler Library, Columbia University

Willard Bartlett Family Papers, which include twenty-four business and personal letters from Dana to Willard and William Bartlett.

Selected papers from the manuscript collections of Allan Nevins, Joseph Pulitzer, the *New York World*, and Edward Morse Sheppard.

Massachusetts Historical Society

Charles Dana Miscellaneous Manuscripts.

Selected letters pertaining to the *American Cyclopaedia* from the collections of John Andrew, Richard Henry Dana, Francis Parkman, and George Bancroft.

Boston Public Library

Charles Dana Miscellaneous Manuscripts.

John S. Dwight Collection, which contains several letters referring to Brook Farm.

Other Collections

Henry C. Carey Papers, in Henry Carey Gardiner Collection, Historical Society of Pennsylvania.

Corporate Minute Books of the Tribune Association, Whitney Communication Corporation, New York, N.Y.
James Harrison Wilson Collection, Historical Society of Delaware.
Bayard Taylor Correspondence, Department of Manuscripts and University Archives, Cornell University Library.

Microfilmed Collections

Henry S. Borneman Papers, microfilm edition, Illinois Historical Survey, University of Illinois.
John Stillman Brown Family Papers, microfilm edition, Kansas State Historical Society.
James S. Pike Collection, microfilm edition, Calais Free Library, Calais, Me.

Newspapers

The *Harbinger*, 1845–49.
The *New York Tribune*, 1848–49 and selected copies through 1862.
The *New York Sun*, 1868–97.
The *Chicago Republican*, 1865–66.
The *Journalist*, 1884–89.
Selected copies of the *New York World*, *New York Times*, and *New York Tribune*, 1880–97.

Books

Adams, Henry. *The Education of Henry Adams*. Boston: Massachusetts Historical Society, 1918.
Alexander, DeAlva Stanwood. *A Political History of the State of New York*. New York: Henry Holt and Co., 1909.
Allmendinger, David F. *Paupers and Scholars: The Transformation of Student Life in Nineteenth-Century New England*. New York: St. Martin's, 1975.
Ayer, N. W. *N. W. Ayer's American Newspaper Annual*. Philadelphia: N. W. Ayer and Son, 1880–97.
Baker, Jean H. *Affairs of Party: The Political Culture of Northern Democrats in the Mid-Nineteenth Century*. Ithaca: Cornell Univ. Press, 1983.
Barnouw, Erik. *The Sponsor: Notes on a Modern Potentate*. New York: Oxford Univ. Press, 1978.

Barth, Gunther. *City People: The Rise of Modern City Culture in Nineteenth-Century America.* New York: Oxford Univ. Press, 1980.

Bender, Thomas. *New York Intellect: A History of Intellectual Life in New York City, From 1750 to the Beginnings of Our Own Time.* New York: Knopf, 1987.

Bernstein, Iver. *The New York City Draft Riots: Their Significance for American Society and Politics in the Age of the Civil War.* New York: Oxford Univ. Press, 1990.

Black, David. *The King of Fifth Avenue: The Fortunes of August Belmont.* New York: Dial, 1981.

Blair, Walter, and Hill, Hamlin. *America's Humor: From Poor Richard to Doonesbury.* New York: Oxford Univ. Press, 1978.

Blumin, Stuart M. *The Emergence of the Middle Class: Social Experience in the American City, 1760–1900.* Cambridge: Cambridge Univ. Press, 1989.

Booraem, Hendrick. *The Formation of the Republican Party in New York.* New York: New York Univ. Press, 1983.

Brockway, Beman. *Fifty Years in Journalism.* New York: Daily Times Printing and Publishing House, 1891.

Burton, Katherine. *Paradise Planners: The Story of Brook Farm.* New York: Longmans, Green and Co., 1939.

Carey, Henry C. *The Harmony of Interests, Agricultural, Manufacturing, Commercial.* New York: M. Finch, 1852.

Carruth, Gorton, and Ehrlich, Eugene. *The Harper Book of American Quotations.* New York: Harper and Row, 1988.

Childs, George William. *Recollections.* Philadelphia: J. B. Lippincott Co., 1890.

Clemens, Samuel L., and Warner, Charles Dudley. *The Gilded Age; A Tale of Today.* Hartford: American Publishing Co., 1873.

Crowe, Charles. *George Ripley: Transcendentalist and Utopian Socialist.* Athens: Univ. of Georgia Press, 1967.

Dana, Charles A. *The Art of Newspaper Making.* New York: D. Appleton and Co., 1895.

———. *Eastern Journeys.* New York: D. Appleton and Co., 1898.

———. *A Lecture on Association, in Its Connection with Religion.* Boston: B. H. Greene, 1844.

———. *Lincoln and His Cabinet; A Lecture Delivered on Tuesday, March 10, 1896, Before the New Haven Colony Historical Society.* De Vinne Press, 1896.

———. *Proudhon and His "Bank of the People."* New York: Benj. R. Tucker, 1896.

————. *Recollections of the Civil War.* New York: D. Appleton and Co., 1899.

Denning, Michael. *Mechanic Accents: Dime Novels and Working Class Culture in America.* New York: Verso Press, 1987.

Dreiser, Theodore. *Sister Carrie.* New York: American Library Edition, 1980.

Durden, Robert F. *James Shepherd Pike: Republicanism and the American Negro, 1850–1882.* Durham: Duke Univ. Press, 1957.

Dwight, Marianne. *Letters From Brook Farm 1844–1847.* New York: Vassar College, 1928.

Emery, Edwin. *The Press and America.* 3d ed. New Jersey: Prentice-Hall, 1972.

Ewen, Stuart. *Captains of Consciousness: Advertising and the Social Roots of the Consumer Culture.* New York: McGraw-Hill, 1976.

Foner, Eric. *Free Soil, Free Labor, Free Men: The Ideology of the Republican Party Before the Civil War.* New York: Oxford Univ. Press, 1970.

Foner, Philip S. *The Great Labor Uprising of 1877.* New York: Monad Press, 1977.

Fox, Richard Wightman, and Lears, T. J. Jackson, eds. *The Culture of Consumption: Critical Essays in American History, 1880–1908.* New York: Pantheon, 1984.

Fredrickson, George M. *The Inner Civil War: Northern Intellectuals and the Crisis of the Union.* New York: Harper and Row, 1965.

Frothingham, Octavius Brooks. *George Ripley.* New York: Houghton Mifflin and Co., 1882.

Gans, Herbert J. *Deciding What's News.* New York: Pantheon Books, 1979.

Gramling, Oliver. *AP: The Story of News.* New York: Farrar and Rinehart, 1940.

Greeley, Horace. *Hints Towards Reform.* New York: Harper and Brothers, 1850.

————. *On Lincoln, With Mr. Greeley's Letters to Charles A. Dana and a Lady Friend,* edited by Joel Benton. New York: Baker and Taylor Co., 1893.

Green, Arnold W. *Henry Charles Carey, Nineteenth-Century Sociologist.* Philadelphia: Univ. of Pennsylvania Press, 1951.

Guarneri, Carl. "Utopian Socialism and American Ideas." Ph.D. diss., Johns Hopkins Univ., 1979.

Hammack, David C. *Power and Society: Greater New York at the Turn of the Century.* New York: Russell Sage Foundation, 1982.

Haraszti, Zoltan. *The Idyll of Brook Farm.* Boston: Boston Public Library, 1937.

Harper, J. Henry. *I Remember.* New York: Harper and Brothers, 1934.

Harper, Robert S. *Lincoln and the Press*. New York: McGraw-Hill, 1951.

Harris, Neil. *Humbug: The Art of P. T. Barnum*. Boston: Little, Brown and Co., 1973.

Harvard University. *Quinquennial Catalogue: 1636–1930*. Cambridge: Harvard Univ. Press, 1930.

Harvey, David. *Consciousness and the Urban Experience: Studies in the History and Theory of Capitalist Urbanization*. Baltimore: Johns Hopkins Univ. Press, 1985.

Haskell, Thomas. *The Emergence of Professional Social Science: The American Social Science Association and the Nineteenth Century Crisis of Authority*. Urbana: Univ. of Illinois Press, 1977.

Hauck, Richard Boyd. *A Cheerful Nihilism: Confidence and 'The Absurd' in American Humorous Fiction*. Bloomington: Indiana Univ. Press, 1971.

Headly, Joel Tyler. *The Great Riots of New York: 1712–1873*. New York: E. B. Treat, 1873.

Hershkowitz, Leo. *Tweed's New York: Another Look*. New York: Anchor Press, 1978.

Higham, John. *From Boundlessness to Consolidation: the Transformation of American Culture, 1848–1860*. Ann Arbor, Mich.: William L. Clements Library Associates, 1969.

———. "The Reorientation of American Culture in the 1890's." In *Writing American History*. Bloomington: Indiana Univ. Press, 1972.

———. *Strangers in the Land: Patterns of American Nativism: 1860–1925*. New York: Atheneum, 1968.

Hoe, Robert. *A Short History of the Printing Press and of the Improvements in Printing Machinery*. New York: R. Hoe, 1902.

Hoogenboom, Ari. *Outlawing the Spoils: A History of the Civil Service Reform Movement, 1865–1883*. Urbana: Univ. of Illinois Press, 1961.

Howe, Daniel Walker, ed. *Victorian America*. Philadelphia: Univ. of Pennsylvania Press, 1978.

Hudson, Frederick. *Journalism in the United States, from 1690 to 1872*. New York: Harper and Brothers, 1873.

Hughes, Helen MacGill. *News and the Human Interest Story*. Chicago: Univ. of Chicago Press, 1940.

Hutchison, William R. *The Transcendentalist Ministers: Church Reform in the New England Renaissance*. New Haven: Yale Univ. Press, 1959.

Isely, Jeter Allen. *Horace Greeley and the Republican Party, 1853–1861*. Princeton: Princeton Univ. Press, 1947.

Jensen, Richard J. *The Winning of the Midwest: Social and Political Conflict, 1888–1896*. Chicago: Univ. of Chicago Press, 1971.

Jones, Gareth Stedman. *Languages of Class: Studies in English Working-class History 1832–1982*. London: Cambridge Univ. Press, 1983.

Juergens, George. *Joseph Pulitzer and the New York World*. Princeton: Princeton Univ. Press, 1966.

Kaplan, A. D. H. *Henry Charles Carey*. Baltimore: Johns Hopkins Univ. Press, 1931.

Katz, Irving. *August Belmont: A Political Biography*. New York: Columbia Univ. Press, 1968.

Keller, Morton. *Affairs of State: Public Life in Late Nineteenth Century America*. Cambridge: Harvard Univ. Press, 1977.

Kelley, Robert. *The Transatlantic Persuasion: The Liberal Democratic Mind in the Age of Gladstone*. New York: Alfred A. Knopf, 1969.

Kinsley, Philip. *The Chicago Tribune, Its First Hundred Years*. Vols. 1–3. Chicago: Tribune Company, 1946.

Kleppner, Paul. *The Cross of Culture; A Social Analysis of Midwestern Politics, 1850–1900*. New York: Free Press, 1970.

Kluger, Richard. *The Paper: The Life and Death of the New York Herald-Tribune*. New York: Knopf, 1986.

Lee, Alfred McClung. *The Daily Newspaper in America; the Evolution of a Social Instrument*. New York: The Macmillan Company, 1937.

Lee, Martin, and Solomon, Norman. *Unreliable Sources: A Guide to Detecting Bias in the News Media*. New York: Carol Publishing Group, 1990.

Leonard, Thomas C. *The Power of the Press: The Birth of American Political Reporting*. New York: Oxford Univ. Press, 1986.

Liebling, A. J. *The Press*. New York: Pantheon Books, 1961.

Low, Seth. *New York in 1850 and in 1890*. New York: New-York Historical Society, 1893.

Lowe, David. *Lost Chicago*. New York: American Legacy Press, 1975.

Lunde, Eric S. *Horace Greeley*. Boston: Twayne Publishers, 1981.

Lynn, Kenneth S. *The Comic Tradition in America*. New York: Doubleday, 1958.

Mandelbaum, Seymour J. *Boss Tweed's New York*. New York: John Wiley and Sons, 1965.

Mangold, George B. *The Labor Argument in the American Pro-Tariff Discussion*. Madison: Univ. of Wisconsin Press, 1906.

Marcus, Robert. *Grand Old Party: Political Structure in the Gilded Age, 1880–1906*. New York: Oxford Univ. Press, 1974.

Marx, Karl, and Engels, Friedrich. *Collected Works*. Vols. 38–40. New York: International Publishers, 1975.

McFeely, William S. *Grant: A Biography*. New York: W. W. Norton and Co., 1981.

Milne, Gordon. *George William Curtis: The Genteel Tradition.* Bloomington: Univ. of Indiana Press, 1956.

Mitchell, Edward P. *Memoirs of an Editor.* New York: Scribner's, 1924.

Mix, James B. *The Biter Bit, or the Robert Macaire of Journalism.* Washington, D.C.: 1870.

Mohr, James C. *The Radical Republicans and Reform in New York During
Reconstruction.* Ithaca: Cornell Univ. Press, 1973.

Morgan, H. Wayne. *From Hayes to McKinley: National Party Politics, 1877–
1896.* New York: Syracuse Univ. Press, 1969.

————, ed. *The Gilded Age, A Reappraisal.* Syracuse: Syracuse Univ. Press,
1963.

Mott, Frank Luther. *American Journalism, A History 1690–1960.* New York:
Macmillan, 1962.

Mushkat, Jerome. *The Reconstruction of the New York Democracy, 1861–
1874.* London: Associated Univ. Presses, 1981.

Nevins, Allan. *The Evening Post: A Century of Journalism.* New York: Boni
and Liveright, 1922.

————. *Hamilton Fish: The Inner History of the Grant Administration.* New
York: F. Ungar Publishing Company, 1957.

New York Cuban Junta, *Facts about Cuba.* Published under the authority
of the New York Cuban Junta. New York: Sun Job Printing Office, 1870.

O'Brien, Frank M. *The Story of the Sun.* New York: D. Appleton and Co.,
1928.

Paine, Albert Bigelow. *Th. Nast: His Period and His Pictures.* New York: The
Macmillan Company, 1904.

Park, Robert E.; Burgess, Ernest W.; and McKenzie, Roderick D. *The City:
Suggestions for Investigation of Human Behavior in the Urban Environment.* Chicago: Univ. of Chicago Press, 1925.

Parrington, Vernon L. *Main Currents in American Thought.* Vol. 3, *The Beginnings of Critical Realism in America.* New York: Harcourt, Brace
and Company, 1930.

Pike, James S. *First Blows of the Civil War.* New York: American News Co.,
1879.

————. *Horace Greeley in 1872.* New York: Powers, Macgowan and Slipper,
1873.

Riis, Jacob. *How the Other Half Lives.* New York: Scribner's Sons, 1917.

————. *The Making of an American.* New York: Grossett and Dunlap, 1901.

Rose, Ann C. *Transcendentalism as a Social Movement, 1830–1850.* New
Haven: Yale Univ. Press, 1981.

Rosebault, Charles J. *When Dana Was the Sun.* New York: R. M. McBride
and Co., 1931.

Rosewater, Victor. *History of Cooperative Newsgathering*. New York: D. Appleton and Co., 1930.

Ross, Dorothy. "The Liberal Tradition Revisited and the Republican Tradition Addressed." In *New Directions in American Intellectual History*, edited by John Higham and Paul K. Conkin, 116–31. Baltimore: Johns Hopkins Univ. Press, 1979.

Ross, Marc. "John Swinton, Journalist and Reformer: The Active Years, 1858–1887." Ph.D. diss., New York Univ., 1969.

Rowell, George P. *American Newspaper Directory*. New York: Geo. P. Rowell and Son, 1869–79.

Schiller, Daniel. *Objectivity and the News*. Philadelphia: Univ. of Pennsylvania Press, 1981.

Schudson, Michael. *Discovering the News: A Social History of American Newspapers*. New York: Basic, 1978.

Seitz, Donald C. *The James Gordon Bennetts, Father and Son*. Indianapolis: Bobbs-Merrill Co., 1928.

Sinclair, Upton. *The Brass Check: A Study in American Journalism*. Reprint. New York: Arno and the New York Times, 1970.

Smith, George Winston. *Henry C. Carey and American Sectional Conflict*. Albuquerque: Univ. of New Mexico Press, 1951.

Smith, Henry Nash. *Mark Twain's Fable of Progress: Political and Economic Ideas in 'A Connecticut Yankee.'* New Brunswick, N.J.: Rutgers Univ. Press, 1969.

Spann, Edward K. *The New Metropolis: New York City, 1840–1857.* New York: Columbia Univ. Press, 1981.

Sproat, John G. *The Best Men: Liberal Reformers in the Gilded Age*. New York: Oxford Univ. Press, 1968.

Stampp, Kenneth M. *The Era of Reconstruction: 1865–1877.* New York: Vintage, 1965.

Stanton, Elizabeth Cady. *Eighty Years and More*. London: T. Fisher Unwin, 1898.

Stone, Candace. *Dana and the Sun*. New York: Dodd, Mead and Co., 1938.

Story, Ronald. *The Forging of an Aristocracy: Harvard and the Boston Upper Class*. Middletown: Wesleyan Univ. Press, 1980.

Strong, George Templeton. *The Diary of George Templeton Strong*, edited by Allan Nevins and Milton Halsey Thomas. New York: Macmillan, 1952.

The Sun's Guide to New York. Jersey City: Jersey City Printing Co., 1892.

Susman, Warren L. *Culture as History: The Transformation of American Society in the Twentieth Century*. New York: Pantheon, 1984.

Swanberg, W. A. *Pulitzer*. New York: Scribner's Sons, 1967.

Swift, Lindsay. *Brook Farm: Its Members, Scholars and Visitors.* New York: The Macmillan Company, 1900.

Tarbell, Ida M. *All in a Day's Work; An Autobiography.* New York: The Macmillan Company, 1939.

Teilhac, Ernest. *Pioneers of American Economic Thought in the Nineteenth Century.* New York: Russell and Russell, 1967.

Trachtenberg, Alan. *The Incorporation of America: Culture and Society in the Gilded Age.* New York: Hill and Wang, 1982.

Tuchman, Gaye. *Making News: A Study in the Construction of Reality.* New York: Free Press, 1978.

Unger, Irwin. *The Greenback Era: A Social and Political History of American Finance, 1865–1879.* Princeton: Princeton Univ. Press, 1964.

Van Deusen, Glyndon. *Horace Greeley: Nineteenth-Century Crusader.* New York: Hill and Wang, 1964.

Walters, Ronald G. *American Reformers: 1815–1860.* New York: Hill and Wang, 1978.

Waters, Robert. *Career and Conversation of John Swinton.* Chicago: C. H. Kerr and Co., 1902.

Weeks, Lyman Horace. *Prominent Families of New York.* New York: Historical Co., 1898.

Werner, Morris. *Tammany Hall.* New York: Doubleday, 1928.

Wilson, James Harrison. *The Life of Charles A. Dana.* New York: Harper and Brothers, 1907.

Wilentz, Sean. *Chants Democratic: New York City and the Rise of the American Working Class 1788–1850.* New York: Oxford Univ. Press, 1983.

Wingate, Charles F. *Views and Interviews on Journalism.* New York: F. B. Patterson, 1875.

Wolfe, Gerard. *New York: A Guide to the Metropolis.* New York: New York Univ. Press, 1983.

Ziff, Larzer. *The American 1890's: Life and Times of a Lost Generation.* New York: Viking, 1966.

———. *Literary Democracy: The Declaration of Cultural Independence in America.* New York: Viking, 1981.

Articles

Bestor, Arthur. "Patent-Office Models of the Good Society: Some Relationships Between Social Reform and Westward Expansion." *American Historical Review* 58 (Apr. 1953): 505–26.

Blodgett, Geoffrey. "The Mugwump Reputation, 1870 to the Present." *Journal of American History* 66 (Mar. 1980): 867–87.

Borden, Morton. "Five Letters of Charles A. Dana to Karl Marx," *Journalism Quarterly* 36 (1959): 314–16.

———. "Some Notes on Horace Greeley, Charles Dana and Karl Marx." *Journalism Quarterly* 34 (1957): 457–65.

Bradford, George P. "Reminiscences of Brook Farm." *Century Magazine* 45 (Nov. 1892): 141–48.

Carey, James W. "The Problem of Journalism History." *Journalism History* 1 (Spring 1974): 3–5.

Carpenter, E. J. "Journalism as a Profession." *Education* 7 (Feb. 1887): 410–15.

Cochran, Thomas C. "Media as Business: A Brief History." *Journal of Communication* 25 (Autumn 1975): 155–65.

Cockerill, John. "Some Phases of Contemporary Journalism." *Cosmopolitan* 13 (Oct. 1892): 695–703.

Curtis, George William, "The Editor's Easy Chair." *Harper's Monthly Magazine* 43 (July 1871): 294–95.

Darnton, Robert. "Writing News and Telling Stories." *Daedalus* 104 (Spring 1975): 175–95.

Downey, Matthew T. "Horace Greeley and the Politicians: The Liberal Republican Convention in 1872." *Journal of American History* 43 (Mar. 1967): 727–50.

Gerber, Richard A. "The Liberal Republicans in Historiographical Perspective." *Journal of American History* 62 (June 1975): 40–73.

Gertz, Elmer. "Charles A. Dana and the *Chicago Republican*." *Journal of the Illinois State Historical Society* 45 (1952): 124–35.

Guarneri, Carl. "Utopian Socialism as a Transatlantic Movement." Paper presented to the Charles Warren Seminar for Boston Area Historians of American History, Harvard University, April 7, 1982.

Gutman, Herbert G. "The Tompkins Square 'Riot' in New York City on Jan. 13, 1874: A Re-examination of Its Causes and Its Aftermath." *Labor History* 6 (Winter 1965): 48–55.

Hale, William Harlan. "When Karl Marx Worked for Horace Greeley." *American Heritage* 8 (Apr. 1957): 20–25, 110–11.

Harmond, Richard. "The 'Beast' in Boston: Benjamin F. Butler as Governor of Massachusetts." *Journal of American History* 55 (Sept. 1968): 266–80.

Hartman, William. "Custom House Patronage Under Lincoln." *New-York Historical Society Quarterly* 41 (Oct. 1957): 440–57.

———. "The New York Custom House: Seats of Spoils Politics." *New-York Historical Society Quarterly* 34 (Apr. 1953): 149–63.

Hazeltine, Mayo D. "Charles Anderson Dana." *North American Review* 185 (July 1907): 510–14.

Keller, J. W. "Journalism as a Career." *Forum* 15 (Aug. 1893): 691–704.

Lilly, W. S. "The Ethics of Journalism." *Forum* 7 (July 1889): 503–12.

Morrison, Rodney J. "Henry C. Carey and American Economic Development." *Explorations in Entrepreneurial History* 5 (Winter 1968): 132–44.

O'Rell, Max. "Lively Journalism." *North American Review* 150 (Mar. 1890): 364–69.

Parton, James. "Newspapers Gone to Seed." *Forum* 1 (Mar. 1886): 15–24.

Peck, Henry Thurston. "Mr. Dana on Journalism." *Bookman* 2 (Nov. 1895): 191–95.

Reid, Whitelaw. "Schools of Journalism." *Scribner's Monthly* 4 (June 1872): 194–204.

Rider, George T. "The Pretensions of Journalism." *North American Review* 135 (Nov. 1882): 471–83.

Savage, M. J. "A Profane View of the Sanctum." *North American Review* 141 (July 1885): 137–53.

Shaw, Donald L. "News Bias and the Telegraph." *Journalism Quarterly* 44 (Spring 1967): 3–12, 31.

Speed, John Gilmer. "Do Newspapers Now Give the News?" *Forum* 15 (Aug. 1893): 705–11.

Sumner, Arthur. "A Boy's Recollections of Brook Farm." *New England Magazine* 10 (May 1894): 309–13.

Swinton, John. "Memoranda as to the Late Charles A. Dana." *Chautauquan* 26 (Mar. 1898): 612.

Taylor, William. "The Launching of a Commercial Culture: New York City, 1860–1930." Unpublished paper in my possession, Mar. 16, 1984.

Walker, John Brisben. "Henry George and Charles A. Dana." *Cosmopolitan* 24 (Dec. 1897): 199–204.

Welter, Rush. "The Idea of Progress in America." *Journal of the History of Ideas* 16 (June 1955): 404–5.

White, Richard Grant. "The Morals and Manners of Journalism." *Galaxy* 8 (1869): 840–47.

———. "The Pest of the Period." *Galaxy* 9 (Jan. 1870): 102–12.

White, Z. L. "A Decade of American Journalism." *Westminster Review* (Oct. 1887): 856.

Index

The Sun Shines for All

was composed in 10½ on 13 Caledonia
on Digital Compugraphic equipment
by Metricomp;
with display type in Goudy Text
by Rochester Mono/Headliners;
printed by sheet-fed offset on 50-pound, acid-free Natural Smooth,
Smyth-sewn and bound over binder's boards in Holliston Roxite B,
and with dust jackets printed in 2 colors
by Braun-Brumfield, Inc.;
designed by Victoria M. Lane;
and published by
Syracuse University Press
Syracuse, New York 13244-5160